a
precarious
peace

Polyglossia: Radical Reformation Theologies

Edited by Peter Dula, Chris K. Huebner and J. Alexander Sider

A series intended for conversation among academics, ministers and laypersons regarding knowledge, beliefs and the practices of the Christian faith. *Polyglossia* grows out of John Howard Yoder's call to see radical reformation as a tone, style, or a stance, a way of thinking theologically that requires precarious attempts to speak the gospel in new idioms. It is a form of theological reflection that blends patient vulnerability and hermeneutical charity with considered judgment and informed criticism. The books in this series will emerge out of conversations with contemporary movements in theology, as well as philosophy, political theory, literature, and cultural studies.

a precarious peace

Chris K. Huebner

Foreword by Stanley Hauerwas

Yoderian Explorations on Theology, Knowledge, and Identity

Herald Press

Waterloo, Ontario
Scottdale, Pennsylvania

Library and Archives Canada Cataloging in Publication
Huebner, Chris K., 1969-
   A precarious peace ; Yoderian explorations on theology, knowledge, and identity / Chris K. Huebner ; foreword by Stanley Hauerwas.

Includes bibliographical references and index.
   ISBN 0-8361-9341-5
   1. Peace—Religious aspects—Mennonites. 2. Mennonites—Doctrines.
3. Yoder, John Howard. I. Title.
   BX8128.P4H83 2006
   262.8'730882897

                              C2006-904249-7

A PRECARIOUS PEACE
Copyright © 2006 by Herald Press, Waterloo, Ont. N2L 6H7
   Published simultaneously in the United States of America by Herald
   Press, Scottdale, Pa. 15683. All rights reserved
Library of Congress Control Number: 2006930988
Canadiana Entry Number: C2006-904249-7
International Standard Book Number: 0-8361-9341-5
Printed in the United States of America
Cover design by Judith Rempel Smucker

12 11 10 09 08 07 06   10 9 8 7 6 5 4 3 2 1

To order or request information, please call
1-800-759-4447 (individuals); 1-800-245-7894 (trade).
Web site: www.heraldpress.com

To Rachel

Contents

Foreword

"Yoder never assumed that he finally knew what peace was." With this claim, Chris Huebner inaugurates a new stage in Mennonite theology and, hopefully, a renewed reception of the work of John Howard Yoder. His claim that Yoder did not know what peace was is not a retreat from the Mennonite commitment to nonviolence, but rather an attempt to help us understand the radical character of Christian pacifism. Accordingly, Huebner argues that Yoder's non-Constantinian approach to Christian theology is not just an expression of his "ethics," but rather, a challenge to the dualisms that continue to haunt mainstream Catholic and Protestant theology. Huebner thereby forces us to see—and force is the right word—that Yoder's critique of Constantinianism is an attack on all forms of "methodologism" that seek to secure an unproblematic account of Christian identity. The "peace" that is Christ's cross is an apocalyptic reality that interrupts and challenges what we had assumed was peace.

Huebner, therefore, teaches us to read Yoder in a manner not unlike how Wittgenstein must be read; that is, after having read them, we cannot help but see the world differently. Yoder and Wittgenstein return us to the "rough ground" where we may not know our way. But nowhere else can we be if we are to avoid the self-deceptive attempt to find safety in abstractions that, at least for Yoder, become ways to avoid following Christ. Thus, Huebner challenges the widespread tendency to make peace and justice ideals abstracted from the gospel. The peace of Christ comes only as a gift, and like all gifts, it can be received to the degree that we have learned to live out of control. Moreover, we can only learn to live out of control by listening to those who challenge our strategies of legitimation.

Huebner develops this way of reading Yoder by putting Yoder into conversation with surprising interlocutors. In truth, Huebner is a philosopher in theological disguise. Accordingly, he is able to help us see how Yoder's work, like that of MacIntyre and Milbank, is a challenge to the epistemological conceits of modernity. Huebner, however, argues that Yoder may well share more in common with the genealogical tradition—that is, with Derrida and Foucault—than with MacIntyre just to the extent that MacIntyre has failed to follow through his own best insights. In a similar fashion, Huebner argues that Yoder provides a more thorough account of what it means to live by gift—and in particular, the gift of friendship—than MacIntyre or Milbank.

One of the ways to recover the "rough ground" is through cultural criticism. Thus, Huebner employs Virilio's work on speed to make the significance of Yoder's account of patience recognizable as a commentary on our cultural pathologies. Indeed, Huebner is even able to show how Yoder might have proved to be an able expositor of the pathology of the images that pervade our culture and shape our lives in a manner we only vaguely understand. Anyone who reads Huebner's reflections and analysis of the habits that shape our lives—and in particular, how those habits threaten to erode the significance of memory for those who have lost the ability to remember—will be stricken by the gentle wisdom that informs his description of those whom he knows he must remember.

I believe that *A Precarious Peace* is a breakthrough book. I simply do not see how the mainstream intellectual cultures, Christian and non-Christian, can ignore this book by relegating it, just as they have tried to relegate John Howard Yoder, to the Mennonite ghetto. Huebner's book should be impossible to ignore not only because of the sources he engages but because he addresses the central philosophical and theological challenges before us. For example, his chapter on martyrdom and knowledge should become required reading for anyone concerned with the ongoing discussion of the difference the church can make for the formation of universities. He offers an alternative to the knowledges of the university that legitimate, for example, the assumption that war is simply part of the way things are.

Yet, as challenging as this book will be for non-Mennonites, it will be no less challenging for Mennonites. Indeed, in many ways *A Precarious Peace* will be more difficult for Mennonites to receive than it will be for mainstream Protestants and Catholics. Just as Yoder never tired of pointing out to Mennonites that farm culture too often turned out to be but another form of Constantinianism, so Huebner is unrelenting in his attempt to unsettle the presumption that Mennonites have "got peace down." That Huebner finds Rowan Williams, the Archbishop of Canterbury, one of his most important theological resources is surely an indication that Mennonites must be ready to recognize that those they once considered hopelessly compromised represent what it means to be the church in contrast to the world.

Some may well read this last remark as an apology for my ambiguous ecclesial status. Thus my self-declared status to be a high church Mennonite. I am what I am, and Huebner is what he is. He is a Canadian Mennonite and I am not. I did have the good fortune to be Huebner's teacher, but I would not want to tar him with my brush. I think this book is a clear indication he is more than capable on his own of getting into trouble without my help. Yet I also think this book is the beginning of a new day in which the burden and the glory of being Mennonite is made an unavoidable reality for all Christians. Thank God!

—*Stanley Hauerwas*
Duke University
July 2006

Acknowledgments

Every book reflects trails of conversations that no doubt fail to do justice to the liveliness of the original discussions themselves. This book bears traces of conversations that span two different locations and arise against the background of somewhat distinct contexts. About half of the essays were originally written while I was a doctoral student at Duke University in Durham, North Carolina. The others were written after I began teaching at Canadian Mennonite University in Winnipeg, Manitoba.

Several of these essays began as paper assignments for graduate seminars at Duke. For their inspiration, encouragement, and support, I would like to thank my professors, Owen Flanagan, Mary McClintock Fulkerson, Alasdair MacIntyre, Dale Martin, Geoffrey Wainwright, and especially Romand Coles and Stanley Hauerwas. During my time at Duke, I was also fortunate to have had a community of close friends and fellow students from whose observations and criticisms I have benefited a great deal. In particular, I would like to thank Richard Church, David Cloutier, Charlie Collier, Rosalee and Sam Velloso Ewell, Amy and Peter Frykholm, Alex Hawkins, Kelly Johnson, Tom and Mary Jo Lehman, Joel Shuman, David Stubbs, Scott and Jenny Williams, and Laura Yordy. I owe a special debt to Peter Dula and Alex Sider, whose intellectual companionship over the years has been so profound I can scarcely imagine thinking without it.

At Canadian Mennonite University (CMU) I have been blessed with an energetic and stimulating group of dialogue partners from a wide range of disciplines. In particular, I would like to thank Paul Dyck, Harry Huebner, and Gordon Zerbe for the influence they have had on much of my recent thinking. More generally, CMU provides a context that has proven to be fertile ground to test out new ideas. And it has proven to be a perfect fit for my nomadic and sometimes unfocussed intellectual interests. CMU is a rarity in that it is a small institution in which teaching can genuinely dovetail with research and writing. My teaching responsibilities at CMU are made rewarding in part because of the company of an exceptional group of students that have found their way into my classes in one way or another. Jennifer Braun, Kevin Derksen, Jonathan Dyck, Jason Peters, Grant Poettcker, Julia Thiessen, and Joe Wiebe have in various ways enriched my work over the past four years. Special thanks are due to Greg Wiebe for help in preparing the index.

Finally, one person's presence spans both of these locations. Rachel Klassen Huebner has been a figure of constancy throughout the time that has gone into this book, and more. For her intuitive and uncanny way of knowing when incisive criticism is necessary and when caring support is needed, I am thankful in ways that are impossible to summarize in a few words. Though I am aware that it is hardly an adequate expression of my appreciation for all that she has given me, I dedicate this book to her.

—Chris K. Huebner
Winnipeg, Manitoba

Chapters of this book appeared in an earlier form in various journals and books. The author and publisher gratefully acknowledge permission to reprint from these publications:

"A Precarious People" was originally published as "For a Healthy Schizophrenia." *Christian Living* 48:6 (Sept. 2001): 5-6.

"Radical Orthodoxy, Radical Reformation: What Might Mennonites and Milbank Learn from Each Other?" was originally published as "What Should Mennonites and Milbank Learn from Each Other?" *Conrad Grebel Review* 23:2 (2005): 9-18.

"Mennonites and Narrative Theology: The Case of John Howard Yoder" was originally published as "Mennonites and Narrative Theology: The Case of John Howard Yoder." *Conrad Grebel Review* 16:2 (1998): 15-38.

"Radical Ecumenism, or Receiving One Another in Kuala Lumpur" was originally published as "Radical Ecumenism, or Receiving One Another in Kuala Lumpur." *Ecumenical Review* 57:4 (2005).

"Can a Gift Be Commanded? Political Ontology and Theoretical Closure in Milbank, Barth, and Yoder" was originally published as "Can a Gift Be Commanded? Theological Ethics Without Theory by Way of Barth, Milbank, and Yoder." *Scottish Journal of Theology* 53:4 (2000): 472-489.

"Globalization, Theory, and Dialogical Vulnerability: John Howard Yoder and the Possibility of a Pacifist Epistemology" was originally published as "Globalization, Theory, and Dialogical Vulnerability: John Howard Yoder and the Possibility of a Pacifist Epistemology." *Mennonite Quarterly Review* 76:1 (2002): 49-62.

"Patience, Witness, and the Scattered Body of Christ: Yoder and Virilio on Knowledge, Politics and Speed" was originally published in *A Mind Patient and Untamed: Assessing John Howard Yoder's Contribution to Theology, Ethics, and Peacemaking*, ed. Ben C. Ollenburger and Gayle Gerber Koontz, 56-74. Telford, Pa.: Cascadia Publishing House, 2004.

"The Agony of Truth: Martyrdom, Violence, and Christian Ways of Knowing" first appeared in *Consensus: A Canadian Lutheran Journal of Theology* (Vol. 31, No. 2), and is reprinted here by permission.

"Christian Pacifism as Friendship with God: MacIntyre, Mennonites, and the Genealogical Tradition" was originally published as a chapter in *Anabaptists and Postmodernity*, ed. Susan and Gerald Biesecker-Mast, 339-355. Telford, Pa.: Pandora Press U.S., 2000.

"Between Victory and Victimhood: Reflections on Martyrdom, Culture, and Identity" was originally published in *Direction* 34:2 (2005): 228-240.

"Putting Ourselves in Question" was originally a sermon preached at Hope Mennonite Church, in Winnipeg, Manitoba, Palm/Passion Sunday, April 13, 2003.

Introduction

Christian theology is exploration. It is ceaselessly on the move. The theologian is an essentially restless figure. Or at any rate, he has—or should have—a difficult time sitting still. If theology's greatest temptation is with the fixedness, the permanence, the unhiddenness of idols, this temptation is given social expression in a life of idle settlement. Christians are sent out into the world armed with nothing more than a conviction that we have been given a word of truth so exceedingly strange that we nailed it to the cross.

The Christian is called forth from the world of the same, the familiar, the known, and sent back into that very same world on a dangerous task that finds her always in search of new ground to unearth, new truths to uncover, and new lies to name. Because truth is hidden, even as it sits before our very eyes, the Christian travels beyond the limits of regulative horizons, crossing fixed boundaries, and is thus ever in search of new ventures and conversation partners. In doing so, theology "inspires endless departures and returns," as the orthodox theologian David Bentley Hart puts it.[1] Because its truth is as much a question of form as content, the theologian wears many masks and works in multiple genres.

The Christian theologian is not an expert or a specialist, neither a proprietor of some bounded domain nor a detached surveyor of a given field of inquiry. At its best, theology reflects a spirit of playful investigation, a spirit that is perhaps best reflected by the work of Karl Barth. This is not to suggest that it is therefore not serious but to maintain that it is as much experimental and improvisational as it is the performance of a given script.

The Christian theologian, like the church more generally, is torn between two worlds, two cities, and thus is always and yet never entirely at home. Although always in some measure involved in conversation with the world, theology is a most unworldly science. Its meditations

17

seem untimely, at least from the perspective of the world's conception of time. Its words cannot but come across as being out of place, at least when they are measured against those officially sanctioned places, the places we desire to have patrolled and policed.

The church, in other words, is a scattered body. And so those who inhabit it are doomed to—or rather graced by—a life of unsettled wandering. Those who are given a home in the church also find themselves in the midst of the wilderness, even wandering multiple wildernesses. In doing so, they provide glimpses of surprising and unpredictable happenings, and so complicate our will to explain and contain. They serve to embody threatening interruptions, and so leave us uncoupled from our will to secure passages of safety.

The church gives voice to irresponsible hopes, and so defies our calculated and effective activity. A hauntingly strange figure in this world of negotiated settlements and contractual bargains, the Christian theologian does not function primarily as a broker of agreement, but seeks to cultivate space for those meaningful disagreements out of which hitherto unrecognized possibilities, new expressions of faithfulness, might emerge.

But if Christian theology is exploration, this presents the theologian with a serious image problem. For explorers typically have a bad name, especially in those places they claim to have discovered. This bad reputation is of course justly deserved in many cases. To speak of exploration is to call to mind notions of conquest and colonization. It conjures up images of brutal confinement, forced "conversions," not to mention torture and rape. And it is one of the great tragedies in the life of the church, both past and present, that it has all too often been complicit in these ventures.

To correct for this, we are tempted to invent new, less controversial and more sanitized, less threatening and more humanized images of theology, images like creative expression and human longing. Images designed to cure theology once and for all of its exploratory urges. But as tempting as such a venture might be, it is also a grave mistake. Put bluntly, these more humanized images leave theology stripped of the ability to articulate how it is *not* at home in the world. They leave the theologian without the means to express the sense in which she is untimely and out of place, and so abandon her to identification with the vast empires and provincial colonies that define the world. So instead of avoiding the exploratory character of theology, it is best to meet it head on. In doing so, it is important to reckon with how it is that the church explores, but explores differently—not least because of its attitude toward difference. This book is an attempt to provide a few gestures toward answering such a question.

In this, as in so many other things, such as an interest in discipline, it is helpful to explore the sense in which the church might be said to resemble the military. Both name a way of life that is ever moving into new territories. Both make claims to new ground. Both exist as if torn between two worlds. But there is a key difference, such that these turn out to be only surface similarities. The military travels violently. Its movement is territorial, as it seeks to capture and control other territories in a preservationist drive for protection and security. It is, in short, the very embodiment of exploration as conquest and colonization. The church, however, because it is given shape by the peace of Christ, travels in an entirely different way. It is equally on the move. It also makes claims to new ground. And yet when Christian thought is true to its call to be the church, its travels exhibit a renunciation of the desire to control.

The movement of the military is guided by an above-ground perspective of surveillance. It utilizes an expansive field of vision that casts its controlling gaze ever wider. The church, by contrast, moves as if from below, from the underground. Its vision consisting of glimpses and brief snatches, never putting itself above the realities it encounters. While the military travels in a territorial vein, the church works to uncouple us from our territorial attachments and longings. Whereas the military sees being torn as a threat, the church might even see it as gift. In other words, the grace of which Christians speak consists precisely in being torn out. It is to be separated from the grip of the world and its powers. It is a cut within the fabric of empire. This is why the church, when it has been faithful, has constituted a threat to the military and the powers it represents. The theologian is thus not so much the hunter as the hunted. And so Christians have often had to resort to worshipping in caves. The church's life is on the run; its theology is delivered on the fly.

Perhaps even more significantly, the military and the church both represent a desire for peace. And yet the peace of which they speak could not be more different. In a military guise, peace is something secured. It is brokered, negotiated, the end result in a chain of calculated, instrumental causes and effects. It is imposed on the world and seeks to tame it, to bring order to a scene of warring chaos. It is, in short, a word of safety, of security, of balance. The peace of the church, however, is a vulnerable exchange of gifts. It is not safe, but dangerous. It does not offer us a comforting message of security and balance, but unsettles our desire for settlement. It is not the effect of a cause, but an unwelcome interruption.

The peace of Christ explodes that which we take to be given. It radically transforms the world as we know it. It is paradoxically more militant, or at least more militantly disruptive, than the military. The tragedy of Christian pacifism is that its vision of peace has largely become captive to sanitized discourses of humanization. It has adopted the military's search for guarantees, its desire to create passages of safety. It attempts to tame and to bring order to that which is deemed wild and out of control. Like the military, Christian pacifism all too often speaks as if it has a monopoly on peace. Its rhetoric assumes that it occupies a position of ownership over peace. The pacifist speaks as if he inhabits a standpoint that is somehow purified of violence, of sin. Or at least he assumes that he is able to keep violence under control.

But if the church were true to its call, it would speak, not of such worldly peace, but of the peace of Christ, which, as gift, is precisely out of control. Christian pacifism is distorted to the extent that it could be spoken of as something owned. The peace of Christ is first of all to be spoken in a confessional vein. It arises from struggle against the background of a recognition that it is always already implicated in some form of violence or another. It is not yet free from sin. The peace of Christ, the church's grammar of peace, is as fragile and vulnerable as it is threatening and explosive. It cannot but exist in the absence of guarantees. It moves without the benefit of strategic calculations designed to bring it about more effectively. It teeters uneasily on the edge. It is, as the title of this book suggests, a precarious peace.

Thus, the theologian who is called to speak the peace of Christ will be found wandering strange new worlds and speaking strange new words. This is also true, perhaps especially, with respect to the new ground we call the ordinary. In other words, one of the key, though largely neglected, tasks of the theologian is to articulate and negotiate the strangeness of that with which we are already in some ways familiar.

The exploration I speak of is not to be confused with an exotic concept of exploration, one in search of something out there. Accounts of the strangeness or otherness of the church regarding the world are often delivered in comforting and self-confirming tones. They tempt us to fix our critical gaze on some other terrain. One such manifestation of this approach is the project of theological liberalism known as "apologetic theology," the task of defending the integrity of theology against its secular, cultured despisers. But it is often present, albeit in a more subtle way, in so-called post-liberal approaches as well. The conception of strangeness and exploration I speak of is not this sort.

Rather, I am interested in exploring theology's role in confronting the strangeness of the everyday. Such an approach attends as much to the silences that define us, to our discursive gaps, as to our explicit words and reasoned justifications. The Christian is one whose ear has been trained to hear the strained inflections of the so-called minority voice. She is one who has learned to become attentive to the little lies we tell ourselves every day, our subtle strategies of self-legitimation. And so she is skilled at identifying the many ways in which our key theological claims work against themselves. At one time, before Christians became uncomfortable with the idea of sin, before being Christian became confused with being happy, this sort of task was understood to be included as part of Christian grammar of sin. But such a grammar has become as strange and foreign as the figure of the theologian itself, not least in those places in which the theologian is said to be at home.

This book, then, is a set of explorations that seeks, from some perspective called "theology," to explore the habits of theology itself. We'll explore its characteristic figures of speech, claims to knowledge, forms of life, and modes of action. This book seeks to explore the strangeness of theology to itself and in so doing to read theology against itself. The Christian theologian is one who embodies a difficult and precarious stance of being simultaneously for and against the church, just as he is simultaneously for and against the world.

The subject of these explorations can be grouped together in three broad categories, which correspond to the three sections of the book: (1) Mennonite theology, (2) problems of knowledge, and (3) questions of identity. More specifically, I offer a reading of Mennonite theology as something that resists establishment, including the establishment of something called Mennonite theology itself. Building on such a reading, I develop a theological account of knowledge that resists ownership, the assumption that one can be said somehow to be in possession of what one knows. And finally, I provide some gestures toward an interpretation of identity that resists territorial urges, the desire to think of identity as being a fixed, stable site, located in one territory or another, whether geographically speaking or otherwise. More generally, and reflecting the title of the book as a whole, these three reflections can be read together as a series of theological explorations on peace as a precarious gift. This names an understanding of peace that works against the grain of much that goes under the name of Christian pacifism.

I have called these particular explorations "Yoderian." This signals a book essentially about John Howard Yoder. And yet it is not a book *about* Yoder if that means an explicit recounting and interpretation of what Yoder said. Rather, it is a book that seeks to explore *what* Yoder said in a way that is attentive to *how* it is that he said it. The value of Yoder's work has as much to do with matters of rhetoric, performance, and form as it does with the specific content of his claims. I do not offer a systematic explanation and defense of Yoder's key positions. And yet it might be said that precisely in this sense, the book is most significantly about Yoder. In other words, it is a book about Yoder that strives to do justice to the fact that Yoder did not develop positions.

Yoder's work was not the articulation and justification of a theological system. His approach to theology is not systematic but conversational and dialogical. It only makes sense against the background of the church, the worshipping and hermeneutical community, in its many complex interactions with and without the world. His writings are thus ad hoc, occasional, and episodic, often elicited as an invitation to speak on an assigned topic or arising out of a particular encounter of some sort. In short, Yoder's work is not a self-generated and self-standing theological enterprise. It does not reflect the dominating presence of an authorial "I," let alone the stance of a professional theologian, even though many mistakenly approach it as though it does. Accordingly, this book seeks to display a certain Yoderian spirit, a style, a way of proceeding theologically. It strives to perform the art of theological exploration as Yoder teaches us to practice it.

Many of the essays do deal directly with various aspects of Yoder's work. Some of them work explicitly to advance readings and develop interpretations of what I take to be some of his more significant contributions. Other essays proceed by bringing his work into conversation with others, particularly others with whom he was not himself engaged in direct conversation but whose voices help to elicit important elements of his work. In still others, however, the name of Yoder is scarcely mentioned at all. At times his voice is completely silent. And yet it ought not to be concluded that Yoder's voice is entirely absent from these discussions. On the contrary, these essays might be more genuinely Yoderian than some of those that deal with his work explicitly. This is because they do not speak from a position of ownership over a completed position that was never there in the first place.

Yoder did not approach the church as a body that is capable of being established. He did not see theology as something that can be owned or territorially located in some determinative way. Accordingly, any attempt to provide an account of these aspects of Yoder's work will be defeated to the extent that it allows traces of his own voice to dominate too loudly—as something established, owned, and located.

The Story in Outline

Disestablishing, disowning, dislocating. This is a story that takes place in three acts, an argument developed in three interrelated parts. In order to set the stage for the discussions that follow, I'll outline the general contours of the story of this book and introduce some of its main characters. At the outset, it should be emphasized that the following theological explorations are offered as a series of reflections on and interpretations of the larger story of the church, the body of Christ. I am especially interested in the struggle of the church to be the church, to faithfully embody the body of Christ in the midst of the temptations named "world." In particular, I examine three key movements of the church, three defining activities or performances: those of disestablishment, of disowning, and of dislocation.

Each of these names a negative moment. They perform an activity of distancing whereby the church expresses its otherness, its difference from the world. And yet they simultaneously name a distance and differentiation that is internal to the very life of church itself. In other words, they explore the character of the church as a kind of dislocated identity. They present a collection of interpretations that seek to give expression to the body of Christ as a strange body that exists in a precarious state of unsettled tornness. They tell a story of the relationship between church and world, focusing in particular on the sense in which the church exists as somehow torn between the very distinction of church and world that defines it. Put differently, they provide an account of the church as it is charged with the task of giving voice to the peace of Christ in a way that does not compromise its precarious nature as gift. They tell a story of a strange and unsettled people who face the difficult and ongoing task of giving expression to a body that does not admit of establishment, a truth that does not admit of ownership, and an identity that does not admit of location.

Each of these moments is developed with respect to a particular subject matter. They are elaborated by way of a discussion of three specific questions: the question of Mennonite theology, the question of knowledge, and the question of identity. Together with the three negative acts mentioned above, these questions constitute the threefold structure of book, its division into three parts: disestablishing Mennonite theology, disowning knowledge, and dislocating identity. In discussing the first question, I explore various aspects of the critique of an establishmentarian stance that might arguably be claimed to lie at the heart of Mennonite theology. Mennonite theology is an inherently precarious and unstable enterprise. Its theological case against establishment can be deployed against the drive to secure the establishment of the very idea of Mennonite theology itself.

I turn next to the question of ownership, and in particular to an examination of the temptation to give expression to a kind of ownership over knowledge, to think of truth as a possession of some sort. In doing so, I gesture toward a theological interpretation of knowledge that resists ownership, if only because it understands knowledge under the category of gift.

I go on to deploy many of these same arguments to explore questions of identity. In particular, I critically examine the temptation to think of identity in territorial terms, as a kind of location or site whose boundaries are assumed to be as clearly identifiable as is the need to protect them against external threats. A theological understanding of identity is at odds with many standard notions of identity. The peoplehood of those who are called Christians is inherently contingent, arising out of an unexpected calling. It is thus not a territorial given to be protected and secured, but is unsettled and diasporic, pulled ceaselessly beyond itself. It will be useful to outline briefly the arguments concerning each of these questions.

Part I grapples with the tension between the establishment and disestablishment of Mennonite theology. The last half of the twentieth century saw increasing energy devoted to the idea of a specifically Mennonite theology. I suggest in chapter 3 that this can be attributed to Harold Bender's attempt to establish a normative statement of the

a way of insulating certain forms of violence from the possibility of meaningful critique and resistance.

Chapter 5 revisits the work of John Milbank. In particular, I examine Milbank's ontology of peace from the perspective of the sharp distinction he draws between the categories of gift and command. I do so by bringing Milbank into conversation with Karl Barth, whose theology might be said to turn on his account of the command of God. What is particularly instructive about this staged encounter is that Barth's understanding of command is not grounded on an assumed distinction between command and gift that Milbank takes to be basic. Indeed, for Barth the command of God is not capable of being grounded at all. Rather, it is utterly contingent, the expression of the unpredictable freedom of God. In other words, Barth develops an account of the command of God as gift, and in particular the gift of Jesus Christ.

Chapter 6 contributes to the discussion of an epistemology of peace by examining the relationship between medium and message in Yoder's work. I argue that the full significance of Yoder's understanding of peace is all too often compromised by an attempt to articulate it through a medium that is somehow implicated in the violent desire for ownership and possession. An example comes from a reading of two otherwise friendly interpretations of Yoder's work offered by Lisa Sowle Cahill and Nancey Murphy.

I focus on the theme of patience in chapter 7. Here I bring Yoder into conversation with the contemporary French war theorist Paul Virilio, together with a recent critique of Virilio's work by the American political theorist William Connolly. I begin with the assumption that it will be instructive to read Yoder's "patience as method" and its peaceable renunciation of controlled effectiveness alongside Virilio's understanding of violence and technology, especially his claim that the essence of violence is speed.

I conclude this discussion of knowledge and ownership in chapter 8 with an account of the epistemological significance of Christian martyrdom. In particular, I set out to explore the traditional Christian claim that the martyr is somehow in a privileged position with respect to the truth. I argue that martyrdom names an approach to truth that is as much about bodily performances as cognitive ideas. More specifically, it is an epistemological performance that unsettles the presumption of ownership that is made when we speak of having or holding beliefs. Martyrdom is not the secondary result of beliefs that one claims to know. It is a key Christian practice that constitutes and makes intelligible a certain nonviolent and dispossessive way of knowing.

Part III turns from a discussion of knowledge and truth to questions of selfhood and identity. It is an exploration of Christian identity as identity in Christ. I suggest that identity in Christ means that Christian identity is necessarily at odds with identity—or at least it is at odds with what might be called "identitarianism." Identitarianism names the assumption that identity is somehow self-identifiable, that we can articulate our own identities. Against such a view, I argue that identity in Christ implies a conception of identity that does not coincide with itself. Just as the precarious peace of Christ disturbs our desire to construe knowledge as a form of ownership, so it works to unsettle our temptation to think of identity as something solid and impenetrable. I am particularly interested in exploring the difference between a sovereign territorial conception of identity and a non-sovereign diasporic understanding of identity.

I begin this task in chapter 9 by focusing on friendship, a theme that is neglected by those who defend either individualism or communitarianism. I take up Aristotle's definition of the friend as another self, and its transformation in the hands of Aquinas into a radically theological account of friendship with God. Through the staging of a three-way encounter between Alasdair MacIntyre, Jacques Derrida, and John Milbank, I argue that Christian pacifism turns on an appreciation of the significance of God's first claiming us as friend.

Chapter 10 continues with the theme of friendship and its blurring of the lines between self and other, this time in the context of the ethics of memory and the challenge posed by Alzheimer's disease. I begin with a discussion of ethics that relies heavily on the notions of memory and identity, an approach that assumes that the first task of ethics is to remember who you are. According to such an approach, ethics does not primarily turn on the development of abstract rational theories or calculative mechanisms that promise to settle all the difficult decisions and choices we might happen to face. Rather, it sees ethics as a work of shared memory, involving the cultivation of historically formed identity, such as my Mennonite grandmother taught her children.

Chapter 11 further explores the theme of diasporic dislocation that was introduced in chapter 7. More specifically, I set out to articulate an account of diasporic identity against the background of an examination of the interplay between image and identity, and the ethics of visual culture more generally. I approach this discussion by bringing together the Canadian philosopher Charles Taylor and the Canadian filmmaker Atom Egoyan. Taylor and Egoyan represent two rival conceptions of the relationship between image and identity. Taylor's work can be described as an attempt to save identity and the self from their demise at the hands of Enlightenment individualism. He attributes the dissolution of identity to a shift that has taken place with respect to knowledge and the self, a turn from participation to representation, from engaging the world to picturing it. He sets out to strengthen identity over against the threats posed by the turn to a world of pictures. The films of Egoyan examine the temptation to seize upon images, to control them as a way of fixing identity. At the heart of Egoyan's work is a kind of struggle over the loss of identity. But his is an identity loss that occurs precisely because of an attempt to strengthen and seize identity, whether by locating it in territorial boundaries or by seeking to capture it with images in one way or another.

I wrap up this discussion of identity and dislocation in chapter 12 by returning to the question of martyrdom. I take up a recent reading of martyrdom by Elizabeth Castelli, which argues that the discourse of the martyr arises out of an exercise of collective memory that strives to settle and fix identity and to found static and solidified conceptions of culture. While Castelli is no doubt correct to identify a significant impulse that motivates many common approaches to martyrdom, I offer an alternative reading of martyrdom according to which the figure of the martyr disrupts given cultural forms and unsettles fixed conceptions of identity. I argue that the martyr performs a kind of uncoupling whereby we are dislocated from those identities and cultural formations that we take to be settled and complete.

Instead of a final conclusion that promises to draw all the various strands of this discussion together into some final programmatic statement of a position, I bring these explorations to a close with a sermon. If the task of theology involves ongoing exploration, it might be suggested that the sermon is its proper form. The word that is the sermon is never finished. Its claims, when they are honest, are not final. Rather, the very form of the sermon works theologically against the desire to bring itself to a close. So I offer a sermon that retraces much of the ground previously covered, albeit in a somewhat different way, which in turn may open up some new questions and possible avenues of exploration. It is a sermon for Palm Sunday, a reflection on the triumphal entry as a renunciation of triumphalism. More generally, it is a sermon that speaks of the passion story in terms of the necessity of putting ourselves in question. It is just such a stance of questioning that I have attempted to pursue in the explorations that make up this book.

The Precariousness of Peace

If there is a common theme that winds its way through these essays and thereby serves as a way of linking them together, however imperfectly, it is that peace is essentially precarious. And so I offer a few additional comments on what I take this to mean. This book is an attempt to name a peace that is somehow divided against itself. It reads peace in a way that is always simultaneously for and against peace. It has no stake in defending some generalized account of peace as such. It is thus as much a critique of certain common conceptions of peace as it is an attempt to articulate a theologically meaningful vision of peace. Peace is often understood as a future goal that we might reach. Sometimes it is assumed to name a state of tranquility and security, whether a utopia or a golden age. At other times, it is understood to express a sense of natural harmony or cosmic balance. In general, it is typically assumed that peace somehow articulates a stance that is purified of violence.

But none of these assumptions adequately reflects that particular and peculiar peace that is the peace of Christ. Among other things, such a peace is spoken from a perspective that recognizes that we are always already implicated in some form of violence or another. One such form of violence is the very desire to domesticate peace itself. Far from being a word of simple comfort and confirmation, the peace of Christ is wildly disruptive. It interrupts and explodes our strategies for exercising control over things. It divests us from the schemes of classification we devise to impose and manage order. One significant implication of such a claim is that the peace of Christ cannot be located in something called the realm of the ethical or the political. Or at least it would be misleading to suggest that it is *merely* ethical or political, if by that is meant that it is somehow other than theological and does not pertain to questions of knowledge or of identity. Rather, the peace of Christ inaugurates a transformed way of life that informs all aspects of life, unsettling the temptation to speak of life as a possession we must strive to have a handle on.

In the most general sense, to speak of the precariousness of peace is an attempt to understand peace as a theological category, and in particular in terms of a theology of gift. Such a theological peace defies the capture that is establishment. It cannot be owned, and it is impossible to locate it decisively. Each of these all-too-common desires—for establishment, for ownership, for location—is the expression of a theological failure that seeks to turn the gift of peace into a given that might be secured in some way.

Once again, it is important to emphasize that all of this is but a way of trying to communicate what I think we still have to learn from John Howard Yoder. In particular, it is an attempt to spell out and grapple with the significance of Yoder's claim that Christian theology is not finally the expression of a preference for peace over against violence, at least if that assumes that peace is somehow intelligible apart from theological reflection and display. As Yoder puts it, "What Jesus renounced is not first of all violence, but rather the compulsiveness of purpose that leads the strong to violate the dignity of others. The point is not that one can attain all of one's legitimate ends without using violent means. It is rather that our readiness to renounce our legitimate ends when they cannot be attained by legitimate means itself constitutes our participation in the triumphant suffering of the Lamb."[2]

To speak of a peace that is precarious is equally an attempt to articulate what Yoder means when he emphasizes the disruptive character of seeing history doxologically: "To see history doxologically demands and enables that we appropriate especially/specifically those modes of witness which explode the limits that our own systems impose on our capacity to be illuminated and led."[3]

The essays that follow should be read as attempting to provide just such a discussion. But for now, it is fitting for a theology that claims to refuse the temptation to utter the last word to give the last word to someone else. So I close with yet another of Yoder's claims that animates the very heart of the theological explorations this book sets out to undertake: "That Christian pacifism which has a theological basis in the character of God and the work of Jesus Christ is one in which the calculating link between our obedience and ultimate efficacy has been broken, since the triumph of God comes through resurrection and not through effective sovereignty or assured survival."[4]

Disestablishing Mennonite Theology

—1—

A Precarious People:
The Ambiguity of
Mennonite Identity

I begin with a seemingly paradoxical assertion: contemporary
Mennonite identity is fundamentally precarious. It is inherently at risk,
necessarily vulnerable to dissolution. It might seem to follow from this
that there is no such thing as Mennonite identity at all. But I do not
think such a conclusion is justified, and I shall attempt to explain why.
Such a series of claims no doubt runs the risk of saying simultaneously
too much and too little. It might be read as cutting an inappropriately
wide swath and thus claiming to say far too much. Or it might come
across as so general that it could not possibly be spelled out in any
meaningful way, thereby amounting to little more than annoying
provocation. And yet both of these risks are worth entertaining as I
seek to describe a Mennonite identity that is at once fragile and robust.

What I mean to suggest in speaking of precariousness is that
contemporary discussions of Mennonite identity are marked by
notable contradictions and ambiguities, conflicts and ruptures that,
when pushed, could be used to call into question the very idea of
Mennonite identity itself. For example, a split exists between the
church's mission agencies and those devoted to social justice. While both
do much good and important work, the very fact that we have institu-
tionalized such a division of labor in the church suggests that the care
of the soul is somehow separate from a concern for the body. The result
is an unfortunate separation between theology and ethics.

This division contributes to an all-too-common difficulty in articulating a Mennonite identity. When pressed to clarify what it means to be Mennonite, it does not take much time before many settle on the commitment to peace. We Mennonites all know that we are committed, whether we like it or not, to an ethic of peaceableness. But we have a much more difficult time explaining why we are so committed, or in describing more specifically what the peace we point to looks like. Add to this the perpetual debate concerning the tension between the Anabaptist vision and contemporary Mennonite reality, and it appears that we are in the midst of a full-blown identity crisis. Mennonites are infatuated with the question of identity, and yet we cannot seem to reach any kind of substantial agreement on what it consists in.

Although this disjointed, almost schizophrenic state of affairs is troubling, I also find something profoundly correct about the seemingly interminable debates concerning the nature of Mennonite identity. It is in sorting out the good from the bad aspects of Mennonite precariousness that I locate some of the greatest challenges and opportunities facing the contemporary church.

I have already alluded to the bad, the separation of an ethic of peace from its larger theological context. In terms of Mennonite identity, it is important to recognize that merely pointing to a commitment to peace is hardly sufficient, even though there are some contexts in which it may be a good place to start. There are many different kinds of peace, not all of them equally desirable. One of the more troubling sorts of pacifism is that captured by the metaphors of harmony and ordered stability. The problem is that the rhetoric of harmony suggests ideals of strength, solidity, resolution, and closure. A harmonic conception of peace implies a social order of strongly unified wholes.

A more theologically robust conception of pacifism calls much of this harmonic idea into question. From a theological perspective, peace is rooted in the gracious gift of God in Jesus Christ. It is not a possession to be protected but a radically contingent gift that must be given and received in a spirit of ongoing vulnerability. The peace of Christ does not seek to make itself more secure and stable. It is radically unstable and risky precisely because it exists as gift. Not only does it recognize that there are no final guarantees for the securing of peace, it understands that the pursuit of such guarantees is just another form of violence. Whereas a harmonic outlook tends to define peace negatively, in terms of the absence of conflict, Christian pacifism can expect to encounter more rather than less conflict, as the history of nonviolent martyrs attests. Indeed, the stories in the *Martyrs Mirror* are among the best examples of a theology that resists the kind of disconnection between mission and justice that besets the contemporary church.

But in overcoming this bad sort of precariousness, we might see an opening for a more positive understanding of a fundamentally precarious Mennonite identity. This has everything to do with the riskiness and vulnerability of peace already noted. When peace is understood as a gift, it contains pressures that work against the temptation to define a supremely stable self-identity. It resists a concentric model of identities and communities, and calls for a vulnerable recognition of difference. The pursuit of a stable identity works against the call to remain charitably open to the stranger.

A Christian conception of peace is better captured by metaphors of fluidity and ambiguity than by those of solidity and stability. But this is not an unconstrained openness. It is important to work at defining our identity. It is just that in doing so, we discover forces that work against the tendency to pin it down too decisively, to control it. Put differently, it is good to seek self-defining first principles. But when those first principles are rooted in the peace of Christ, it is also crucial to remember that they are essentially fragile. Such is the paradox of Mennonite identity.

For many, this understanding of identity is essentially negative. It is seen as something we should run from. Discussions about the "Anabaptist vision" and "contemporary Mennonite reality" often proceed as expression of a desire to sharpen up Mennonite identity, to make it more tightly coherent. To borrow a metaphor from the philosopher Stanley Cavell, this experience of Mennonite ambiguity cuts abrasively against us, as if we are being "chafed by our own skin."[1] But I am suggesting that we need not be so chafed. Indeed, I hope to gesture in the chapters that follow toward a way of seeing the value in the essentially precarious faith that defines us.

At its best, the Mennonite church exists as a kind of ongoing political experiment. The church is a social body that is constantly seeking new alternatives to worldly conceptions of power. In this sense, it is important to recognize that the Mennonite church has always existed in the midst of dual pressures toward closure and openness. It is doomed to being simultaneously conservative and liberal. Of course, this is also to say that it can be neither conservative nor liberal. To use more biblical terminology, the church is called to practice binding and loosing.

The problem I see in looking at the contemporary Mennonite church is that some congregations are dedicated practitioners of binding, while others are experts at loosing. Very rarely does one find both in one place. This is yet another form of bad precariousness that becomes possible when theology has become separated from ethics. If we can find a way to overcome these problematic breaks and dualisms, we may be able to recognize the more positive sense of fragmented identities that grows out of the call to love our enemies. If not, we will continue the trend toward being domesticated by the wider world. My hope for the future of the Mennonite church thus turns on the ability to cultivate a more fluid and ambiguous conception of identity. We can only preserve a meaningful understanding of Mennonite identity by losing it in the sense of a faith that is fundamentally precarious.

—2—

Radical Orthodoxy, Radical Reformation: What Might Mennonites and Milbank Learn from Each Other?

The movement known as Radical Orthodoxy springs from a recognition that much contemporary theological reflection, let alone first-order Christian speech, is theologically empty. In particular, it suggests that theology ceases to be theological when it becomes an attempt to make the world safe for theology and theology safe for the world. In doing so, it seeks to diagnose the sense of false humility characteristic of such an approach as but another violent attempt to secure power in a secular landscape of barren positivities. By contrast, Radical Orthodoxy presents itself as an audacious attempt to reclaim the world for theology and to reclaim theology for the world.

Breaking out of the narrow confines theology imposes on itself in its characteristically modern moments, Radical Orthodoxy seeks to recover nothing less than the entire world as the appropriate subject of theological investigation. Radical Orthodoxy articulates a new vision of hope for the world. The scope of its theological vision is daunting, as it seeks a comprehensiveness—"a commitment to all or nothing"[1]—that passes beyond the universal, since it reads the universal as but a moment inscribed within a larger dance with particularity, a duality that is only meaningful against the background of an economy of scarcity, mastery, and control. As it seeks to "read the signs of the times . . . in terms of the grammar of the Christian faith," Radical Orthodoxy is nothing if not unashamedly bold and daringly ambitious.[2]

Radical Orthodoxy flies in the face of any liberal safe-making strategies, making it a risky endeavor. It is risky because it refuses the temptation to anchor theology to a self-legitimating ground of some sort. But this is not a "reactive" sense of risk that assumes conflict to be ontologically basic and seeks control and security in a dangerous situation that always threatens to overwhelm us. Rather, it is a riskiness understood on grounds internal to theology itself. It follows from the logic of creation *ex nihilo* that theology, to be theology, must unhook itself from any external non-theological vehicle designed to guarantee its successful arrival upon some pre-given scene.

The theology of Radical Orthodoxy is one that radically refuses all positivities, all strategic and regulative reductions, whether rationalistic or fideistic, ecclesial or psychological. Any such attempt to ground theology on a neutral footing is finally the expression of a possessive, territorial drive to secure power that contradicts the gratuitous exchange of gift-giving and receiving that is the logic of creation. This attempt to refuse the temptation to tame or domesticate the essential contingency and riskiness of theology makes the work of Radical Orthodoxy bold. Its radicalism is thus perhaps best seen in the sense in which the comprehensiveness and the essential riskiness of theology are brought together, as a master discourse that is at the same time a discourse of non-mastery.[3]

How, then, might Mennonites engage this project? Boldness and audacity are not the sorts of words one usually associates with Mennonites. And yet Mennonite theology also grows out of a vision of theological radicalism that resists the temptation to absolutize itself in some given conception of space and/or time. What is it that Mennonite theology might have to learn from Radical Orthodoxy? How can Mennonites receive the gifts that John Milbank and others associated with the movement have to give?

I shall suggest that Milbank can be used to identify certain problematic tendencies associated with contemporary Mennonite theology. At the same time, however, I shall identify a few critical counter-gifts to be offered in return. A Mennonite theology that has properly learned what Radical Orthodoxy has to teach can in turn offer resources from which to mount a criticism of certain aspects of Milbank's work. Not only is it instructive to read radical reformation against the background of Radical Orthodoxy. It is equally important to read Radical

Orthodoxy against the background of radical reformation. The conception of theological radicalism claimed by both is best understood when each of them properly receives and returns these critical gifts.

What Might Mennonites Learn from Milbank?

Perhaps the most striking feature of contemporary Mennonite theology when it is read against the background of Radical Orthodoxy is its almost systematic evasion of theology. While defenders of Radical Orthodoxy, along with Stanley Hauerwas and others, have warned against the dangers of distinguishing between theology and ethics, Mennonite theology often appears to be based largely on a choice of ethics over against theology. Theology is reduced to an ethic of pacifism that is often appropriately described in the terms used by the political philosopher John Rawls to summarize his theory of justice, namely that it is political, not metaphysical.

Peace is abstracted from its larger theological home, idealized, and turned into a criterion through which to adjudicate all subsequent reflection, theological or otherwise. But this is to do to peace what Duns Scotus and the late-medieval nominalists, on the Radical Orthodoxy reading, have done in elevating being to a higher station over God. Mennonite theological reflection is developed as though it is secondary to a prior non-theological concept—in this case, peace—and therefore ceases to be theological in any meaningful sense. Peace is reinterpreted as a univocal concept, as Mennonites seemingly latch on to any reference to peace, with little or no apparent appreciation of the sense in which the very meaning of peace differs markedly from one variety of pacifism to another. From this perspective, Mennonite theology goes wrong when it focuses too exclusively on the question of peace and violence, as it often does; and in doing so, its discourse on peace is empty of any theological content whatsoever.[4]

At the same time, one often gets the impression that peace is reified and treated statically, as a kind of possession that we Mennonites somehow have privileged access to, such that we are charged with the task of distributing it effectively to others. In Milbank's terms, this is to understand peace as if it exists in an economy of scarcity. Assuming a short supply, such peace becomes interpreted as a more secure investment or insurance against a prior danger.[5] But this is to miss the sense in which Christian theology presumes an economy of generous plenitude and excess. To assert the ontological priority of peace is to see it as an excessive and freely given charitable donation. Christians are thereby called to "cease to be self-sufficient in the face of scarcity" and instead to embody an exchange of gift-giving and receiving that flows out of the excessively gracious self-giving of God. [6]

Put differently, Mennonite theology often seems to operate under a conception of peacemaking that names a process of bringing order to what is disordered in *this* world, whereas for Milbank, peace names a fundamentally different ontology. Christian worship, and in particular the forgiveness of sins, thus constitutes the interruption of a new order—simultaneously a counter-politics and counter-ontology—into the world of the secular.[7]

Most importantly, a theological conception of peace is not reactive. It is not primarily understood as a response to conflict, so we should not speak as if violence is something to be "overcome." Instead of understanding peace as a reaction to violence, Milbank reads the story of creation *ex nihilo* as an alternative vision of the world, which turns on the idea of original peace. Peace is ontologically prior to violence. It cannot be secured, and thus cannot flourish in a capitalist economy of self-interest, debt, scarcity, and contract. Rather, it is at home in an economy of charitable donation and thus exists only as unnecessarily given and received. To participate in Christian worship is to be within a logic of gift-giving and receiving, a generosity of participation in the gracious self-given and excessive reality of God.

Closely related to this, it might be suggested that Mennonite theology has much to learn from Radical Orthodoxy's re-reading of the so-called tradition. Milbank notes that "Radical Orthodoxy, if catholic, is not a specifically Roman Catholic theology. Although it can be espoused by Roman Catholics, it can equally be espoused by those who are formally 'protestant,' yet whose theory and practice essentially accords with the catholic vision of the Patristic period through to the high Middle Ages."[8] And yet Mennonite theology all too often skips directly from the New Testament to the sixteenth century. Or when it does engage this catholic vision, it is often categorically rejected as involving nothing more than an elaborate legitimation of violence. But we do well to remember that patristic and medieval sources are part of our tradition too. In doing so, we might further learn from Milbank and others that we do not have to read patristic and medieval theology as it has been read against the background of the Reformation. Perhaps more accurately, we do not need to read medieval theology against the background of the Enlightenment invention of the distinction between natural and revealed religion or between reason and tradition. In particular, it is not to be read in a way that projects onto it a series of dualities, such as faith and reason, nature and grace, or the spiritual and the political.

Milbank suggests that before the Enlightenment, faith and reason were not the names of essentially distinct realms, but rather differing degrees of intensity of participation in the mind of God.[9] In a similar vein, he shows that the common interpretation that attributes to Aquinas a two-tiered account of nature and grace as distinct stages must give way to an appreciation of the sense in which Aquinas saw nature as always already graced. More generally, the medieval metaphysics of participation and analogy might help resist the tendency to overemphasize peace to the extent that it becomes non-theological, an object or possession to be secured and distributed, as noted above. Discipleship could then be understood, not as a simple copying of Jesus' acts, but rather as a participation in the very body of Christ itself, a body that is simultaneously metaphysical and political.

The third lesson that Mennonites might learn from Radical Orthodoxy draws on Catharine Pickstock's suggestion that Radical Orthodoxy is not to be regarded as "a discrete edifice which purports to be a stronghold" but as "a hermeneutic disposition and a style of metaphysical vision; and it is not so much a 'thing' or 'place' as a task."[10] In particular, it is a hermeneutic of worshipful dispossession or theological deterritorialization. It resists any strategy of "spatialization" that might reduce the gifts of knowledge understood as divine illumination to an objectified given to be secured and protected through a kind of policing of borders.[11] In a similar vein, I want to suggest that it is equally important to understand Radical Reformation as naming a hermeneutic or style rather than a distinct entity or thing. This point has, of course, already been made by John Howard Yoder, but its significance is often missed.

Yoder suggests that Radical Reformation names a certain habit of thinking, a kind of dialogical vulnerability, that cultivates a "constant potential for reformation and in the more dramatic situations a readiness for the reformation even to be 'radical.'"[12] This is equally a style of metaphysical vision that is perhaps best described as apocalyptic, as Stanley Hauerwas has attempted to show by building on Yoder's claim that "people who bear crosses are working with the grain of the universe."[13] Though in different ways, both Radical Orthodoxy and radical reformation name a theological style that refuses the rhetoric of spatialization or self-absolutization and ceases to think of theology as an entity or territory that must be policed through the erection and protection of boundaries.

One of the implications of this understanding is that it becomes rather odd to speak of such a thing as Mennonite theology at all. The characteristic styles of Radical Orthodoxy and radical reformation call into question the assumption of Mennonite theological distinctiveness as resting on concentric habits of thinking, or as grounded in an underlying territorial conception of theological inquiry.[14]

What Might Milbank Learn from Mennonites?

Having just called into question the assumption that there might be such a thing as a distinctively Mennonite theology, I now identify three critical counter-gifts that Mennonites might give to Milbank. Each could suggest that Mennonites might be equipped to learn from Milbank in a way that surpasses what Milbank has learned from himself. The first such gift centers on the voice of the theologian. Despite his call to recast theology as an ecclesial Christian practice, Milbank also privileges the voice of the theologian in a way that suggests a residual commitment to specialization and professionalism. This is a kind of reactive heroism he otherwise calls into question as one more instance of a secular economy of security and possession.

This can be illustrated by contrasting two quotes by Milbank. First, in one of my favorite passages from *Theology and Social Theory,* he writes: "In a rhetorical perspective, the story of the development of the tradition—for example, in the case of Christianity, a story of preachings, journeyings, miracles, martyrdoms, intrigues, sin and warfare—really *is* the argument for the tradition."[15] Second, from the opening lines of *The Word Made Strange,* Milbank suggests that "today, theology is tragically too important," such that "the theologian feels almost that the entire ecclesial task falls on his own head: in the meager mode of reflective words he must seek to imagine what a true practical repetition would look like."[16] This second claim strikingly cancels out the insights of the first. It gives the impression that theology is brought *to* Christian practice and not found anywhere within it, despite whatever flaws it may have.

For all his talk of ecclesial practice, Milbank finally suggests that theology is an intellectual exercise overseen by the theologian. He gives the impression that authority is not internal to practices themselves, but is rather imposed externally from the perspective of an authority figure of some sort who inhabits a theoretical space that transcends the practice in question. By contrast, I see the Radical Reformation as an attempt to understand theology in a way that resists such a basic privileging of the theologian or any such turn to theory, emphasizing rather, the many members who make up the body of Christ. To quote from Yoder once again, "The agent of moral discernment in the doxological community is not a theologian, a bishop, or a pollster, but the Holy Spirit, discerned as the unity of the entire body."[17]

This conception of the unified body turns crucially on the practice of patience, and here I locate a second lesson Milbank might learn from Mennonites. This is a vision of the church as a counter-epistemology that is not preoccupied with epistemic justification. The church practices the epistemological virtue of patience required for genuine engagement with the other in a process of open conversation, often referred to as the Rule of Paul. This mode of knowledge unfolds in fragments and ad hoc alliances, slowly proceeding through the hard work of an open conversation whose parameters cannot be defined prior to a concrete encounter. It seeks to hear all the relevant voices in a conversation and resists the violent tendency to silence anyone by virtue of the way the debate is constructed in advance of actual engagement.

This epistemology resists closure, refusing the lie of the total perspective and the search for a purified form of speech. It recognizes that language about God is not finally limited to our current vocabularies. Moreover, it encourages the active pursuit of conflict in conversation, being willing to engage in self-criticism. In short, this theological inquiry lingers timefully and patiently, resisting the temptation to self-absolutization. Milbank sometimes suggests something similar, as when he writes that "consensus happens, unpredictably, through the blending of differences, and by means of these differences, not despite them."[18]

But at the same time, Millbank exhibits a rhetorical preoccupation with speed of delivery that suggests implicitly the overcoming of patience. This is perhaps best exemplified in the way he differentiates a Christian counter-ontology of peace from a secular ontology of violence by means of the sharp, almost over-general contrasts he draws between their competing logics. It is also exemplified in his tendency to trace everything to the one basic mistake of the Scotist elevation of being over God. I do not suggest that in so doing Milbank does not identify theologically problematic claims. But the way Milbank develops his interpretation as a kind of unrestrained rhetorical hyper-narrative reveals a preoccupation with speed, efficiency, and possessive mastery that he otherwise calls into question.

It is also possible to read Milbank's understanding of pedagogically justified violence from the standpoint of speed. He defends the possible necessity of recourse to violence in "bringing a defaulter to his senses" rather than risk the possibility that this will not happen in ongoing, timeful "open conversation." The value of Mennonite theology—to the extent that it is meaningful to speak of such a thing—is that it proceeds patiently. It enters vulnerably into the world of another, rather than employing an accelerated and possessive hermeneutics of mastery and control.

There is a lingering commitment to instrumental causality that appears in Milbank's work despite his thoroughgoing rejection of instrumentalism as one of the defining features of secular reason. Particularly interesting from the perspective of Mennonite theology is how this appeal to instrumental causality tends to appear at precisely those moments where Milbank argues that an ontology of peace does not entail a commitment to pacifism. For example, he writes, "The *purpose* of ecclesial coercion is peace" and suggests that violence can be justified insofar as it "contribute[s] to the *final goal* of peace."[19]

Claims such as these suggest that pedagogical coercion is justified because it is effective in bringing about an independently specifiable end. Accordingly, there is a sense in which Milbank's rhetoric underwrites a securing of agreement that conflicts with his account of consensus arising through an exchange of difference. Equally striking is that at crucial points, Milbank is rather silent about the activity of God. As noted above, much of his theology turns on an account of *poesis* as human participation in the creative activity of God. But when discussing the possibility of ecclesial violence and the cultivation of peace, it sounds curiously as if the "fate of the counter-kingdom" falls squarely on human shoulders.

Milbank argues that "one way to secure peace is to draw boundaries around 'the same,' and exclude 'the other'; to promote some practices and disallow alternatives. Most polities, and most religions, characteristically do this. But the Church has misunderstood itself when it does likewise."[20] In this he is exactly right. But my concern is that his discussion of pedagogical coercion and legitimate violence sounds too much like just this kind of ecclesial failure.

A commitment to nonviolence need not be to "fetishize freedom," as Milbank appropriately worries it might.[21] Nonviolence is best read as an attempt to take more seriously the possibility of participating, however imperfectly, in God's gratuitous economy of peaceable plentitude and excess. It is one thing to recognize retrospectively that we are always already implicated in some form of violence, and to struggle collectively to disentangle ourselves—or rather, open ourselves to the possibility of being disentangled—from it. It is quite another thing, however, to justify in advance the enactment of violence as bringing about a certain desired effect, even one as important as the truth about God. For the most profound truth about God—and that which Christian nonviolence most significantly turns on—is that God's continued survival is not dependent on us.

So the Mennonite commitment to nonviolence might serve as a third lesson, despite the fact that it has so often been interpreted in a manifestly untheological way. It represents an ongoing commitment to just the kind of ecclesial practice that might itself be the most profound argument for the tradition, an argument that is significant precisely in that it does not seek to secure itself by invoking the heroic voice of the theologian.

The Risk of Mennonite Theology

In conclusion, I return to the themes of comprehensiveness and risk with which this discussion began. Mennonites have often understood themselves to be somehow necessarily at odds with boldness and comprehensiveness, but here we have misunderstood ourselves. On the contrary, it might be suggested that a Mennonite commitment to practicing nonviolence exemplifies an even more thoroughgoing commitment to the comprehensiveness of all or nothing. Our theology does not have the safety net of an appeal to coercive violence to fall back on when consensus does not happen through the unpredictable blending of differences.

In a similar vein, Mennonite theology appropriately embodies the essential riskiness of a theological vision. Its appreciation of theological riskiness can be seen in its refusal of the temptation to make Christianity necessary, and in its embodiment of an ethos of conversational vulnerability that cultivates a readiness for radical reformation. Thus, in a sense, a radical reformation stance turns out to display just the kind of radicalism called for by Radical Orthodoxy—sometimes more consistently than the defenders of Radical Orthodoxy themselves. But it is important to recognize that the apparent sense of accomplishment captured in such claims comes at a price. For such a reading of the radical reformation can only be sustained when it stops focusing too exclusively on violence and peace *as such* and understands peace in more substantively theological and ontological terms. Among other things, this calls into question the very idea of a distinctive Mennonite theology to be articulated and defended in the first place.

—3—

Mennonites and Narrative Theology:
The Case of John Howard Yoder

One of the more significant outcomes of Harold Bender's now classic statement of the "Anabaptist Vision" at the American Society of Church History in 1943 has been its ability to generate interest in the question of a specifically Anabaptist and Mennonite theology.[1] Indeed, Bender might be credited with having established the very idea of a Mennonite theology, at least in the sense of an academic and broadly systematic theological vision to be situated alongside other denominational voices. And although Bender is to be credited with creating a space for Mennonite voices in the larger theological conversation, this is a dubious, or at any rate ambiguous, legacy. In short, it leaves us with the burden of having to articulate and defend something called "Mennonite theology," a roughly homogenous whole whose boundaries are in need of policing in some way. It tempts us to think of Mennonite theology in terms of a set of criteria designed to determine who's in and who's out. To put it bluntly, methodology becomes a substitute for ecclesiology.

In the previous chapters I have argued that such a territorial orientation exists in tension with other non-territorial impulses of the Anabaptist and Mennonite tradition. I claimed that some of the more important aspects of Mennonite theology are those that militate against the very idea of a specifically Mennonite theology. This leaves us in the precarious position of having to be simultaneously for and against Mennonite theology. In this chapter I take up this theme of the ambiguity of Mennonite theology by examining Mennonite interest in the category of narrative that dominated much of the discussion among

Mennonite theologians at the end of the twentieth century.[2] Although no firm consensus emerged, many Mennonite theologians seemed, for a time, to agree that the category of narrative captures in a meaningful way many of the characteristic emphases of the Anabaptist Mennonite tradition. Indeed, it often appeared that the burden of proof lay with those who would question the value of narrative.

In the context of these discussions about Mennonites and narrative theology, the work of John Howard Yoder figures prominently. The work of Yoder was appealed to more than any other Mennonite theologian in order to provide support for the claim that Mennonite theology is best understood as a version of narrative theology. However, aside from the significant presence of his voice in the work of Stanley Hauerwas,[3] Yoder is conspicuously absent in the work of others commonly associated with the movement of narrative theology, such as Hans Frei, George Lindbeck, Ronald Thiemann, William Placher, and, more recently, Gerard Loughlin.[4] Similarly, it is important to note that Yoder did not himself enthusiastically embrace the label of narrative theologian. At the same time, he did not explicitly eschew it either. In light of this complicated set of dynamics, an explanation of the relationship between Yoder and the narrative theologians is in order.

This chapter is an attempt to provide such an explanation, and in so doing to address the larger question of the nature and possibility of a specifically Mennonite theology. In short, I shall argue that Yoder's ambiguous stance regarding narrative, his apparent willingness to be simultaneously for and against narrative theology, is crucial to the very heart of his theology. Moreover, I shall suggest that this ambiguous style has everything to do with Yoder's approach to the question of a specifically Mennonite theology. I will develop such a reading of Yoder and others by way of an examination of the relationship between the category of narrative and questions of ecclesiology, of what it might mean for the church to be the church.

At the outset, it is important to acknowledge that others have raised questions about the suitability of narrative as a category for expressing Anabaptist-Mennonite theological commitments. What separates my argument from this group, however, is that I raise concerns about narrative theology for precisely the opposite kinds of reasons. Stated briefly, the standard case against narrative theology tends to locate Yoder in continuity with the movement of narrative theology. It argues that both are problematic because they are too particularistic, and hence sectarian and insular. Narrative is thus supplanted in favor of a more universal, often humanistic move in the direction of something called public theology.[5] In contrast, I suggest that narrative theology is problematic from a Mennonite perspective because it is *insufficiently* particularistic. But this particularity does not render Mennonite theology sectarian or insular for reasons that have been most adequately articulated by Yoder.

The Rise of Narrative Theology: A Polemical Overview

In providing an account of the characteristic emphases of narrative theology, it is appropriate to begin with Hans Frei's *The Eclipse of Biblical Narrative*. Frei's appeal to the category of narrative is best described as an attempt to claim integrity on behalf of the text itself. He sets out to rescue the Bible from its subservience to external or extra-biblical interpretive and justificatory categories, such as authorial intent or actual historical fact, to which it had been subject since the rise of critical exegesis in the eighteenth century. In doing so, Frei claims that there is no intelligible distinction to be made between the biblical narrative and its proper subject matter. He argues in support of the revival of the genre of "realistic narrative" that closes the gap between stories and the lived reality they represent by envisioning the world as itself informed or absorbed by the biblical story.[6]

Frei can be seen as defending a New Critical conception of textual essentialism or absolutism, according to which meaning is located solely in some conception of the text itself.[7] Although it is said that Frei's later work is marked by a greater appreciation for the church as the proper context in which the Bible is to be read,[8] it nevertheless appears that the role of the church in biblical hermeneutics is much less significant than some of his defenders claim. In short, Frei's appeal to the church amounts to the claim that the church reads the Bible as a narrative unity. In other words, the church functions merely to provide an example of a theoretical conception of biblical narrative that has been defined in abstraction from the practices of the church itself. This is suggested in Frei's claim that "the literal sense is the paradigmatic form of such intertextual interpretation in the Christian community's use of its scripture."[9]

But while this claim places a greater emphasis on the church than Frei had in his earlier work, he still does not accord a significant role to the church in the actual process of interpretation itself. Rather, when he appeals to the practices of the church it is at a second-order level, in order to justify his understanding of the integrity of the text itself. Thus, it seems that Frei's understanding of narrative remains, in the end, a theoretical version of textual absolutism.

Others have followed Frei's lead in turning to the category of narrative as an alternative to some alleged errors of modernity. However, while Frei's defense of narrative is undertaken primarily in the context of the question of biblical hermeneutics, subsequent discussions have expanded the appeal to narrative to address other areas of theological inquiry as well. Perhaps the most widespread of these more extended applications turns to narrative in order to consider methodological and epistemological issues. Such an approach is similar to Frei's anti-apologetic stance in that it resists the subordination of the Christian narrative to external sources.

One favorite example given in support of the narrative approach is to suggest that epistemological foundationalism is an inappropriate methodology for Christian theology. In particular, narrative theologians oppose the tendency to privilege certain categories that lie outside the Christian tradition, such as experience or natural reason.[10] Instead, relying heavily on the work of the American philosopher W. V. O. Quine, narrative conceptions of theological method defend a version of epistemological holism or coherentism.[11] According to a coherentist theory of knowledge, epistemic justification does not consist in an appeal to external sources, but is rather a function of that which is "internal to the Christian framework."[12]

Narrative epistemology understands justification in terms of the interrelationship of coherence among the system of beliefs that constitute the Christian faith.[13] Although its understanding of narrative is less exclusively restricted to the Bible, it is nevertheless closely related to Frei's account of the integrity of the text. In both cases, the emphasis is on the internal logic of the narrative itself.

One of the more significant moves beyond Frei by those who seek to develop a narrative epistemology is to place greater emphasis on the role of the church. In short, the turn to the church is offered as a corrective to the idealism or intellectualism reflected in the appeal to narrative considered in its own right. But as with the work of Frei himself, it is not clear that the appeal to the church ends up making the difference it is said to make. For example, Thiemann argues that the primary context for the meaning of theological concepts is supplied by their "use in Christian community."[14] At the same time, however, he places so much emphasis on the internal logic of the "web of interrelated *beliefs*"[15] that it sounds like the church is merely a vehicle for the transmission of a narrative whose justification is somehow independent of actual ecclesial practices.

Perhaps the most significant account of the role of the church in the context of narrative epistemology is provided by George Lindbeck's cultural-linguistic theory of doctrine, which stresses the primacy of the church as the communal context in which Christian theology gains its intelligibility.[16] However, it has recently been argued that even Lindbeck significantly undervalues the role of the church.[17] In particular, Gerard Loughlin has suggested that Lindbeck distinguishes between doctrinal form and content in a way that presupposes "an unstatable proposition which underwrites the equivalency of formulations,"[18] and which suggests that "creed and Scripture, rule and text," or in other words narrative and ecclesiological practice, are ultimately not mutually constitutive of one another in the way Lindbeck claims.[19]

In a similar vein, Lindbeck's rhetoric often implies what might be called a "derivative" ecclesiology, whereby a conception of church is somehow derived *from* Scripture. This suggests both a priority and a finality of the biblical narrative, each of them equally reductive, such that the church merely proceeds from the story of Christ rather than being somehow co-inherent with the story itself.[20] Thus, as with Frei's appeal to the category of narrative within the context of biblical hermeneutics, it appears that, despite some initial appearances to the contrary, the primary significance of narrative epistemology consists in an idealist or theoretical appeal to the integrity of the story as an entity unto itself.

A similar claim to move beyond theory is often thought to be reflected in the work of those who have appealed to the category of narrative in order to develop an account of personal identity. According to a narrative interpretation of identity, persons are not atomistic individuals made up of a series of isolated actions, ideas, or events. Rather, personal identity is itself structured as a narrative unity. That is to say, one's identity consists in the larger narrative that tells the story of one's life. For example, as Frei suggested in the context of a discussion of the identity of Jesus, "a person's identity is constituted (not simply illustrated) by that intention which he carries into an action," the sequence of which is best captured by narrative.[21] Similarly, Michael Root has suggested that action and identity are intelligible only in the context of a "web of interlocking patterns" that in turn must be displayed in the larger context of a narrative account of a life lived as a whole.[22] In short, it is suggested that a narrative interpretation of identity is able to preserve concrete individuality without reducing it to mere subjective ideas and experiences.

Again, it is important to raise the question of social location at this point, and in particular the role of the church. Among those who have appealed to the category of narrative in developing accounts of identity, the emphasis on concrete social location is perhaps most clearly associated with the work of Hauerwas. However, it is instructive to note that while Hauerwas has come to place greater emphasis on embodiment in concrete relationships such as friendship or ecclesiology more specifically, this comes at the same time that the category of narrative has seen a more diminished role in his theology. Nevertheless, within the larger movement of narrative theology, such identity-constituting stories are presented as somehow sufficient and left to stand alone. Once again, story seems to exist in abstraction from any sort of concrete ecclesial instantiation.

Mennonites and Narrative Theology

Although many of these same emphases can be found in Mennonite discussions of narrative theology, they nevertheless take on a somewhat different shape as a result of the need to emphasize such characteristic Anabaptist emphases as discipleship, peace, and the church. First, one notes that Mennonite discussions of narrative theology are deeply rooted in the narrative of Jesus as the normative story for the Christian faith.[23] This is not to suggest that the more mainstream accounts of narrative theology pay no attention to the story of Jesus.[24] Nevertheless, the normativity of the Jesus story is given a central place in the Mennonite appeal to narrative theology, whereas the wider movement of narrative theology is less exclusively preoccupied with matters of Christology. In a related manner, Mennonite discussions of narrative theology tend to place a greater emphasis on response to the story, in particular by means of an appeal to the notion of discipleship. For example, whereas Thiemann emphasizes that "the structure, content, and fulfillment of a promise depend *solely* on the initiative of the promiser,"[25] J. Denny Weaver stresses the ethical implications of the Jesus story, claiming that the "narrative identifies Jesus in a way which makes discipleship an inherent dimension of identifying with Jesus."[26]

This might be put differently by reflecting on the status of particular doctrinal emphases within the discussion of narrative theology. From the perspective of Mennonite theology, it is significant to note that narrative theology tends to neglect such characteristic Anabaptist themes as a christologically rooted pacifism and an account of apocalyptic eschatology that stresses an important distinction between church and world. Rather, it appears that those who defend a narrative understanding of doctrine tend more toward the mainstream than a Mennonite theology would be comfortable with. For example, while Lindbeck's cultural-linguistic theology might appear compatible with an apocalyptic distinction between church and world at some levels, his discussion is nevertheless haunted by persistent concern not to ghettoize theology. He takes pains to avoid a separatist theology by stressing that the kind of linguistic competence he is defending is to be "sought in the mainstream."[27]

Perhaps the most significant Mennonite appeal to narrative theology is reflected in its concerns for particularity, difference, and otherness, especially as they are understood against the background of a distinction between church and world. In short, Mennonite discussions of narrative theology tend to stress the otherness of the church, claiming that it is informed by a narrative that is fundamentally different than that of the world.[28] Although this bears some affinity to the kind of anti-apologetic stance emphasized by Frei, Mennonite accounts of narrative theology are typically more attentive to the concrete ecclesiological implications of such claims to narrative particularity. For example, Harry Huebner has suggested that the narrative of Jesus constitutes an alternative story with ecclesiological implications, so that the "key task of the church *vis-à-vis* the nation is to speak its own language, re-narrate its own story, re-member its own savior and re-embody its own ontology of peace and justice."[29]

Although a concern for particularity makes narrative theology attractive for some contemporary Mennonite theologians, it is also the primary focus of objections in other Mennonite discussions of narrative theology. As noted above, the standard Mennonite objection to narrative theology claims that it is precisely such particularity that renders it dangerously sectarian and insular.[30] In short, it is suggested that narrative theology is so concerned with protecting its own story that it results in the oppressive exclusion of others. For example, Scott Holland has suggested that "it is not enough for the theologian to master the stories of her religion's canon; she must be attentive to the plots and narrative turns in the other's story even as she attempts to write her community's evolving story."[31]

It is argued that narrative theology has reinforced a tendency to privilege the particular character of the church in a way that is theologically problematic. Implicit in such objections to the Mennonite appeal to narrative theology is the claim that the traditional Anabaptist distinction between church and world ought not to be understood in the particularistic sense that those influenced by narrative theology take it to be. Instead of stressing the particularity of the church as an entity distinct from the world, the standard objection argues for the importance of a more public theology, which sees the church as one body among others.[32] Arguing in favor of such a position, Duane Friesen claims that it is not enough to "simply repeat the Christian narrative and urge the practice of virtues that follow from that narrative."[33] Rather, he maintains, "if Christians are not to be sectarian, they must enter the arena of rational discourse with persons of other viewpoints, employing the analysis of whatever academic or practical discipline is appropriate in speaking to the issues confronted in the *polis*."[34]

I mean at this point only to highlight the fact that the question of theological and ecclesiological particularity is a prominent one within contemporary Mennonite theological circles, underlying the arguments both for and against the appeal to narrative theology. The key to the resolution of this debate no doubt turns significantly on the question of how to interpret the eschatological distinction between church and world. In the remainder of this chapter, I shall attempt to shed some light on this matter by bringing these discussions of narrative theology into conversation with Yoder.

Yoder as Narrative Theologian?

Turning to the theology of Yoder, it is appropriate to begin by noting his various explicit references to the terminology of "narrative" or "story," since it is to these that one might appeal in order to make a case for characterizing Yoder as a representative of narrative theology. Here we find Yoder at times endorsing the category of narrative, at times questioning it, and often situating himself somewhere in between. In what is perhaps his strongest endorsement of the category of narrative, Yoder suggests that the character of the church's self-understanding is to be understood as narrative rather than deductive.[35] As Yoder himself puts it, "The narrative quality of the church's doing ethics provides both that the decision shall always be in the situation and that the moment of decision shall never be isolated but rather finds itself oriented and, in fact, driven along by the momentum of the memories of the communal story."[36]

Similarly, Yoder uses the terminology of narrative to stress the retrospective character of ecclesial rationality, claiming that the church's "procedures of evaluation come after, not before, assent. They operate within the community's story, not from Athens or 'from nowhere.'"[37] At the same time, however, Yoder often uses the terminology of "narrative" in a much more cautious and ambiguous sense. For example, after noting the contingent and historical sense of the Evangel, or Good News, he recognizes that "it is often narrative too," but quickly adds a cautionary warning, stressing that "to make much of that as a special additional issue in our contemporary discussion would be a red herring."[38] Finally, there are cases in which Yoder raises explicit objections to the category of narrative. For example, he argues that it is wrong to claim that "less liberal words" (such as "narrative," "virtue," and "community") are "safer from abuse" than such "worldly" terms as "egalitarianism" or "freedom" that he sees fit to use on certain occasions.[39] Similarly, he objects to the sense in which the category of narrative tends to become a "new kind of universal," whereby it is claimed that there are "narrative forms, lying deeper than the ordinary events and sufficient to explain them."[40]

Taking all of these references together, it is evident that Yoder exhibits a pragmatic willingness to use the terminology of narrative or story in certain cases. Nevertheless, he resists appealing to the general category of narrative and according it primacy in a way that is more characteristic of those associated with the narrative theology movement. In order to more properly explain Yoder's relationship to narrative theology, however, it is necessary to move beyond his explicit references to the terminology of narrative to a more extensive consideration of his theology as a whole so as to contrast it with the account of narrative theology provided above.

Perhaps the most recurring theme in Yoder's theology is his depiction and critique of "Constantinianism." In short, Yoder argues that the history of Christianity must be read in light of a deep and lasting,

though often subtle, shift that took place with respect to the relationship between church and world, and which he claims is best associated
with the reign of Constantine.[41] Whereas pre-Constantinian Christianity was that of a minority church existing in a world that was largely
hostile toward it, Yoder claims that the Constantinian shift resulted in
an alignment of the church with the ruling political regime of the day.[42]
In other words, Constantinianism represents a fusion of church and
state, clergy and emperor, Bible and sword, God and civil authorities,
or the general continuity of Christianity with the wider world. As
Yoder himself describes it, the structure of Constantinianism is rooted
in the "basic axiom" that "the true meaning of history, the true locus
of salvation, is in the cosmos and not in the church. What God is really
doing is being done primarily through the framework of society as a
whole and not in the Christian community."[43]

It is important to recognize the sense in which Yoder identifies the
Constantinian temptation as existing even in a supposedly post-
Constantinian context, in which the church is officially separate from
the state. Short of the actual institutional alignment of church and
state, Yoder claims that Constantinianism continues where there is
merely a formal identification of the church with the prevailing political
establishment, as in American public discourse. It is equally present
when the church is enlisted in support of a program of deseculariza-
tion, as in the "people's democracies" of Eastern Europe. And one
hears echoes of Constantinianism where eschatological hope is construed
in terms of the triumph of some future regime, as in certain Latin
American neo-Marxist revolutionaries.[44]

What is characteristic of all these strategies is that they compromise the lordship of Christ by identifying God's cause in some way
with the powers of the political establishment.[45] Accordingly, Yoder
calls for the church to resist such a Constantinian temptation by
embodying the counter-establishment character and corresponding
critical stance called for by the "politics of Jesus." He maintains that it
is only through its concrete presence as an alternative community that
the church can truly serve as a witness to the world.[46]

While most commentators appropriately recognize the essentially
political character of Yoder's account Constantinianism, his discussion
of what might be called "epistemological" or "methodological" Constantinianism is often overlooked. But the tendency to neglect this
aspect of his work risks giving rise to a significant misunderstanding of

his theology as a whole. Indeed, Yoder would resist the very distinction between the political and the epistemological itself, attributing it to just the kind of establishment stance that serves to relativize the concrete significance of Jesus.[47] In other words, he suggests that such methodological dualisms are themselves the product of the Constantinian privileging of the wider wisdom.

Along with the rise of such distinctions as that between the visible and invisible church, Yoder claims that the Constantinian shift also lies behind such characteristic dualisms as nature and grace, internal and external, collective and individual, and public and private.[48] But given the profoundly counter-establishment stance of the church, Yoder maintains that a non-Constantinian approach must challenge the very terms of the debate which set the stage for discussions within mainline theology.[49] He refers to this sort of stance as a rejection of "methodologism." Yoder defines methodologism as a theoretical or meta-level approach whereby theology is understood as having primarily to do with the question of the proper elucidation of and interrelationship between an allegedly agreed upon collection of central concepts or loci. In addition, methodologism assumes that such concepts can in principle be justified to anyone on the basis of the internal logic of the system itself.[50] The methodologist thus inhabits what the philosopher Thomas Nagel has called "the view from nowhere."

In contrast to such an approach, Yoder claims that the concrete body of the church precedes any methodology or epistemology, since there is no non-neutral or non-particular place from which to produce a general method or system. As Yoder himself puts it, "The life of the community is prior to all possible methodological distillations."[51] Raising the stakes even higher, he claims that meta-level appeals to method or system always run the risk of a particular form of idolatry, which restricts the recognition of God to a particular terminology.[52]

Although his rejection of methodologism has obvious affinities with the recent movement in moral philosophy that has come to be known as "anti-theory,"[53] it is more appropriate to see Yoder as rejecting the options of both theory and anti-theory. Against the theorists, he refuses to detach ethical concepts from concrete social practices. But he denies that such an emphasis on the priority of ethical practices entails the rejection of higher order reflection on practices altogether, as anti-theorists typically conclude. This is perhaps most clearly suggested by Yoder's claim that theology is to be located first of all within the concrete practices of the church community. It need not take the form of a formally coherent system and does not presuppose a prior method. Rather, Yoder suggests that theology is an ad hoc or fragmentary enterprise, always perpetually on the way, addressing individual problems as they arise.[54]

Methodological reflection is useful only as it is rooted in specific practices of the church and constrained by the question of whether those practices faithfully embody practices of Christian discipleship. Or as Yoder himself puts it, "Methodological analysis is helpful to illuminate problems of structure, but it is not the prerequisite for the community's right or capacity to reason morally."[55] To emphasize the prior significance of methodology would be to compromise the church's primary call simply to be the body of Christ.

So far, Yoder's account of the church has remained largely in the background. But in order to more fully appreciate his non-Constantinian theology, it is important to examine his ecclesiology more specifically. Perhaps the most significant aspect of Yoder's understanding of the church in the present discussion is his claim that the church is a sociological, cultural, and political entity in its own right.[56] In contrast to logic he finds implicit in H. Richard Niebuhr's typology in *Christ and Culture,* Yoder claims that the distinction between church and world does not imply that the church is somehow to be contrasted with culture, or that one is political and the other is not. Rather, he insists that the church constitutes a new cultural option, a different kind of politics.[57]

Too often, it seems, the political character of the church is compromised in the name of an eschatology that postpones the concrete instantiation of the body of Christ, awaiting the promise of some future fulfillment. But Yoder's apocalyptic eschatology of church and world heightens rather than lessens the political and embodied character of the church. Pointing to the missionary function of the church, he suggests that it is to be a model or foretaste of God's plan for all of creation. He argues that the Christian eschatological vision consists in the character of the faithful Christian community.[58] In other words, Yoder contends, "the church is called to be now what the world is called to be ultimately."[59]

Yoder claims that the church is called to embody specific practices that together define its character as a particular kind of political community. To take just one example, Yoder notes that the practice of breaking bread together is an "act of economic ethics."[60] It is not merely a symbolic or memorial act, but rather, it is a central practice of the Christian body by which its members are banded together in a form of economic solidarity that transcends individualism and the notion of private property.[61] In other words, such an economic ethics is not derived *from* the Eucharist. Rather, Yoder stresses that "bread eaten together *is* economic sharing."[62] The Christian community is a sharing community precisely because it is defined in part by the practice of breaking bread together.

Another important ecclesial practice that Yoder takes to define the character of the church is that of reading Scripture. Although Yoder often emphasizes that his conception of the church is grounded in Scripture, he nevertheless denies that the biblical text is an autonomous entity that somehow stands alone.[63] Similarly, he denies that ecclesiology can simply be derived or abstracted *from* Scripture, as though it were somehow just there, waiting to be recognized by any unidentified reader. Rather, he claims that the Bible is ecclesiologically mediated, such that it can only be said to have meaning, let alone exist in the first place, within the context of the church.[64] In particular, he emphasizes the sense in which the church exists as a "hermeneutic community" in which the Bible is read and appropriated by the gathered community.[65] In a manner reminiscent of the version of reader-response criticism associated with Stanley Fish, Yoder states:

> To speak of the Bible apart from people reading it and apart from the specific questions those people reading need to answer is to do violence to the very purpose for which we have been given the Holy Scriptures. There is no such thing as an isolated word of the Bible carrying meaning in itself. It has meaning only when it is read by someone and then only when that reader and the society in which he or she lives can understand the issue to which it speaks.[66]

Yoder argues that the interpretation of Scripture is a communal exercise that is properly located in the context of the church. In other words, he denies that the enterprise of reading Scripture can be undertaken by just anyone in any particular context. Rather, the reading of Scripture is a disciplined activity, according to which readers must have been properly initiated by receiving prior training in the particular practices of the church, such as binding and loosing, or that of breaking bread discussed above. As Yoder himself puts it, "Only one who is committed to the direction of obedience can read the truth so as to interpret it in line with the direction of God's purposes."[67]

If it is misleading to suggest that Yoder derives his conception of the church *from* Scripture, it is equally problematic to claim that he moves from the church as a hermeneutic community *to* the Bible. There is no such causal relationship running in either direction according to which either term may be identified as primary to and productive of the other. Rather, Yoder takes church and Scripture to be fundamentally interdependent. Whereas the faithful community may be rooted in Scripture, it is equally the case that Scripture has no existence apart from the church that contextualizes and continues to embody it. Bible and church do not name a series of discrete entities, each with its own autonomous ontological status. On the contrary, it is more appropriate to see them as interparticipatory or mutually constitutive.

Closely related to Yoder's account of the interrelationship between church and Scripture is his understanding of Christian discipleship. Building on his rejection of the claim that the Bible can simply be read as though it were somehow intelligible in and of itself, Yoder argues that the understanding of Scripture consists in its performance or dramatic enactment. Quoting from the early Anabaptist writing of Hans Denk, he claims that a person cannot know Christ unless one also follows after him in life.[68] Indeed, it might be suggested that Yoder's work as a whole is based on the assumption that it is problematic to separate questions of Christology from the life of Christian discipleship.

Yoder is suggesting that Scripture is inseparable from the collective performance and practices of the members of the Christian community.[69] That is to say, the church provides the stage on which the biblical story is animated through the lives of its members. Again, it is important to recognize that Yoder's understanding of discipleship is not to be rendered in terms of a fundamental causal relationship. No deep gap exists between Christ and his followers that must be bridged with some kind of causal explanation. To be a disciple is not to live a life that is patterned after or that merely corresponds to the *example* of Christ. Rather, discipleship consists in a kind of sacramental or liturgical participation in the very body of Christ itself. Similarly, Yoder claims that there is no deeper category such as "humanity" to which patterns of discipleship are somehow added. On the contrary, for Christians, discipleship is itself ontologically basic.[70] No collection of abstract principles might be derived from the example of Christ and consequently applied to the lives of individual Christians. Rather, discipleship is the concretely and corporately embodied participation in the very particular shape of God's plan as revealed in the incarnation of God in Christ.

In spite of Yoder's emphasis on particularity and the otherness of the church, however, he insists that his account of a non-Constantinian theology is not sectarian. In particular, he has argued, against those who would charge him with sectarianism, that the category of sectarian is itself the product of "the standard epistemological context of establishment."[71] More specifically, Yoder claims that those who advance the sectarian objection, such as James Gustafson, endorse a methodological framework that forces a zero-sum choice between sectarian authenticity and public intelligibility.[72] What is problematic about such a methodology, however, is that it presupposes the existence of a unitary and universally accessible system of evaluative criteria. Or at the very least it assumes that there is a single public arena for debate.[73] Against such an assumption, Yoder maintains that the very idea of the public is itself a particular standpoint, representing a "view from somewhere," and thus laden with its own distinctive presuppositions. In Yoder's own words, "There is no 'public' that is not just another particular province."[74] Yet Yoder's critique of establishment epistemology tends to be obscured by those who advance the sectarian objection, as they focus on his understanding of "political" non-Constantinianism in abstraction from the kind of "methodological" non-Constantinianism discussed above. Accordingly, those who charge Yoder with sectarianism end up simply begging the question, criticizing him by reproducing the very standpoint that he explicitly rejects. Unless it meets his account of "methodological" non-Constantinianism head-on, such an objection remains ultimately beside the point.

But even if the sectarian objection did not beg the question against Yoder's rejection of establishment epistemology, it is still significantly flawed, since his theology does not "exclude the other" as his objectors claim. First, he has consistently stressed the missiological sense in which the church is "for the world."[75] Second, Yoder argues that it is one of the marks of the Constantinian shift that the outsider is no longer privileged as "the test of whether one loves one's neighbor."[76] And he defends the radicalism of Christian love over against such a

Constantinian stance, claiming that Jesus redefines the very notion of "neighbor" to include enemies and outsiders. Not only does Constantinianism dissolve the outsider by turning to the sword in order to make the church into "everyone,"[77] but so-called public theology appears to betray a Constantinian temptation by stipulating and policing the terms of "public" debate under the guise of "neutrality." With his understanding of the concrete and embodied character of the Christian community, however, Yoder does not have to provide guarantees that all will necessarily speak a common language.[78] Indeed, there are no such guarantees, and there may be times when meaningful communication is not possible. But that is to be expected if language is indeed the kind of value-laden and community-dependent thing that sociologists, linguists, and philosophers of language have for years been telling us it is.

It might be argued that it is Yoder, rather than those who defend a nonsectarian account of public theology, who holds a more significant respect for the "otherness" of "the other." In stark contrast to Yoder's emphasis on concreteness and embodied specificity, the defenders of public theology continually appeal to the general category of otherness and the abstract terminology of alterity in such a way that it is never clear who in particular it is that is being named as "other." Although he may be more forthcoming and honest about exactly where he is located, Yoder's theology does not preclude dialogue with the other. Rather, it gives the other a name and recognizes her or his particularity in a way that is the first mark of genuine conversation.

Reconsidering Yoder's Relationship to Narrative Theology

In order to address the question of Yoder's relationship to narrative theology more specifically, it might be helpful to highlight some of the main points suggested by the preceding juxtaposition of their respective positions. While it might be claimed that they share a common opponent, namely the "apologetic" nature of much modern theology that seeks to authenticate itself by means of an appeal to external, non-theological sources, there are nevertheless significant differences that remain. First, whereas narrative theologians such as Frei appeal to the category of narrative in order to defend the integrity of the text itself, Yoder is critical of such versions of textual absolutism. He argues instead for the mutual constitution of church and Scripture. In contrast to a narrative conception of biblical hermeneutics in which Scripture might be said to stand alone, Yoder denies the possibility of abstracting the Bible from the church.

Moreover, his understanding of discipleship draws attention to the importance of dramatic enactment or performance of biblical hermeneutics, which is all too often missing in narrative theology.

Whereas narrative theology stresses the intelligibility of the biblical narrative in and of itself, Yoder's understanding of the hermeneutic community requires active participation by the members of the body of Christ. The story of Christ cannot neatly be separated from those actors who participate in, and in fact partially constitute, his very body. Accordingly, he would be equally critical of the narrative interpretation of personal identity. For Yoder, identity does not consist merely in the story of one's life, but rather it involves a concrete interconnectedness in embodied social relationships. In other words, his understanding of the nature of the church suggests that identity is itself partly constituted by participation in ecclesiological practices and the relationships with others that such practices both require and sustain.

Also, among those who claim to move narrative theology beyond its origins in the context of biblical hermeneutics, there remains an emphasis on the internal logic of the story. This itself ends up sounding rather abstract in comparison with Yoder's understanding of theology as situated within the context of the church. Whereas Yoder might share with narrative theology the rejection of epistemological foundationalism, his account of non-Constantinian theology is not merely anti-foundationalist but rather might be said to reject the enterprise of epistemology altogether. In other words, he is equally as critical of the appeal to coherent systems or webs of interrelated beliefs that narrative theologians defend as he is of the axiomatic and deductive hierarchies of foundationalism. Thus, from the perspective of Yoder, narrative theology simply reproduces the methodologist stance, defending the narrative structure of the Christian story in abstraction from the concrete practices of the embodied church. The problem with narrative theology is not that it is too particular, as the defenders of public theology claim. Rather, from a Yoderian standpoint, narrative theology is problematic to the extent that it is insufficiently particular, standing above, or perhaps beside, but in any case not adequately rooted in the life of the church.

Finally, given Yoder's understanding of the apocalyptic distinction between church and world, it is important to question the sense in which narrative theology might remain too close to the so-called mainstream. Methodologically speaking, it appears that narrative theology is closely wedded to establishment epistemology, since coherentism or some other form of holism is currently one of the more preferred positions among the card-carrying members of the professional epistemological guild. A more explicit, and hence more troubling instance of the establishment stance of narrative theology, however, is Lindbeck's appeal to the mainstream as a way of avoiding the ghettoization of theology. From a more political perspective, however, it is difficult to tell where narrative theology is to be situated with respect to the establishment culture, primarily because it has remained rather silent on such matters. But that fact in itself likely counts as a significant reason against it.

Yoder has convincingly argued that one of the characteristic features of mainline theology is its tendency to refrain from explicit involvement in political matters. Accordingly, with its emphasis on methodological questions and its relative silence about ethical and political matters, it appears that narrative theology continues to endorse just the kind of sharp distinction between method and politics that Yoder denies. Thus, unless and until it comes clean on such matters, it is fair to assume that narrative theology bears the burden of proof as to the question of its capitulation to the wider wisdom of the mainstream.

Although I have argued for an interpretation that stresses several points of discontinuity between Yoder and narrative theology, it is important to distinguish between stronger and weaker versions of that position. Put succinctly, the strong version states that there is an essential incompatibility between Yoder and narrative theology or that the category of narrative is problematic in and of itself. The weaker version, however, maintains that there are significant tensions between their respective positions but does not claim that Yoder's theology necessarily rules out the category of narrative altogether. For reasons internal to Yoder's position itself, it is important to recognize that it is the weaker version that most adequately characterizes the relationship between Yoder and narrative theology. First, Yoder's rejection of methodologism includes an objection against those forms of categorical or terminological essentialism that identify a particular term or concept as acceptable or problematic for Christian theology as such. Second, the weaker argument for the discontinuity between Yoder and narrative theology affords a better explanation of his own use of the terminology of narrative.

As noted above, Yoder appeals to the category of narrative in certain cases, while at the same time objecting to the sense in which a conception of theology might be built upon it. In short, he refuses to accord narrative the primary status that it has for those who defend a version of *narrative* theology. Thus, while recognizing his own occasional use of the terminology of narrative or story, the main purpose here has been to stress the important points of divergence or discontinuity between Yoder and the movement of narrative theology. To construct a theology around any such concept or category would be to compromise the concrete social and political character of the church as the body of Christ.

Conclusion

I return again to the question of a specifically Mennonite theology. Focusing on the case of Yoder, I have argued that there is substantial discontinuity between Mennonite and narrative theology that is often overlooked. I have tried to suggest that contrary to the assumptions of many contemporary Mennonite theologians, narrative theology is problematic from the standpoint of Mennonite theology as Yoder sees it. Although this is not to suggest that the category of narrative is somehow problematic in and of itself, it is nevertheless important to draw attention to the differences between Yoder and narrative theology in order to counter the tendency within Mennonite theological circles to interpret Yoder as a narrative theologian. In other words, the category of narrative is as problematic as it is helpful. As such, a properly Mennonite stance should be neither wholly for nor against it. And yet the Mennonite theologians discussed above seem to operate on the basis of precisely such an all-or-nothing set of alternatives.

Those who draw enthusiastically on the work of Yoder in order to address the question of a specifically Mennonite theology should be more careful than they characteristically have been about appealing to narrative theology. Instead of supplementing Yoder's theology as they had hoped, the appeal to narrative theology might actually undermine some of his most significant points. But such a warning applies even to those who would raise critical questions about Yoder as a voice for Mennonite theology, since they equally tend to associate him with the movement of narrative theology. If the argument of this chapter serves to prevent or at least complicate such assumptions about the relationship between Mennonites and narrative theology, then it will have achieved its main purpose.

—4—

Radical Ecumenism, or Receiving One Another in Kuala Lumpur

Stanley Hauerwas likes to stir up trouble by suggesting that every Christian tradition comes equipped with an arsenal of favorite words that it should be prohibited from using. As Hauerwas himself puts it, "Anglicans should never be allowed to say 'Incarnation' because they usually mean by that 'God became human and said, "Say, this is not too bad!"' In like manner Methodists should not be allowed to use the word 'experience' because they usually mean that salvation consists in having the right feelings at the right time and in the right place. Rather than our confrontation with God being an occasion for challenging our endemic narcissism, the emphasis on experience thus only underwrites our fatal narcissism."[1]

What Hauerwas means to highlight here is the way such key words tend to function as a kind of self-confirming shorthand that inhibits genuine theological inquiry and meaningful dialogue more generally. They say at once too much and too little. They imply that Anglicanism and Methodism are *only* about incarnation and experience, or that these traditions can be reduced to categories like incarnation and experience *in general*. The same could be said for Lutherans about grace, Catholics about natural law, Pentecostals and Orthodox about the Spirit, and Mennonites about peace. As a result, they fail to communicate matters of rich and substantive detail that genuine communication involves. Such approaches are condemned to a kind of self-enclosed circle of silence. Or if there is a kind of speech present, it is that of a monologue, not a dialogue that is vulnerable to correction from another.

Hauerwas maintains that there is an intimate connection between this impulse toward abstract generality and what amounts to an essentially idolatrous desire for self-confirmation. This is a specifically theological problem. The idealistic and nonspecific character of such categories creates conditions for easy speech, which in turn underwrites a desire to fix or secure speech about God. Such reductionist strategies cannot but deny the radically contingent character of the Christian God. Hauerwas thus argues that Christian speech, in order to remain meaningfully Christian, needs to be made more difficult. It needs to return to the concrete and messy rough ground of ordinary first-order discourse that speaks, not merely in terms of general categories like experience and incarnation *as such,* but specifies in more nuanced detail what such categories consist in or look like.[2] He suggests that genuine theological dialogue is possible only when Methodists are able to articulate a theology without knee-jerk appeals to experience, and Anglicans without immediate recourse incarnation.

Hauerwas's concern about easy speech as a theological problem has been echoed by Rowan Williams. Much of Williams' work is an attempt to articulate and model an approach to theology that remains vulnerably open to the possibility of being put into question. He sets out to diagnose the lie of "a total perspective" and its desire for theoretical resolution, conceptual neatness, or tidiness.[3] Williams argues that theology all too often takes the form of a "concealing discourse" that "sets out to foreclose the possibility of a genuine response."[4] Instead, he calls for a conception of theology as honest discourse that "permits response and continuation [and] invites collaboration by showing that it does not claim to be, in and of itself, final."[5] Williams writes, "That the Church repeatedly seeks to secure a faith that is not vulnerable to judgment and to put cross and conversion behind it is manifest in every century of Christian history. But in so doing, it cuts itself off from the gift that lies beyond the void of the cross, and imprisons itself in the kind of self-understanding it can master or control. . . . The more God becomes functional to the legitimizing either of ecclesiastical order or of private religiosities, the easier it is to talk of God; the easier it is to talk of God, the less such talk gives place to the freedom of God. And that suggests that there is an aspect of dogmatic utterance that has to do with making it *harder* to talk about God."[6]

Hauerwas and Williams draw attention to what one might call the paradox of theological language, and of dialogue more specifically. They both emphasize the difficult character of Christian speech, and claim that such difficulty is an intrinsic and not merely contingent feature of the Christian faith. On the one hand, they maintain that Christian discourse must be dialogical. It must take one beyond the comfortable confines of the self. On the other hand, they might equally be read as attempting to frustrate dialogue. Much of their rhetoric takes the form of a conversation stopper, or at least a temporary suspension designed to force one to reconsider one's position in light of certain unstated assumptions, such that the conversation cannot keep going as it has up to that point. This is because they recognize that we tend to use words we have control of or a certain mastery over, that our speech is often informed by images of possession.

This lust for ownership is a problem because Hauerwas and Williams claim that Christianity frustrates our desires for mastery, possession, and control. They encourage their readers to seek out dialogue partners and yet seek to make them suspicious that their conversations might be cheap. This is because they recognize that if dialogue is an attempt to reach agreement, it must cultivate meaningful space for radical disagreement, so that agreements are not artificial, as if secured in advance of actual encounter. They encourage the humble stance of vulnerable openness to other voices, yet at the same time speak from the perspective of the militant who sets out to rupture existing orders and preferred linguistic conventions. This is why their work is episodic and tentative, though no less lacking in conviction. It is why they often speak in fragments and identify loose connections rather than unified and tightly ordered wholes.

These concerns of Hauerwas and Williams are nicely summarized by what the Marxist literary theorist Terry Eagleton has recently referred to as radical character of the Christian tradition. Eagleton differentiates the stance of the radical from that of the conservative and the liberal in terms of how they approach the question of the monstrous: "For the conservative, monsters are other people; for the liberal, there are no monsters, only the mistreated and misunderstood; for the radical, the real monsters are ourselves. . . . If we are to escape the sealed circuit of the self, or the equally windless enclosure of self and other, we have to have sympathy for the other precisely as monstrous, to feel the blinded Oedipus or crazed Lear in their very rebarbative inhumanity. And this demands an answerably 'inhuman' compassion, which is far from agreeable. For the Judeo-Christian tradition, this inhuman form of compassion is known as the law of love."[7]

Ecumenical Dialogue and the Problem of Easy Speech

I begin with these allusions to Hauerwas, Williams, and Eagleton because they help to bring into focus my reflections on the 2004 plenary session of the Faith and Order Commission of the World Council of Churches held in Kuala Lumpur. It is to their theological reflections on language and dialogue that I have found myself returning again and again in an attempt to make sense of this particular instance of ecumenical conversation. The great promise of ecumenical dialogue is that it disrupts the monothematic, reductionist, and self-confirming tendencies to which the above comments point. At its best moments, it frustrates our desire for conceptual neatness and disturbs our self-confirming strategies of legitimization. It confronts us with the limitations and narrowness of our preferred theological formulations and so helps us to recognize the lure of theoretical closure or resolution. It can help to diagnose the often subtle logic of possession and ownership that infects our speech, if only by demonstrating that theological speech is much richer than those assertions that we comfortably claim as "our own." In so doing, it encourages a stance of collaboration and vulnerable receptivity to other voices that renders dialogue meaningful.

And yet, while ecumenical dialogue rightly serves to complicate our theological discourse, it walks a fine line in doing so. Even as it encourages an appreciation of the difficulty of Christian speech, there is a sense in which it risks giving rise to certain monothematic and tidy tendencies of its own. Indeed, it might be suggested that the promise of ecumenism is in a strange way bound up with precisely the sorts of problems Hauerwas, Williams, and Eagleton identify. When taken as a whole, ecumenical conversations often contain glimpses of the dialogical virtues noted above. But from a case-by-case perspective, looking at specific statements and contributions, one often gets a sense of the corresponding vices.

The meetings in Kuala Lumpur contained many instances of genuine theological dialogue. But I also find myself wondering about the temptation to deploy certain favorite words and functional, self-legitimating descriptions in representing our various traditions. Driven by a desire to make a meaningful contribution on behalf of one's tradition, to ensure that its distinctive voice makes it to the table, and perhaps equally a sense of obligation that this is the role we are expected to fill, there appears to be an all-too-easy temptation to make carica-tures of ourselves. From the other end, in an attempt to be maximally inclusive, to say something that everyone can identify with, statements often read as a checklist of all the favored categories Hauerwas points to. The unfortunate result in both cases is that we end up saying very little, if anything at all, that a reasonably informed dialogue partner might not already be able to anticipate. Needless to say, this does not make for much of a conversation. On the one hand, there is a deadening sense of being stuck in a repetitive cycle of introductory niceties that make it difficult to move on to the more interesting and important matters of nuanced detail. On the other hand, behind the surface posture of hospitality, one can often hear the shrill ring of single-issue, special-interest-group political maneuvering that runs counter to any meaningful conception of ecumenical unity.

After the meetings in Kuala Lumpur, I was asked on numerous occasions to identify questions and concerns growing out of the discus-sions that are of special interest to Mennonites. In doing so, it is tempting to assume that Mennonites ought to be especially concerned with some of the recent interest being paid to questions of peace theology, or perhaps with the ongoing attention given to the topic of baptism. Or at any rate, such is often the unstated expectation lying behind the question itself. The problem with such an approach, however, is that it focuses on peace and/or baptism in a way that encourages a sense of ghettoization and thus inappropriately limits the scope of Mennonite participation in the larger dialogue. Even more importantly, this would result in an unfortunate misconception with respect to the questions of peace and baptism themselves. To focus on the categories of peace and baptism in this way implies that they are somehow prior to other theological commitments without which they are unintelligible. In this regard, many of the more interesting questions for Mennonites occur, not in the discussions of peace theology and baptism, but in those texts and conversations in which peace and baptism are not explicitly mentioned.

Such an ability to concentrate on certain theological themes in abstraction from others is no doubt encouraged, if only implicitly, by the way the various Faith and Order statements and discussion topics are approached in isolation from one another. For example, to address questions of ethnic identity, nationalism, and unity in abstraction from the study of ecclesiology gives the impression that these important matters are not themselves directly bound up with the question of the church. It can be read as suggesting that so-called ethical and political matters are somehow secondary to properly or purely theological concerns, that they are implications *derived from* prior theological commitments and not themselves the proper subject of theological reflection. More specifically, they imply that ecclesiology is not itself somehow involved in questions of identity, that church does not name way of life that is different than that of nations and ethnicities. In like manner, to consider the question of theological anthropology in a separate document from that of baptism suggests that baptism is not itself an anthropological matter, that it does not have a bearing on what it means to be human. More specifically, the desire for generalized anthropological claims runs the risk of obscuring the way in which baptism is a kind of death to the self. It involves a relativization of the human, a radical redefinition of humanity by means of a serious reckoning with inhumanity or the monstrous that Eagleton finds in the Christian tradition.

Taken together, this sort of fragmentary presentation and arrangement of the various documents and studies can suggest that ecclesiology and baptism are somehow properly doctrinal concerns, whereas ethical and political matters belong to a different domain. This results in an unfortunate separation of doctrine and ethics, thought and practice, or belief and life. It must be acknowledged, of course, that this is in many ways inevitable, given the need to focus on a particular topic or area of debate, and that not every implication can be captured in any one document. And it is important to note that the concerns I have been raising deal primarily with matters of form rather than the actual content contained in the various studies. But I do mean to draw attention to the way that the form of the discussion has significant, though often subtle, implications for questions of content, often working against the grain of the actual content of the studies themselves.

In addition, the kind of approach I have been describing allows for picking and choosing, making it possible to ignore certain implications that might be perceived as uncomfortable or particularly challenging. Put differently, I worry that topical fragmentation gives rise to a sort of piecemeal ecumenism, whereby one finds oneself passionately taking up certain issues of the ecumenical conversation while ignoring others. Such a phenomenon was perhaps most strikingly present during the discussion of the study on nationalism and ethnicity, where many openly wondered whether this was worth discussing at all. As an analogue to Hauerwas's quip about favorite words, it might be suggested that various Christian traditions tend to have their own favorite ecumenical documents.

Perhaps even more significant than this concern about the risk of ecumenism indirectly promoting reductionist, easy speech, Hauerwas's comments help to draw attention to the fact that the ecumenical movement is marked by its own favorite words. Among the many thousands of words uttered during the ten days of official meetings in Kuala Lumpur, none were more ubiquitous than *unity* and *context*. Indeed, there was rarely a comment that did not either appeal to some particular contextual location—whether denominational, geopolitical, economic, racial, or gender-based—or justify itself in some way by means of an appeal to the ecumenical goal of visible unity.

The Nature of the Unity We Seek

Unity is, of course, a well-known theme and is in many ways definitional of the ecumenical movement as a whole. But after so many different appeals to unity, one wonders whether it is concretely specifiable in any intelligible way. That the goal of the ecumenical movement is something called unity is a given. But what that unity consists in is another question altogether, and in many ways the more interesting and difficult one. Many assume that it involves some sort of explicit agreement and focus on the task of securing universal assent. But others might follow Williams in arguing for the ongoing need to cultivate conditions for meaningful forms of disagreement and dissent.

Sometimes the notion of unity is invoked in a manner that seems to rely on concentric metaphors, suggesting a series of expanding circles converging around a common core. One can also detect nonconcentric models of unity that prefer images of cross-cutting connections and multiple points of convergence and overlap in the absence of a common center. One frequently encounters notions of unity that might be described as territorial or spatial, calling to mind a static and quantitative site around which a border can be drawn and which is subject to regulation as if from the outside. Others argue that the church names a nonterritorial reality that is better understood in temporal and qualitative terms, as a kind of ongoing differential movement in time over against which there is no outside, as we are always already in the midst of it. Finally, it often seems like the goal of unity is motivated by an assumed need to unite as a front against a common foe, such as secularism. Here it is assumed that unity names a kind of strength, and often, that the absence of full unity is merely a temporary stumbling block that we can overcome by cultivating better ways of communication and working together.

But one might also raise some significant questions about the assumption that the task of unity is a future reality that exists, if at all, as an achievement of ours. Here it might be suggested that unity is both more profoundly real, though as a gift or promise, and at the same time unrealizable, precisely because we who seek to claim it are part of the problem, as Eagleton's stance of the radical suggests. Here it could be argued that the most meaningfully Christian sense of unity in not one that arises out of a sense of strength, but one that is able to recognize weakness. I mention these various conceptions of unity because each of them was echoed in one way or another in the presentations and conversations in Kuala Lumpur. In light of this, it seems that more explicit discussion about the very idea of unity itself is called for. Almost fifty years ago, John Howard Yoder addressed a consultation of the Faith and Order Commission highlighting a series of implicit assumptions about the notion of ecumenical unity and calling for further discussion on "the nature of the unity we seek."[8] My sense is that Yoder's call is just as pertinent today as it was then, if not more so.

One notable development that has taken place in the intervening fifty years is the rise to prominence of the concept of contextualization. No doubt partly due to the important contributions of liberation theology, such a development is rightly premised against the background that the church has been complicit in various forms of oppression. Christianity has all too often been the expression of an establishment stance that excludes any legitimacy to minority voices. And yet it might be suggested that such appeals to contextualization insufficiently break with the kinds of violence they seek to identify and oppose.

Slavoj Zizek likes to point out, in his typically extreme style, that certain feminist accounts of the particularity of women's experience are formally identical to the conceptions of racial difference that character-ized the apartheid regime in South Africa. Zizek is suggesting that such an "identitarian" notion of difference makes it possible to assert new voices only at the cost of making it difficult, if not impossible, to develop and sustain any meaningful criticism and resistance. Referring to the example of the Holocaust, Zizek claims, "You cannot say that the Nazis were telling one story and Jews were simply telling another. You cannot say that the only sin of the Nazis was that they repressed the other story; it's not strong enough."[9]

In addition, it might be argued that the notion of context continues to underwrite the logic of mastery, possession, and ownership highlighted by Hauerwas, Williams, and Eagleton. Many of the appeals to contextual location throughout the meetings in Kuala Lumpur were too strong in that they seemed to imply a particularist notion of identity that encloses the self within some defined set of particular experiences. Not only does this give the impression that our understanding of context is unproblematic and straightforward, but it suggests that we are somehow the owners of our experiences, that we have a kind of mastery over them. At the same time, it threatens to turn conversation into a kind of boundary-defining exercise, such that discourse becomes little more than an exercise of positioning ourselves strategically and judgmentally over against others. In this way, context risks becoming yet another version of the functionalism of theological speech that Williams identifies. It also serves to exclude the stance of the radical that Eagleton points to because it obscures the possibility of recognizing that we ourselves might be the monsters. This is not to suggest that meaningful dialogue and the genuine critical engagement must strive to be contextless. But it is to say that something goes wrong, theologically speaking, when our framework for discussion takes its orientation too narrowly from some particular context or another.

Some might worry that the main problem with the emphasis on context is that it exists as a kind of barrier to the ecumenical goal of unity. But my attempt to highlight the favorite words *unity* and *context* is not meant to suggest that they are necessarily in competition with one another. On the contrary, I am concerned about the way in which certain notions of context and unity can coalesce to form what amounts to a false sense of unity that threatens the very promise of ecumenism, or at least the church of which it speaks.

I worry that certain aspects of the recent ecumenical movement—and in particular, some of its rhetorical figures of speech regarding the worldwide church, both global and local—sound suspiciously similar to the discourse of globalization, or more specifically, of global capitalism. Many recent theorists of globalization demonstrate its subtle ability to offer itself as a kind of universality that is not threatened by difference, but rather turns on difference, encouraging the existence of particular identities even as it relativizes any critical purchase they might have against the capitalist logic of endless consumption. As one such theorist, Alain Badiou, puts it, "Capital demands a permanent creation of subjective and territorial identities in order for its principle of movement to homogenize its space of action; identities, moreover, that never demand anything but the right to be exposed in the same way as others to the uniform prerogatives of the market. The capitalist logic of the general equivalent and the identitarian logic of communities or minorities form an articulated whole."[10]

The church is no doubt a global body in many ways, existing as it does beyond national boundaries. But it is equally clear that it has no place for the possessive logic of capital. Accordingly, I suspect one of the more significant challenges that the ecumenical movement will face in years to come will be to distance itself from the destructive dance of unity and context that Badiou and others identify as characteristic of global capitalism.

In this regard, it would be interesting to consider the significance of the fact that these meetings were held in Kuala Lumpur, a city that resonates with symbolism linking it to the new global world order. It is perhaps even more interesting to consider that the chosen theme for the meeting was drawn from Paul's letter to the Romans: "Receive one another, as Christ has received you, for the glory of God" (Rom 15:7). What makes this choice particularly noteworthy is the irony that Zizek and Badiou appeal to Paul precisely as an alternative to globalization. Badiou, for example, finds in Paul's move beyond Jew and Greek a "militant discourse of weakness" that exceeds the closures of identitarian particularity and instead constitutes a "nomadism of gratuitousness," a "universalism [that] supposes one be able to think the multiple not as a part, but as in excess of itself, as that which is out of place."[11]

For Badiou, difference is neither canceled nor patronizingly tolerated and strategically deployed as a potential source of income, but suspended by a more radical universalism that cuts diagonally through every particular identity. In other words, Pauline unity is the disturbing and interruptive unity of resurrection, which "exceeds its real contingent site, which is the community of believers such as it exists at the moment."[12] And yet I sensed in Kuala Lumpur a certain tendency to speak of receiving one another in a way that often sounded like the kind of non-interruptive tolerance that is characteristic of global capitalism. I suspect this is related to the apparent assumption that the theme verse is best read from left to right. This suggests that it is our receiving one another that will bring about the glory of God. Such a reading places its hope precisely in the "community of believers such as it exists at the moment." Not only does this presume that the ecumenical goal of unity somehow rests exclusively on our shoulders, but it also reflects a progressivist assumption that we will achieve our goals if only we become better educated and work hard enough.

But I wonder if Romans 15:7 might equally be read from right to left. This would have the implication of reading receptivity as a specifically theological notion. Here the act of receiving one another is not dependent on us alone, but is rather a gift that flows from the excessive glory of God. This is not the unity of receiving parts into a larger whole. Rather, it is a unity that interrupts each identity as it pulls each of us excessively beyond ourselves. Here unity is as much something that happens in spite of us as because of us. Indeed, it enables us to recognize that we ourselves are often the most significant roadblocks to the unity that comes to us as a gift. In other words, unity consists significantly in the stance of the radical mentioned above.

Conclusion: Toward a Radical Ecumenism

If in these reflections on the Faith and Order Commission's meetings and the state of the ecumenical movement more generally I have concentrated more on the risks than the promise of ecumenism, it is only because of a desire to take its promise seriously. Ecumenical dialogue should not shy away from the need to grapple with its own risks and weaknesses. Indeed, what I find promising about ecumenism is its ability to cultivate an openness to such a sense of risk. But at the same time, there often appears to be a sense of frustration with what is taken to be a failure to achieve the desired goal of visible unity. The unity of which we speak appears to be fleeting. It shows itself in glimpses and brief snatches that we are unable to grab hold of and control so that we might be able to "move it in the right direction," as Yoder puts it.[13] But perhaps this is as it should be, at least for the ecumenical movement in which the unity spoken of is that of the church.

A theological conception of unity is radical precisely in that it is out of our control. It unsettles us and takes us uncomfortably beyond our desires for mastery, possession, and ownership. And so I close with a gloss on the quote by Eagleton, cited above, offering it as a gesture toward what might be called radical ecumenism: For conservatives, ecumenism is an instrumental and strategic task of bringing the other to our side; for liberals, ecumenism is an expression of the givenness of a unity that is merely misunderstood, such that the work of unity is an exercise in developing better lines of communication; for the radical, unity is an unwarranted and often unwelcome gift that defies and interrupts our sentimental and self-legitimating strategies of closure and reduction. During my time in Kuala Lumpur, I heard many instances of liberal ecumenism and several expressions of conservative ecumenism, but I experienced little evidence of radical ecumenism. Or rather only a few fleeting glimpses.

Disowning Knowledge

—5—

Can a Gift Be Commanded? Political Ontology and Theoretical Closure in Milbank, Barth, and Yoder

In his landmark work *Theology and Social Theory*, John Milbank unleashes a wild and epic narrative that promises to chart a theological path "beyond secular reason" in both its modern and postmodern varieties.[1] Milbank's argument unfolds with a sweeping, critical genealogy of contemporary thought, displaying the many senses in which secular rationality grounds its very being in violence. This names the assumption that violence is ontologically basic. It sees conflict as a given that is somehow central to any state of affairs. The work of secular reason is thus essentially instrumental and bureaucratic as it seeks to impose order on some inherently conflictual reality.

Theoretical inquiry, on this model, does not so much seek to eliminate violence—it is a given, after all—as to bring it under control. It sets out to tame the violence of the world and thereby to use it to bring about some desired end. The general aim of Milbank's genealogy is to demonstrate that the secular and its ontology of violence is not a given but an invention. He argues that things were not always this way and, perhaps more importantly, that they need not be now.

Many have assumed, because of his rhetoric of the secular, that Milbank's primary aim is to develop an elaborate apology for theology over against its secular despisers. His work is often read as an attempt to defend theology from some secular threat that is understood to be located on a field external to theology. But such an assumption significantly misconstrues his argument and thereby blunts its polemical edge. For Milbank's real targets are the theologians, or at least those who claim to speak in the name of theology. In other words, *Theology and Social Theory* is based on the conviction that much (if not all) of what passes itself off as Christian theology and ethics is really a kind of pseudo-theology.

Milbank argues that too much contemporary theology situates itself, whether unwittingly or intentionally, on the terrain of secular reason and its attendant vision of original violence. Against this tragic state of affairs, he launches a variously pronged campaign for the need to reclaim a specifically theological understanding of theology and ethics. His aim is not to articulate a theology that is able to meet secular reason on its own terms. This is the sort of apologetic orientation he identifies as problematic. Rather, he sets out to save theology from its own secular tendencies.

In this effort, Milbank's work echoes that of Karl Barth, whose task was to rescue the church from its self-imposed captivity to theological liberalism. Like Milbank, Barth's work is a diagnosis of liberalism's evacuation of theological substance in favor of secular form, and in particular, the sense in which such a split is complicit in the preservation of secular power, that is, the modern nation-state. Both Barth and Milbank develop elaborate theological enterprises that are addressed first of all to the need to keep theology properly theological. And yet there are some significant differences. This chapter explores some of those differences against the background of their common goal of articulating what might be called a post-secular political theology.

In Milbank's case, the call to keep theology theological is expressed largely in terms of a counter-ontology that is at the same time a counter-politics. He speaks of this as an ontology of peace. According to Milbank, a theological understanding of being asserts, not the priority of a violence that needs to be contained, but a peace that is excessive and thus beyond containment. In sum, an ontology of peace asserts the "gratuitous creative giving of existence" and its expression in an ongoing harmonic interplay of differences.[2]

Much of Milbank's work that has appeared since *Theology and Social Theory* might be read as an attempt to develop and refine this understanding of a Christian political ontology. It is instructive to note that he now speaks less in terms of an ontology of peace and more in terms of an "ontology of the gift."[3] This is not to suggest that he has abandoned peace in favor of the gift. Rather, Milbank is making the theme of gratuitous donation even more central by claiming that the best resources for understanding his political ontology of peace can be found in the logic of gift and gift-exchange.

Among other things, Milbank suggests, in a series of passing comments, that the logic of gift involves a rejection of the notion of command.[4] This is noteworthy because it is precisely the notion of command that occupies a central place in Barth's attempt to keep theology theological. Given his construal of ethics in terms of command and obligation, it is often suggested that Barth's ethics is problematic to the extent that it retains the structure of the Kantian categorical imperative and in particular its theoretical formalism.[5] More significantly, it is argued that this residual separation of form and content compromises Barth's theological critique of the modern nation-state. This is because a commitment to Kantian formalism makes ethics and politics a largely theoretical matter in a way that renders the church incapable of addressing matters of substantive political change.

On the other hand, it is noteworthy that Barth develops his account of the command of God in the context of gift, and in particular the specifically theological context of the gracious gift of God in Jesus Christ. Such a combination of command and gift has led some to suggest that Barth's ethics is actually significantly anti-Kantian such that it can be defended against the charge of ethical and political impotence.[6] But it is at this point that Milbank's recent work on gift is most relevant. On the basis of his claim that the notions of command and gift are fundamentally incompatible, Milbank's ontology of the gift constitutes an objection even to the so-called anti-Kantian interpretation of Barth.

According to Milbank, any appeal to the notion of command is problematic, even Barth's attempt to re-narrate the notion of command in a specifically theological context of the gift. In other words, Milbank would agree with Barth on the need to re-narrate political theology within a specifically Christian context. Like Barth, he endeavors to do theology in a way that remains genuinely theological all the way down. But he argues that Barth himself failed to achieve this goal just to the extent that he retained a commitment to the notion of command.

The question of a specifically Christian political ontology can thus be approached by examining the role of command and gift in the theologies of Barth and Milbank. In order to do so, I will present Milbank's recent work on the logic of gift as an objection to Barth's understanding of the command of God as gift, attempting to sort out the relationship or non-relationship between command and gift by analyzing their disagreement. At one level, I shall suggest that it is appropriate to see Barth and Milbank as offering rival and in fact contrary answers to the question, "Can a gift be commanded?"

Yet in a significant sense, the debate between Barth and Milbank must remain unresolved as it stands. But this argument can finally be made only by turning to the work of a third theologian who champions the need for a specifically Christian political ontology, namely, John Howard Yoder. On the one hand, I shall suggest that Milbank is correct to draw attention to the sense in which Barth's ethics retains a significant sense of Kantian formalism. On the other hand, I will argue that Yoder offers a way of reading Barth that enables him to be defended against Milbank's objection.

Indeed, Yoder's contribution to this debate makes it possible to suggest that it is finally Milbank who remains wedded to the essentially violent conception of bureaucratic rationality and theoretical closure that speaks from a position of mastery over God. There is thus a sense in which Barth and Milbank end up calling each other's work into question. In short, by turning to Yoder in order to re-narrate the debate between Barth and Milbank, I hope to show that despite their own best insights, they both retain a disposition toward the violence of theoretical closure in a way that is theologically quite problematic. Or at least it is problematic if a specifically Christian political ontology is concretely grounded—and thereby ungrounded—by the specific particularities of the Christian story they both try to highlight.

Rethinking Barth's Divine Command Ethics

Barth's ethics can be understood as an attempt to combine the notions of command and gift. Nigel Biggar maintains that Barth's account of the divine command is only part of a larger ethical system that also includes God's gift of grace in Jesus Christ. In particular, he argues against the Kantian interpretation noted above, claiming that Barth's conception of the command of God differs significantly from Kant's categorical imperative precisely because it is not strictly formal. Whereas Kant attempted to provide a purely rational basis for ethics, Biggar contends that Barth's account of the divine command is intelligible only in the context of a concrete relationship with God.[7] In contrast to Kant's appeal to an abstract moral principle, then, he suggests that Barth consistently refused to separate "what is commanded from the person of the commanding God."[8]

As Barth himself would put it, the problem with the Kantian categorical imperative is that it is a version of general ethics. It is based on the presumption that there is "an ethical question in itself and for itself, as if it were not first posed by the grace of God."[9] Barth's ethics, however, does not presuppose any generalized anthropology, nor does it begin with abstract theoretical questions such as the relationship between the right and the good. Rather, his account of the divine command is to be understood as an attempt to develop a special ethics, one that is specifically Christian.

For Barth the divine command is only intelligible in the context of the doctrine of election.[10] The command of God is rooted in the gracious gift of Jesus. It is "issued by God's grace to the elect man Jesus Christ, and again by God's grace already fulfilled by this man."[11] It is thus in and through Jesus that a relationship with God becomes possible such that the command of God can be put to humans in the first place.

At the same time, it is important to recognize how Barth argues that the divine command is *itself* gift: "The particularity of theological ethics does not consist in the fact that it is 'theonomous' ethics, that it understands the command of the good as God's command. The same thing is done elsewhere with seriousness and emphasis. But its peculiarity and advantage consist in the name of Jesus Christ with which it can state the basis and right of the divine claim."[12] In other words, the command of God is given in the gift of Jesus Christ. In arguing for a specifically Christian ethics, Barth is thus not merely claiming that the divine command presupposes the election of Jesus Christ, but is also making the more politically and ontologically radical claim that Jesus is the gift through which the command is given. The command of God is both rooted in and based on the gift of Jesus Christ.[13]

To put this differently, Barth's account of the relationship between command and gift might be understood as an alternative to the excessively rationalist and formalist approaches often characterized as "ethical theory" represented by Kant. Unlike Kant, Barth does not seek to identify the command as a single principle that is able to stand on its own and thus provide the foundation for an ethical theory. Nor does he understand the relationship between command and gift as one of form (command) and content (gift) or cause (election/gift) and effect (command). Rather, the command of God cannot be separated from the gracious gift of God in Jesus Christ. In the election, command and gift have become one. "The man, Jesus, who fulfils the commandment of God, does not *give* the answer, but by God's grace He *is* the answer to the ethical question put by God's grace."[14] There is thus, for Barth, no distinction to be made between command and gift. There is only a "commanding grace,"[15] the "command of the grace of God."[16]

A Milbankian Critique

By drawing attention to this inextricable interweaving of command and gift in Barth's ethics, it is surely correct that Barth's conception of theological ethics differs from that of Kant. But what such an account does not provide is a justification for Barth's use of the notion of command in the first place. Therefore, Barth remains open to an objection based on the work of Milbank, namely, that his ethics is problematic because he appeals to the notion of command at all. In developing Milbank's position, it is important to recognize that he shares with Barth the fundamental presupposition that theological ethics is irreducibly particular and rejects any kind of general ethic.[17]

Drawing upon Milbank in order to mount an objection to Barth is thus to construct a critical conversation that is essentially internal to the Barthian project. It suggests that Barth fails to follow his own best insights to their own proper conclusions. Barth would no doubt be in complete agreement with Milbank's general conclusion that "Christian morality is a thing *so* strange that it must be declared immoral or amoral according to all other human norms and codes of morality."[18] But Milbank would nevertheless maintain that Barth has failed to properly locate the difference between Christian theology and the secular. For according to Milbank, one of the defining characteristics of a secular ontology of violence is the very notion of command that figures so prominently in Barth's theology.

In particular, Milbank argues that the notion of command is abstract and general in a way that compromises the concrete specificity of the gift. He begins with a discussion of the Kantian claim that a command is morally prescriptive only when it falls under the category of a general law of "what should *always* be done."[19] But what is even more problematic about the logic of command, according to Milbank, is that such an ethic presupposes an essentially "reactive" context. The appeal to a universal moral command is occasioned by some *prior* threat or evil that is to be overcome, such as an external threat of violence, internal weakness, economic scarcity, or death.[20] In other words, the moral command must be made universal in order to *contain* the threat of a prior evil to which it is a response. Or as Milbank himself puts it, "The demand for uniformity is paradoxically an emergency measure to sustain a unity of a thoroughly abstract kind."[21] Similarly, he suggests that the language of command is intelligible only in the context of a moral psychology that presupposes a conception of the autonomous self, whose agency is fundamentally independent of both the command and the commander.[22]

In sharp contrast to the abstract and universal notion of command, Milbank claims that "a genuine gift is excessive since it is not required, and it occasions not a loss but a gain in subjectivity for the giver which is reinforced by the counter-gift of gratitude from the recipient."[23] A gift is not occasioned by some prior context that makes it somehow necessary. On the contrary, it is purely contingent, an unnecessary exception. It is thus always specific and particular, irreducible to any prior logic according to which it might be subsumed under a more general and abstract notion or principle.

Christian theology understood in terms of an ontology of the gift is, according to Milbank, best understood by reflecting on the creation story, which is at the same time the story of the incarnation. Since God did not have to create, since God did not have to become bodily present in Jesus, theology is to be understood as contingent and gratuitous all the way down. There is no *prior* context, reactive or otherwise, to which God's gift can be construed as a response. In a similar vein, the divine gift thus defies the possibility of theoretical containment or closure. Rather, the gracious gift of God in Jesus Christ is itself ontologically and politically primary.[24] Christian theology, in other words, is concretely rooted in the context of the church as the very body of Christ. Accordingly, Milbank suggests that in an ontology of the gift, there is no "self" whose agency exists in abstraction from the body of Christ. No self is prior to and thus capable of receiving the gift of God. Rather, according to Milbank, the self simply *is* gift, and thus only exists insofar as it is made "eucharistically manifest" in and through the body of Christ.[25]

Having thus set up a sharp contrast between the notions of command and gift, Milbank concludes by suggesting that "the genuine gift can in no way be anything commanded."[26] In short, he claims that the logic of gift subverts that of command, and vice versa. This claim most directly captures how his work might be read as an objection to Barth. Although he agrees with Barth's theological emphasis on the gift, Milbank would maintain that Barth's understanding of the gift is contaminated and thus ultimately compromised by his attempt to combine it with the notion of command.

Milbank would be critical of Barth's theology because it is insufficiently particular. Indeed, Barth's failure in this regard may be a suggestive example of just how difficult it is to escape the secular temptation of abstract reason or theoretical closure that seeks to gain a handle on Christian speech and thus to exert a kind of leverage over God. Although Barth's emphasis on gift appears to hold out the promise of a concrete and materially specified conception of theology, his appeal to the notion of command ultimately withdraws that promise by introducing a theologically unjustified element of generality. In other words, Barth's ethics ultimately fails to live up to his own claim to provide a specifically Christian alternative to general ethics.

In arguing that Christian theology is only intelligible within the context of the concretely embodied and materially specific church, Milbank may be seen as extending an objection that has been raised against Barth by other theologians who are equally sympathetic to his overall project of developing a specifically Christian ethics.[27] In the context of the present discussion, Barth's insufficient ecclesiology is suggested by his claim that the divine command involves a direct transaction between God and humans that requires no interpretation or mediation.[28] It thus appears to be legitimate for Milbank to ask whether Barth's failure to accord a more substantial role to the church in moral formation calls into question the emphasis on specificity and concreteness with which he begins his discussion of ethics. But while Milbank may be correct to argue that a specifically Christian ethics requires a more significant account of the church, his own account of the radical incompatibility between the logic of gift and that of command still needs to be examined more closely.

For such an examination it will be instructive to turn to the work of John Howard Yoder. At the outset, it is important to recognize that on one level Yoder confirms Milbank's objection to the absence of concrete ecclesiology in Barth. But while he thus shares Milbank's emphasis on the contingent specificity of the church over against the Barthian command, Yoder also provides a way of reading the debate that favors Barth's discussion of the relationship of command and gift over against that of Milbank.

Beyond Command and Gift: The Contribution of John Howard Yoder

Yoder's argument in support of the non-Constantinian character of the church is well known. In short, he claims that the church is to be seen as a sociological, cultural, and political entity in its own right. It is only by embodying such an alternative community that the church can truly serve as a witness to the world.[29] But more important is his account of what might be called "methodological" or "ontological" non-Constantinianism. Indeed, Yoder would no doubt resist the very distinction between the political and the ontological itself as just the kind of theoretical dualism that serves to relativize the concrete political significance of Jesus.

Yoder would argue that one of the most problematic aspects of the Constantinian subordination of the church to the wider world is the "methodologist" construal of theology. Here theology becomes a theoretical discipline that is concerned primarily with the question of the proper elucidation of and logical interrelationship between certain central concepts.[30] Such an approach betrays a desire to contain Christian discourse, to master or to own it as if it were a possession of some kind. Yoder argues that this cannot but compromise the particularity of the church. Accordingly, he claims that the concrete body of Christ precedes all epistemological and conceptual discussions. As Yoder himself puts it, "The life of the community is prior to all possible methodological distillations."[31] In fact, he warns that meta-level or theoretical discussions of conceptual matters always run the risk of a particular form of idolatry, which ends up restricting meaningful speech about God to some one vocabulary or another.[32] Let us call this the idolatry of theoretical closure.

Returning to the debate between Milbank and Barth, it is now possible to understand Barth's ethics of the gift and command in a way that does not render him susceptible to Milbank's objection. Whereas some defend Barth against the Kantian interpretation by claiming that he combines the notions of command and gift in a way that they can be incorporated into some larger theological system, Yoder's theological rejection of methodologism allows us to take Barth at his anti-systematic word.[33] Although Barth's ethics may not be sufficiently rooted in the concrete practices of the church, it is concretely rooted in the person and work of Christ.

Barth was not interested in theoretical questions concerning the essential compatibility or incompatibility of concepts such as command and gift. Rather, as Hans Frei has pointed out, Barth's theology is best understood as a work of narrative re-description: "He took the classical themes of communal Christian language molded by the Bible, tradition and constant usage in worship, practice, instruction and controversy, and he restated them or redescribed them, rather than evolving arguments on their behalf."[34] Barth's primary concern is not with questions of the logical compatibility of particular concepts such as command and gift in and of themselves, as though they somehow carry their meaning along with them. Rather, what matters crucially to him is the task of providing them with a christologically disciplined re-narration.

It is thus problematic to describe Barth's ethics in terms of a combination of command and gift, since the very grammar of that way of putting it presupposes that the concepts of command and gift are intelligible in and of themselves. This assumes that their meaning remains relatively fixed throughout his theological re-narration. On the contrary, their meaning is fundamentally altered, most significantly to the extent that they are now unintelligible apart from the concrete reality of Jesus.

Like Yoder, Barth's fundamental point is that Jesus Christ is prior to any particular terminology that could be used to talk about him. Accordingly, the question of which vocabulary to use is largely a contingent matter. Although he does attempt to develop an account of ethics by appealing to command and gift, Barth would not claim that it is therefore necessary to construe Christian ethics by using that particular terminology. This is not to suggest, however, that theology can appeal to any set of categories without discriminating judgments of any kind. Rather, the crucial point made by Yoder and exemplified by Barth's work is that the particular concepts used in theological discourse are under constant negotiation and are always subordinate to more concrete theological matters, whether the practices of the church, as in Yoder, or Jesus Christ himself, as in Barth.

From the standpoint of such an anti-systematic reading of Barth, what is most striking about Milbank is that he appears committed to a version of conceptual essentialism that appears to be in tension with his understanding radical theological contingency. Having argued for the importance of contingency and concrete particularity on theological grounds, it is problematic for Milbank to claim that Christian ethics is necessarily committed to the logic of gift as opposed to that of command. By contrasting command and gift so sharply, as fundamentally or essentially opposed, Milbank appears to be taking meaning as fixed in a way that it should not be if it is rooted in concrete theological practices. Accordingly, Milbank's argument presupposes the very distinction between form and content that his emphasis on the materiality of the church is designed to call into question. He is offering a meta-level argument that the concepts or logics of command and gift are necessarily opposed, in order to establish an account of contingency grounded in concrete practices.

Milbank's position hinges on the claim that Christian ethics operates according to a logic of gift that is fundamentally at odds with the logic of command. But if theology is as radically concrete and contingent as he takes it to be, it should not be reducible to any one set of concepts. Rather, that contingency should extend to the concepts used to explicate theology as well. Accordingly, Milbank might himself be guilty of the kind of violence referred to above as theoretical closure. By restricting his specifically Christian political ontology to the terminology of gift against command, his rhetoric bears traces of a desire to capture and contain, suggesting an underlying concern for theoretical closure. In other words, his genealogical critique of mastery, possession, and control is itself infected by a will to mastery, possession, and control, as he appears to impose limits on meaningful speech about God in just the way that Yoder has warned against.

In defense of Milbank, however, it might be objected that his argument is not conceptually abstract or theoretical in a way that ignores practices altogether. For his discussion of the ontology of gift is no doubt an attempt to explicate the logic that he takes to be implicit in such ecclesial practices as the Eucharist. My criticism of Milbank does not require him to be committed to such a strong theoretical approach. Rather, I am suggesting that in spite of his emphasis on these concrete ecclesial practices, or rather precisely because of it, Milbank retains too significant a role for theory.

Thus, in light of the theological rejection of methodologism provided by Yoder, it may be Milbank who fails to fulfill the promise of theological concreteness, and not Barth. The radical character of the Eucharist is not that it presupposes the logic of gift over against that of command, but rather that it resists the possibility of being fully captured by any set of concepts or any logic whatsoever.

Conclusion

By defending Barth against Milbank in this way, however, it is important to stress that I am not advocating the superiority of Barth's theology to that of Milbank as a whole. For I take it that Milbank's original objection to Barth still stands. Accordingly, it is best to see Barth and Milbank as mutually critiquing one another. In short, it is possible to understand each of them as showing that there are aspects of the other that remain in tension with the emphasis on contingency and radical theological particularity that they both share. The problem with Barth's theology is that it fails to accord the church a more substantial role in moral formation. At the same time, Milbank's theology is problematic in being based on a version of conceptual essentialism that tends toward abstraction. It makes conceptual matters more important than the actual practices of the church they are supposed to explain.

But that is only half the story. What is perhaps most important is the sense in which the debate between Barth and Milbank is best understood from the standpoint of Yoder. Yoder is in general agreement with Barth and Milbank in arguing that theology is irreducibly concrete and particular, but he goes much farther than either of them do on their own. And while Yoder's work confirms the criticisms implied by Barth and Milbank against each other, what is even more important is the sense in which he shows that their respective positions actually require one another. Although Yoder's theology is as radically christological as that of Barth, he argues that Christology is unintelligible apart from the concrete practices of the church in a manner not unlike Milbank. At the same time, however, he shows that such an account of ecclesial practices also requires the rejection of methodologism that Milbank continues to employ, an insight that Barth exemplified in practice, despite his inadequate ecclesiology. Yoder's account of a theological political ontology that resists the lure of theoretical closure is thus superior to that of both Barth and Milbank. Yoder provides both an explanation of and a solution to the problems characteristic of Barth and Milbank in a way that remains in fundamental continuity with their own shared understanding of the need to keep theology properly theological.

Finally, Yoder shows that the question "Can a gift be commanded?" that was originally posed by means of an account of the debate between Barth and Milbank is itself indicative of the problem. The very presumption that theology consists primarily in the analysis of such theoretical questions suggests that a decisive shift has been made away from the embodied practices that constitute the body of Christ. From the standpoint of Yoder, therefore, the debate between Barth and Milbank is best understood as a pseudo-debate. Their disagreement regarding the relationship between command and gift is ultimately interminable as it stands, because problematic assumptions have been incorporated into the very terms of the discussion itself. In the end, albeit in very different ways, Barth and Milbank are both unable to overcome the temptation toward the abstraction of theory. The promise of Yoder's work, by contrast, is that he offers a more complete attempt to return theology to its proper context in the church as the very body of Christ and thereby moves it decisively beyond theory.

—6—

Globalization, Theory, and Dialogical Vulnerability: John Howard Yoder and the Possibility of a Pacifist Epistemology

This chapter explores how the message of the peace of Christ is negated when it is articulated by a medium that is somehow implicated in the expression of violence. At the outset, it is important to emphasize that such an approach assumes that the question of how conversations about peacemaking should take place is much more than just a formal or methodological one. Theoretical and methodological discussions are not neutral, but rather are bound up with substantive ethical and political matters internal to the question of peace itself. Yet the significance of this crucial point is somehow missed by many of the most vocal advocates of Christian pacifism.

As a response to this tragic state of affairs, I offer these reflections on the state of recent peace theology. At the risk of oversimplification, I suggest that contemporary discussions of peace are compromised by a continued, though often subtle, deployment of a series of methodological distinctions—between practice and theory, ethics and theology, politics and knowledge. These distinctions are typically enlisted in an attempt to capture the basic meaning of peace, to make it easier to understand, and thus to bring it under some sort of conceptual control.

But I aim to make peace more complicated, to offer a vision of peace as an essentially difficult notion. I argue that peace is beyond capture, methodologically or otherwise. This involves an examination of the kinds of questions to which the peace of Christ is offered as an answer. Who is included or excluded from these discussions by definition, in virtue of the kinds of questions being asked? More generally, what is the ethical and political import of those categories through which we express the meaning of peace?

Globalization, Peace, and the Question of Theory

The importance of these questions is in many ways heightened by the recent phenomenon of globalization that defines the context for this particular discussion.[1] Among other things, globalization names a series of relatively recent and interrelated changes in technological, economic, and geopolitical realities: the possibility of near-instant worldwide communication, the emergence of the world market, and the diminishing significance of the nation-state.[2] But it is also important to recognize that globalization applies to matters of knowledge and theoretical inquiry as well, and it is with these sorts of questions that I am primarily concerned.

Globalization is not merely a technological, economic, and geopolitical question; it is a philosophical and theological issue as well. Frederic Jameson notes that the rise of globalization is closely related to the decline of nineteenth-century intellectual structures and disciplinary classifications.[3] This involves a heightened awareness of the explicitly political nature of all discourse, or what I have referred to as the interrelationship between medium and message. Against the background of globalization, the modern fascination with abstract and purely theoretical system building seems at best a naive pursuit carried on by disengaged intellectuals, and at worst an attempt to undergird the imperialist project of universalizing Eurocentric culture.[4]

The discussion that follows asks whether Christian pacifism fares any better. I will argue that too much of what is offered in the name of pacifism presumes such a modern intellectual and epistemological orientation and thereby remains implicated in a kind of epistemological violence. But I will suggest that the work of John Howard Yoder provides a way of understanding Christian pacifism that is not susceptible to these sorts of problems. Moreover, I will demonstrate that many sympathetic interpreters and defenders of Yoder's work have failed to appreciate the full significance of his pacifism for questions of epistemology and method. Situating Yoder's pacifism against the background of some recent discussions of globalization helps to illuminate his important but often misunderstood commitment to epistemological pacifism. But before turning to a discussion of Yoder more specifically, I need to say a bit more about the relationship between globalization and the enterprise of theoretical system building.

Globalization highlights the sense in which the production of knowledges and the practices of particular communities go hand in hand and thus cannot be distinguished as form and content. Knowledge and moral inquiry exist in concrete political space. This is not to suggest that political practices somehow determine the nature of particular knowledges. Nor is it to suggest that ethical inquiry has no critical purchase on concrete forms of life. Both assumptions are equally reductive. They both imply that we may choose straightforwardly between theory and practice. On the contrary, there is a complex inter-relationship between knowledge and politics or theory and practice that cannot be neatly codified into discrete components or realms. For the very idea of codification betrays a tendency to exactly the kind of pure theory that discourses of globalization so helpfully call into question. Accordingly, if we must continue to use the language of theory and practice, it is best to speak of theories as embodied in social practices or of practice-informed theories.

Christian pacifism is thus not to be understood merely as a conclusion to some ethical theory that legitimizes and prohibits various activities and justifies particular political structures. It is also—at the same time, in the same place—a particular style of thinking or mode of discourse. In addition to the way of life it calls for, Christian pacifism involves a corresponding epistemology, a different way of thinking about knowledge.

The "reality" of globalization demands awareness of the sense in which knowledge is imported and exported across borders.[5] Theories travel, as Edward Said so helpfully puts it, and they do not remain neutral or unchanged as they move from place to place.[6] Some people have welcomed this apparent overcoming or blurring of nationalistic boundaries, while others have warned of its disturbing consequences. Put bluntly, it is unclear whether globalization represents the overcoming of the colonialist habits of Eurocentric thinking or their ultimate triumph. I suspect the truth is somewhere between these two extremes. Moreover, this crucial ambiguity is somehow central to the very question of globalization itself, in that it suggests that there is finally no such thing as globalization as such. Rather, multiple discourses of globalization serve vastly different purposes. Some operate in complicity with the ever-expanding forces of corporate culture, while others are deeply resistant to the evils of capitalism.[7]

Accordingly, we should be careful how we pose the question of peacemaking in a globalized world. Although we might look to certain discourses of globalization for possible resources to enhance the discussion of Christian pacifism, it is important to be aware that globalization is not a straightforward notion. How theories travel has everything to do with the very substance of the theory itself. In particular, much of what I shall say suggests that Christian pacifism is best understood as traveling nomadically or diasporically, holding no territory, and moving in an ad hoc and episodic manner. Yet all too often the travels of pacifism end up looking more like those of yet another conqueror, proceeding systematically in the pursuit of more and ever greater control. Both ways of traveling cross borders and involve multiple exchanges with various others.

But *Christian* pacifism, as opposed to, say, humanitarian pacifism, can be exchanged only insofar as it is received as a gracious gift from God that is in turn offered to others in a way that is best captured by the notion of witness. When pacifism travels not as witness but as an attempt to secure power and control by means of argument, the conflict between medium and message tends to become most strikingly apparent.

Yoder and the Epistemology of Peace

These brief comments can be fleshed out through an extended interpretation of Yoder's epistemology of peace. Central to my reading of Yoder is an account of what I have called "methodological non-Constantinianism." In addition to his better-known depiction of ecclesial or political non-Constantinianism, according to which the church embodies a counter-politics to that of the world, Yoder's work also includes a counter-epistemology that provides an alternative to general assumptions about what knowledge is and how it might be attained. The church is called to embody peaceableness, which includes, among other things, the refusal of state power and its assumptions about the need to secure its territory. In the same way, Yoder advocates an epistemology of peace that assumes that the truth about God is not something that can be possessed or secured through some kind of theory of justification. It can only be witnessed, which is to say, vulnerably given and received as a contingent gift. Accordingly, there is something about Yoder's ad hoc, dialogical, and unsystematic way of proceeding that is central to his very understanding of peace itself.

In other words, how one reads Yoder makes all the difference in the world. But that makes it all the more important to consider why Yoder is so often misread, even by many who consider themselves to be defending his work. His work is misunderstood because he challenges the very terms of the debate that many of us who read him continue to employ. Unable to break fully with the intellectual habits of the mainstream, many interpret Yoder by appealing to categories whose status he calls into question. To paraphrase Richard Rorty, Yoder's work is often read as if it is an attempt to provide new, nonviolent answers to old questions, whereas it is more appropriate to see him as suggesting that we would be better off not asking those questions anymore.[8]

The questions themselves, the very categories of the epistemological mainstream, constitute a significant part of the conception of violence that Yoder explores. Indeed, Yoder concludes one of his earliest books, *The Christian Witness to the State,* by suggesting: "It is normal for the newcomer to a debate which is already in process to accept the prevailing definitions of terms and choose one of the existing sides, whereas the wiser approach is to question the definitions."[9] This general hermeneutical principle should be kept in mind in any reading of Yoder's work. To take a standard example, Troeltschian categories of church and sect, or Reinhold Niebuhr's distinction between nonresistance and nonviolent resistance, both have the effect of limiting the acceptable alternatives to being either violent or politically irrelevant. But instead of developing new answers to the questions asked by Troeltsch and Niebuhr, the way so many others do, Yoder's pacifism goes much deeper by calling into question the very terms of the debate whose parameters Troeltsch and Niebuhr define.

One general manifestation of Yoder's resistance to the epistemological mainstream is his refusal to develop a systematic elaboration of his position or to offer a basic introduction to his work. He refused to write in a way that gave the impression of starting from scratch, arguing that there is "no scratch from which to start."[10] At the same time, he refrained from offering any "final reading," preferring instead to look for possible new interpretations and potential antagonisms. Indeed, one of the most striking features of Yoder's work is that it embodies an appreciation of radical contingency with respect to both the beginnings and endings of theological inquiry.

This vulnerability is perhaps best exemplified by Yoder's dialogical practice of writing under assignment. He typically proceeded by responding to an invitation to speak and not on the basis of a desire to generate and defend a position against all possible objections.[11] This was an attempt to resist the way in which starting from scratch renders inquiry monological rather than dialogical. The search for a final reading is equally monological, since it fails to prepare one for the ongoing possibility of reformation. Such monological forms of inquiry are violent in the sense that they make inquiry invulnerable to critique at the hands of other dialogue partners. As Yoder himself put it, "The foundational appeal [of starting from scratch] remains, after all, a mental power play to avoid my being dependent on your voluntary assent, to bypass my becoming vulnerable to your world in your otherness."[12]

Monologue tries to secure power by sidestepping vulnerability and articulating one's standpoint as if others do not exist, as if no other relevant participants are in the discussion. But one of the constant points of emphasis throughout Yoder's work is that it is never a question of whether critical and dissenting minority voices exist. Rather, the question is whether one is willing to take those voices seriously. He writes, "There never was a homogenous moral language; it only seemed that there was because the other voices were not heard."[13] The fragmentary and occasionalist style of Yoder's work is often recognized. What tends to be underappreciated is that this way of proceeding is firmly rooted in his understanding of Christian pacifism. Both the temptation to start from scratch and the rhetoric of finality can be seen as forms of epistemological violence in the sense that they constitute a retreat from vulnerability. They undercut the possibility of radical reformation, which Yoder has always read as a call to cultivate a fallible stance of openness to the possibility of radical critique at the hands of other interlocutors.

This stance is further exemplified in Yoder's consistent emphasis on the way violence is reflected in a preoccupation with effectiveness. Indeed, it is precisely this general critique of the orientation toward expedience, or what has been called the "anxiety of influence," that distinguishes the kind of theological or christological pacifism Yoder depicts from the other varieties of pacifism, whether rooted in universal principles or instrumental calculations.

As Yoder himself puts it, "That Christian pacifism which has a theological basis in the character of God and the work of Jesus Christ is one in which the calculating link between our obedience and ultimate efficacy has been broken, since the triumph of God comes through the resurrection and not through effective sovereignty or assured survival."[14] When pacifism is understood as involving a rejection of efficacy, it becomes much broader than the standard understandings that typically construe it as an alternative to some sort of physical or structural violence. In particular, it extends far beyond what is commonly called the ethical or the political (designations Yoder would never use) to include methodological and epistemological questions of the very way inquiry is conducted.

Just as Yoder's reading of the politics of Jesus involves the renunciation of the temptation that it is up to us to ensure that history comes out right, so his understanding of epistemology rejects the pursuit of effectiveness in terms of theoretical dualisms or abstract principles that seek to master contingency. In other words, Yoder's work reflects a widespread attempt to avoid the temptation to secure guarantees that would establish the necessary givenness of its own key claims. And it is important to appreciate that this is motivated by reasons internal to Christian theology itself.[15] The problem with methodological dualisms such as church and sect or subject and object is that they define the available alternatives *in advance* of actual engagement with others and the concrete social contexts they inhabit. Perhaps even more important, they relativize the concrete historical significance of Jesus.

To use Yoder's terminology, epistemology all too often functions as an attempt to put "handles" on history in order to move it in the right direction.[16] Echoing Michel Foucault, Said, and others, Yoder's work grows out of an appreciation of the inextricable interrelationship between politics and knowledge. He recognizes that epistemologies, just as much as concrete political maneuvers, can be expressions of violence, especially insofar as they can underwrite attempts to secure power or exercise forms of control over others.

This kind of epistemological violence is what Yoder refers to in his later writings as "methodologism." Methodologism assumes that there is some one methodology or some preferred idiom for the expression of the Christian life. One notable example that Yoder offers is the assumption, most commonly associated with Stanley Hauerwas, that Christian ethics must employ the language of the virtues rather than that of rights.[17] Another is the claim that narrative is the preferred medium for expressing the truth of the gospel message. Against such assumptions, Yoder argues that the church must not be committed to a single method, epistemology, or idiom. It is not that narrative and the virtues are wrong. They are just not the only ways of expressing the concrete reality of the church.

There are various epistemologies, some of which may be more useful than others for certain specific purposes. But all epistemologies must remain subordinate to the faithful practices of the church as a body of disciplined followers of Jesus. As Yoder himself puts it, "Pluralism as to epistemological method is not a counsel of despair but part of the Good News. Ultimate validation is a matter not of a reasoning process which one could by dint of more doubt or finer hair-splitting push down one story closer to bedrock, but of the concrete social genuineness of the community's reasoning together in the Spirit."[18]

How *Not* to Read Yoder

These reflections are offered against the background of what I take to be two characteristic shortcomings associated with what might be called the "standard approach" to Christian pacifism. The first short-coming privileges the *what* at the cost of the *how*. It focuses on the content of Christian pacifism, understood as an autonomous ethical position, and fails to appreciate that epistemology and method are equally implicated in the question of peace and violence. It is primarily concerned with understanding the message of peace and proceeds in abstraction from questions concerning its proper medium. Such an approach typically proceeds by constructing a comparative typology that seeks to outline the varieties of pacifism as a subset of the wider ethical inquiry into the various approaches to the question of violence more generally. Christian pacifism becomes only one answer to some kind of basic question (e.g., When is it permissible to go to war?) that admits a spectrum of different answers, both violent and nonviolent. But it fails to pay adequate attention to the sense in which the questions themselves are not morally neutral but have significant implications for *how* the debate is conducted. In other words, the spectrum itself might need to be called into question.

The second shortcoming, by contrast, tends to focus on the *how* at the cost of the *what*. Such an approach takes the character of pacifism for granted and concerns itself with epistemological and methodological questions. It begins with the gospel message of peace as a given and concentrates on developing a medium that will more effectively spread the word. In doing so, it recognizes the ad hoc and dialogical character of Yoder's work but treats it as a shortcoming to be corrected and overcome. It suggests that Yoder did himself a serious disservice by not developing his understanding of Christian pacifism in a more thoroughly systematic form. The problem with Yoder's pacifism, according to such a reading, is that it is insufficiently developed with respect to the question of epistemology and method. It is assumed that the Christian alternative of peace will not be taken seriously as a legitimate ethical option unless and until it is developed in a systematic fashion. The problem with such an approach is that it suggests that epistemology is somehow ahistorical and apolitical. Moreover, it overlooks the sense in which methodological and epistemological issues have significant implications for the question of the nature (the *what*) of pacifism itself.

Both of these shortcomings are closely related to the question of how to read (or not read) Yoder. Indeed, they are captured in some instructive misreadings of Yoder's work that are worthy of closer scrutiny. What is perhaps most instructive about these misreadings is that they get so much else right. They are not the same old Niebuhrian attempts to reject Christian pacifism out of hand, but rather they are friendly to the overall commitment to peace that Yoder's work represents.

The first such shortcoming is nicely exemplified by Lisa Sowle Cahill. In the preface to *Love Your Enemies: Discipleship, Pacifism, and Just War Theory*, Cahill writes:

> The challenge to decide about violence, especially state-supported and institutionally perpetuated violence, has been with Christians from the beginning. Christians are not only believers within a religious community, but citizens and members within social, cultural, and political communities. The pluralism of their identity has always posed the problem of where they are to place their allegiance, or how they can reconcile competing allegiances and responsibilities.[19]

In a similar vein, Cahill claims that "the questions of the sect or the church, Scripture or philosophy, conversion in Christ or natural law, the formation of an inclusive community of moral discourse or of a witness against the wider society" are "perennial questions for Christian ethics."[20]

It is important to acknowledge that there are many things Cahill gets right. She recognizes that Christian pacifism is best understood as an embodied way of life rather than a set of action-guiding principles. She also rightly emphasizes the extent to which Christian discussions of peace and war turn on debates about eschatology. But setting up the general debate between Christian pacifists and just warriors in this way remains problematic from the perspective of Yoder, whose work she discusses later in the book. To put it bluntly, Yoder does not believe in "perennial questions for Christian ethics." He appreciates radical historicity and theological contingency too much for that.

To identify "challenges which have been with us from the beginning," as Cahill does, looks suspiciously like just another way of assuming that there is a scratch from which to start. More specifically, by suggesting that there are perennial questions for Christian ethics, Cahill appears to overlook the significance of the Constantinian shift that Yoder takes to be central to his reading of the history of Christian attitudes to war and peace. In short, for Yoder, the kinds of questions Cahill identifies become intelligible only after the fusion of the church and the world, only after the "identification of the civil authority as the bearer of God's cause," represented by the reign of Constantine.[21] Thus, despite her sincere attempt to take Yoder more seriously than many of her predecessors do, Cahill sets up the discussion in such a way that she cannot help but misread him. In particular, she reads Yoder as an attempt to offer new non-Constantinian answers to certain perennial or basic questions, whereas Yoder claims that those questions and the range of alternatives they present as acceptable are themselves the product of a Constantinian perspective.

To generalize, we must not read Yoder as an attempt to provide an answer to the somehow given dualistic question of church and sect. Indeed, we must not read Yoder as if what he writes is a response to any perennial questions. His work is ad hoc, addressing a particular crisis or moment of clarification, responding to a specific invitation to speak, or sometimes constituting a direct engagement with another's work. It is fundamentally dialogical, and it is significant that almost always a specific dialogue partner or context for discussion is mentioned in his published writings. Accordingly, the best way to read Yoder's work is to recognize the concrete social contexts in which his discourse operates. Different contexts often saw him articulate himself in vastly different registers. It is equally important to recognize the other interlocutors who were posing questions and receiving his answers.

Yoder must not be read as if he were defending a self-standing position of some sort. He must not be read as if he were speaking in a single, unified voice across the range of his numerous pursuits. To do so is to make his work seem abstract and systematic in a way that cannot but distort it in significant ways. Indeed, such a sidestepping of these concrete and significantly contingent factors may even be an instance of (even if not explicitly intended as) a form of epistemological violence. In any event, it misses the important fact that Yoder's dialogical way of proceeding is motivated by an attempt to embody an alternative, pacifist epistemology.

The second misreading can be found most clearly in the work of Nancey Murphy. Again, it is instructive to note that Murphy's interpretation of Yoder is a friendly one. Indeed, Murphy's work, much more than the prefatory comments of Cahill on how to approach "the question of war and peace," is offered in defense of Yoder's pacifism. Unlike Cahill, Murphy explicitly recognizes that Yoder's work is unsystematic. But it is at this point that she steps in to offer her assistance. Murphy suggests that Yoder's account of Christian pacifism has not received the widespread attention it deserves because he failed explicitly to develop it in a systematic manner.[22] She tries to remedy this relative neglect of Yoder's Christian pacifism by developing it on the basis of a broadly coherentist epistemology and the notion of a research program developed by the Hungarian philosopher of science, Imre Lakatos.[23]

Although Murphy is friendly to the spirit of Yoder's work, she actually ends up working against Yoder by distorting his understanding of pacifism in certain crucial ways. Like Cahill, though from the opposite end of the how/what spectrum referred to above, Murphy fails to appreciate that Yoder's ad hoc, nonsystematic way of operating is crucial to the very substance of his pacifist theological position.[24] In other words, Murphy's gift of a more sophisticated epistemology is one that Yoder does not want to receive. In effect, she cancels Yoder's understanding of the priority of ecclesiology to epistemology by reasserting the Enlightenment dogma of epistemological primacy. Murphy defends Yoder's politically non-Constantinian understanding of pacifism by drawing on the methodologically Constantinian resources of system and theory, thereby reintroducing the dualism between the political and methodological into his work. In offering a systematic correction to Yoder's work, she is thus compromising the very radicalism of his account of Christian pacifism.

By contrast, we must take Yoder at his word, in a way that Murphy apparently does not, and read his work as a particular style or stance rather than a formal or systematic argument.[25] Just as *The Politics of Jesus* is an attempt to display that the doctrine of Christology cannot be abstracted from the life of disciplined imitation of Christ as sustained by ecclesial practices, Yoder's work as a whole is to be read as a series of thick descriptions of social practices, such as baptism and communion, forgiveness and community discernment, that collectively define a particular stance or way of life called church. More specifically, the stance he describes is that of missionary existence rooted in the diaspora identity of a scattered minority, which is in many ways most clearly exemplified by the social history of the Jews, and in particular Jeremiah's call to "seek the peace of the city where I send you."[26]

The history of Jewish diaspora existence exemplifies a way of speaking to the world that refuses to privilege and reify the world's terms. Among other things, this involves giving up the temptation to take charge of the world.[27] It also involves the rejection of methodological dualisms or the disposition to develop a generalized epistemology that defines the acceptable standards of what is and is not justifiable in advance of actual practice and engagement with concrete dialogue partners. Accordingly, it involves the rejection of any distinction between the *how* and the *what* that both Cahill and Murphy read into Yoder's work, albeit in quite different ways.

All of this relates to what Yoder refers to as the theoretical project of putting handles on history, as noted above. In one of the more important passages of *The Politics of Jesus,* Yoder writes:

> One way to characterize thinking about social ethics in our time is to say that Christians are obsessed with the meaning and direction of history. Social ethical concern is moved by a deep desire to make things move in the right direction. Whether a given action is right or not seems to be inseparable from the question of what effects it will cause. Thus, part if not all of social concern has to do with looking for the right "handle" by which one can "get a hold on" the course of history and move it in the right direction.[28]

But according to Yoder, the faithful witness of the church involves giving up the Constantinian assumption that it is up to us to guarantee that history comes out right. Thus, against the standard post-Troeltschian understanding of political theology, Yoder argues that the church must understand itself in terms of the "functional necessity of just being there with a particular identity" and thereby conceive of its task as providing an example to the world of an alternative politics and an alternative epistemology.[29]

Witness is the most important medium for expressing the message of Christian pacifism. The truth of Jesus can only be witnessed to by way of invitation and example, and is best understood as an exercise of gift-exchange. It cannot be secured or justified on the grounds of a generalized theory of knowledge. By attempting to develop a systematic defense of Yoder's pacifism, Murphy has apparently missed the full significance of this point, which I suspect is closely related to her apparent failure to pick up on the important emphasis on diaspora in Yoder. In other words, Murphy fails to appreciate that the peace of Christ is to be given and received as a gift.

Radical Reformation and Dialogical Vulnerability

In order to make Yoder's epistemology of peace more clear, I want to highlight two positive examples of what this looks like in an attempt to complement the more negative approach undertaken thus far. The first is Yoder's interpretation of radical reformation as a kind of epistemological virtue of vulnerability. Peppered throughout Yoder's writings is the claim that radical reformation is not merely a historical designation or a marker for some particular church group. Rather, it is a call to remain open to the possibility of radical criticism. Yoder puts it most strongly in the introduction to *The Priestly Kingdom*: "In contrast to other views of the church, this is one which holds more strongly than others to a positive doctrine of fallibility. Any existing church is not only fallible but in fact peccable. That is why there needs to be a constant potential for reformation and in the more dramatic situations a readiness for the reformation even to be 'radical.'"[30]

A radical reformation stance involves a dedicated willingness to subject one's own standpoint to criticism and a corresponding attitude of vulnerable openness to new and potentially hostile voices. In other words, Yoder's claim that it is not finally up to us to guarantee that history comes out right can be translated into epistemological terms as the reminder that it is not up to us to secure the truth of the Christian faith. Indeed, Yoder suggests that the slide into violence of the post-Constantinian church results from a more general failure to take seriously the possibility of such self-criticism. Hence, he links the violence of the

Constantinian church to an epistemological attitude of closure. The Constantinian church tended to understand tradition statically, as a kind of deposit, the truth of which is to be protected and secured. By contrast, Yoder reads tradition dynamically, as an ongoing and constantly changing argument extended through time.[31]

Yoder's dynamic conception of tradition does not downplay the significance of disagreement. On the contrary, he highlights the centrality of disagreement, emphasizing the fallibilist sense in which communities and traditions must remain vulnerably open to questioning through ongoing engagement with rival traditions of inquiry.[32] Thus, Yoder's discussion of radical reformation is to be read as an attempt to narrate peace as an epistemological virtue. That, in turn, fosters a conception of discourse that is vigilantly open to the possibility of revision over against an ultimately violent conception of inquiry that tends toward mastery, control, and closure.

The Practice of Patience

Closely related to this way of reading radical reformation is Yoder's emphasis on the methodological significance of patience. In short, patience functions as a second epistemological virtue alongside that of the vulnerable cultivation of a readiness for radical reformation. Together, they are two of the more important skills that contribute to his understanding of epistemological pacifism. Yoder argues that patience is necessary because conversation takes time and hard work. It is especially important in the interest of hearing all the relevant voices and resisting the violent tendency to silence anyone by virtue of the way the debate is constructed in advance of actual engagement. Yoder has long been a critic of the way this kind of silencing of the "lesser voice" of Anabaptism takes place by the privileging of mainstream questions in certain ecumenical discussions.[33] To avoid this, he encourages the cultivation of "ecumenical patience" that accepts "willingly and not just grudgingly the fact that we are conversing with people who have been educated other than ourselves, in ways that we think theologically wrong, yet which are for them the present framework of their integrity and accountability."[34]

The necessity of patience is also captured in his discussion of the ecclesial practice of the "Rule of Paul," an attempt to embody a context for conversation in which "everyone who has something to say can have the floor."[35] The kind of patience Yoder recommends is thus not idle or passive, but rather, an active pursuit of conflict in the sense of being willing to engage in self-criticism, as noted above. Such epistemological patience is characteristically ignored by those who seek to avoid taking seriously the fallibility of their own central claims.

Finally, Yoder notes that the virtue of patience is implied in his rejection of methodologism. As Yoder himself puts it:

> Such "patience" is at work in my suspicion of the drive of many for a single master method and of the "foundationalist" claim to a privileged point of departure. My meeting the interlocutor on his own terms is not merely a matter of accepting the minority's conversational handicap, although it is that. It is also a spirituality and a lifestyle. So I discuss war in just-war terms with nonpacifists. I discuss the exception making with the casuists, rather than sweepingly denouncing casuistry as do Karl Barth, Jacques Ellul, and some Lutherans.[36]

Methodologism—whether in the sense of perennial questions, the idea of a privileged moral idiom, or the attempt to put handles on history—is an attempt to short-circuit the hard work of conversation, to sidestep the messiness of engagement, and thus an attempt to master contingency in the name of the essentially violent pursuit of effectiveness and expedience. By contrast, the epistemological virtue of patience is part of a concerted attempt to refuse such reductive strategies and to embody a counter-epistemology as an alternative to that of the wider world.

Conclusion

In summary, we can learn much about the character of Christian pacifism by attending to Yoder's epistemological and methodological reflections. It is just as important to pay attention to how he proceeded in his work as it is to what he says. Indeed, if Yoder's pacifism is to be properly understood at all, there can be no distinction between the what and the how. The ad hoc and dialogical character of his work is as important to his understanding of peace as are his arguments against the Constantinian alignment of the church and world. Yet contemporary readings of his pacifism all too often project a distinction between form and content back into his work. This has the unfortunate effect of diminishing the radicalism of his understanding of peace.

To return to the question of globalization, I am suggesting that Yoder's epistemology of peace is nicely situated with respect to peacemaking in a globalized world. The discourse of globalization often functions as a reductionist attempt to capture the whole world under the single idiom of capital, which can be seen as an attempt to master contingency. One of the great contributions of Yoder's work, however, is to illustrate the sense in which Christian theology, including much that sees itself as pacifist, is often complicit in such a violent attempt to impose order on the contingent world. Moreover, this violent tendency toward mastery and control is not merely a political or economic phenomenon but is involved in the production of knowledges and theories as well, as Yoder's rejection of methodologism so helpfully shows. One of the main tasks of peacemaking in a globalized world is to be especially attentive to these matters.

It is appropriate to return to the theme of traveling theory. Yoder articulates a conception of Christian pacifism that travels in a way that does not attempt to take control of the world, whether politically or epistemologically. It is important to be attentive to the rhetoric of export that one often hears lurking below the surface of contemporary discussions of Christian peacemaking. From the perspective of Yoder, such a rhetoric must be resisted. The peace of Christ cannot be transported heroically across any and every border in a way that safely eludes the danger of serious distortion.

This is not, however, to suggest that the peace of Christ must stay put. Rather, it is to emphasize that the offering of the gift of peace is a decidedly complicated matter. It resembles a delicate and nuanced art more than a mechanistic program. The peace of Christ cannot be bureaucratized and domesticated, just as it cannot finally be secured. Rather, peace can only be given by way of witness. This, of course, is Yoder's name for an epistemology that is both vulnerable and patient. Such an approach does not attempt to smooth over difference but appreciates the messiness and contingency of the world and revels in the many conversations that this condition allows. To gesture toward the possibility of just one such conversation, I close with the Palestinian postcolonial theorist Edward Said, who captures much of what I have been trying to say about Yoder:

A part of something is for the foreseeable future going to be better than all of it. Fragments over wholes. Restless nomadic activity over the settlements of held territory. Criticism over resignation. The Palestinian as self-consciousness in a barren plain of investments and consumer appetites. The heroism of anger over the begging-bowl, limited independence over the status of clients. Attention, alertness, focus. To do as others do, but somehow to stand apart. To tell your story in pieces, *as it is*.[37]

—7—

Patience, Witness, and the Scattered Body of Christ: Yoder and Virilio on Knowledge, Politics and Speed

> The war-machine is not only explosives, it's also communications, vectorization. It's essentially the speed of delivery. . . . Pure War, not the kind which is declared.
>
> —Paul Virilio

Among the many strange twists and turns that John Howard Yoder takes in his wild and wide-ranging reflections on theological nonviolence, two crucial and closely related moments are his understanding of patience as method and his interpretation of the scattered, diasporic body of Christ. The connection between these two key aspects of Yoder's work merits further exploration. I do this by bringing Yoder into conversation with the contemporary French war theorist Paul Virilio. Recognized for his penetrating analyses of the proliferation of violence in the contemporary cultures of Western capitalism, Virilio is best known for his interpretation of violence as speed.

Virilio helps us see that to understand violence and war we must look beyond mere conflict. More important than explosions, bunkers, troop deployment, and other instances of overt conflict, Virilio claims that violence involves a way of organizing political space and its characteristic modes of knowledge. We must move beyond war to an

115

examination of what he calls the "war-machine," beyond a focus on violent activities in and of themselves to an understanding of the conditions that make violent activity possible and the changing conditions that have made it extreme, total, and ubiquitous.

It is at this point that Virilio highlights the epistemological and political priority of speed. He develops this claim through a reading that stresses the connection between technological developments involving the commodification of knowledge as information and the rapid and wide-ranging developments in the techniques of surveillance. Because of the largely unquestioned triumph of these forms of power, Virilio argues that violence has come to organize the very way we think, including the way we have come to think about peace.

Although Virilio's analysis of the contemporary war-machine is valuable in its own right, I am particularly interested in exploring his interpretation of violence as speed and the bearing it has on contemporary peace theology. Virilio explodes our limited understanding of peace, demonstrating that it is much more complicated and multifaceted than is often assumed. Peace is not simply the contrary of violence in some straightforward way, as if they can be located on the same plane or placed on opposite ends of the same spectrum. Moreover, our understanding of peace and violence is limited if we think of them as political implications that are drawn from theoretical claims to knowledge in a secondary sort of way. Rather, Virilio's readings of the war-machine show that political matters are intimately bound up with questions of knowledge themselves. He demonstrates, in other words, that knowledge is always already political.

Since violence is reflected in the very way we think about thinking, it follows that peace must name a simultaneous counter-politics and counter-epistemology that radically shifts the terms of the debate. To return to the metaphors above, it occupies a different plane and inaugurates an entirely new spectrum of possibilities. This is hinted at in Virilio's examination of situations in which there is an absence of overt violence, such as the state of mutual deterrence between nation-states or technologies that are able to minimize destruction and human casualties.

The crux of Virilio's position is that these are *not* to be understood as advances toward peace. Rather, they are developments in the shifting reality of war. In a similar vein, he suggests that the discourse of peace must refrain from humanitarian abstractions such as development or the common assumption that violence grows out of limits imposed on free access to information, that violence is the result of miscommunication. In short, Virilio maintains that these liberal interpretations of peace fail to break sufficiently with the kinds of militaristic epistemological and political categories that breed and sustain violence.

The most general lesson of Virilio's work is that a peaceable alternative to violence requires a radical reconfiguration of what might be called the knowledge-politics complex. It is at this point that Virilio is helpful for understanding the meaning of peace in Yoder's theology. In particular, Yoder is best understood as identifying many of the same conditions of violence and attempting to provide the same kind of double-sensed reconfiguration of knowledge and politics that Virilio calls for. Most importantly, reading Yoder's work against the background of Virilio highlights the significance of Yoder's appeal to the practice of patience as a way of resisting the violent logic of speed. It also helps explain how his conception of epistemological patience is related to his notion of the body of Christ as a scattered, diasporic body.

Such an approach to Yoder stresses that his interest in questions of peace and violence goes all the way down. Interpretations of peace and violence do not rest on some neutral methodological ground. It is necessary to emphasize this because too many interpretations of his work continue to distort his account of the gospel message of peace by forcing it into political and epistemological categories whose status he calls into question as instances of violence. For example, Yoder's understanding of peace is often obscured by those who read him with the assumption that we already know what peace is. This is particularly problematic when peace is taken to name some identifiable state of affairs or some kind of ideal that it is up to us to bring about.

Many continue to enlist Yoder's name in support of an apologetic strategy designed to defend Christian pacifism against those who doubt its capacity to be effective. In doing so, undue stress is placed on the potential of the church to *transform* society.[1] It is suggested that the church can be a "potent force" that has the "power to shape history," claiming that a better future can thus be *secured,* albeit nonviolently.[2] Among other things, I am suggesting that reading Yoder as a conversation partner with Virilio is valuable precisely in that it helps to avoid this kind of ongoing preoccupation with effectiveness.

By way of situating and anticipating the discussion that follows, I offer three claims that guide my interpretation of Yoder's work more generally. First, like Barth, Yoder refused to let the doubters set the agenda for Christian theology. Second, Yoder consistently rejected the kind of instrumentalist thinking that such an apologetic approach exemplifies as contributing to just the kind of violent operation of power to which the church is called to witness an alternative. He did not seek a new nonviolent way of transforming society or securing the future. Rather, he claimed that the peace of Christ involves a rejection of the possessive logic of security and social control. A key part of Yoder's theology is his critique of the Constantinian project of outfitting history with handles designed to move it in the right direction. The pacifism of Christian discipleship thus crucially involves giving up the assumption that it is up to us to make history come out right.[3]

Third, and perhaps most important for the purposes of the present discussion, it is important to recognize that Yoder never assumed that he finally knew what peace was. This is perhaps most clearly exemplified in what might be called the negative orientation of his theology, the sense in which his work consists in a series of exercises dedicated to unthinking the necessity of violence. Many of his writings can be described as an attempt to delegitimate theological strategies designed to guarantee the securing of power.

His profoundly critical theology functions as an ongoing critique of the will to seize power, and in particular those expressions of power that turn on what he described as "seizing godlikeness."[4] To the extent that he worked in a more positive fashion, it is important to recognize that Yoder did not write a systematic treatise on the nature of Christian pacifism, but rather, engaged in an ongoing series of experiments in understanding the peace of Christ. His work is thus necessarily fragmentary and ad hoc. It is episodic, exploratory, and experimental. He offered a collage, a series of sketches designed to reveal certain tendencies, not a final or total perspective on the very nature of peace as such. My attempt to bring Yoder into contact with Virilio is offered in this same spirit, as an experimental sketch that Yoder did not himself provide. It is not an attempt to bring us one step closer to the final word on peace, but at attempt to reveal further tendencies that too often go unnoticed by those readers of Yoder's work who continue to filter his understanding of peace through existing political and epistemological categories.

Violence and Technical Knowledge: Speed as the Essence of War

The basic tendency that Virilio identifies is the close relationship between violence and speed. As Virilio himself puts it, "The war-machine is not only explosives, it's also communications, vectorization. It's essentially the speed of delivery. . . . Pure War, not the kind which is declared."[5] Building upon and at the same time calling into question Marxist interpretations of the politicization of wealth, Virilio calls for a more thoroughgoing recognition of the political character of speed.[6] Indeed, he suggests that violence is primarily a function of speed and only secondarily connected with wealth. That is because wealth is itself the product of the kind of power and mobility speed engenders.

More specifically, Virilio claims that the logic of violence as speed is best understood in terms of the shift from geopolitics into chrono-politics. Violence unfolds and develops in a transformation from a geographical analysis of space to the merging of space-time.[7] This is reflected in the increasing technologization of the war-machine. For example, Virilio identifies three stages in the expanding power of weapons systems.[8] The first instruments of the war were those of obstruction: "ramparts, shields, the size of the elephant." The war-machine originally hinged on the deployment of bunkers, walls, and other physical fortifications designed to define and manage space and thereby to inhibit the movement of one's enemies. The next stage arrives with instruments of destruction, from the development of artillery to the invention of the nuclear bomb, and reaches its apex in the false peace of nuclear deterrence. Finally, Virilio claims that war reaches still a different stage with the deployment of weapons of communication.

Contemporary war is thus best characterized as a kind of virtual "infowar" or "cyberwar," whose primary mechanism is the information bomb. Infowar involves the widespread participation of the media and the deployment of technologies of mass communication of the kind that make the phenomenon of terrorism possible.[9] Virilio writes, "Yesterday's war was a *totalitarian* war, in which the dominant elements were quantity, mass, and the power of the atomic bomb. Tomorrow's war will be *globalitarian,* in which, by virtue of the information bomb, the qualitative will be of greater importance than geophysical scale or population size. . . . Not 'clean war' *with zero deaths,* but 'pure war' *with zero births* for certain species which have disappeared from the bio-diversity of living matter."[10]

As the logic of violence unfolds and intensifies, war is becoming

less and less about territory and more about the management of information. In its earlier stages, war was about the defense and takeover of
geographical space. Now the army only moves in once the battle is
already over. In each new stage of weapons development, space is
compressed by a newfound capacity for speed. This gives rise to what
Virilio calls the "aesthetics of disappearance." The merging of technology and violence gives rise to a new gnostic "mortification of the
flesh."[11] As violence grows and intensifies, the city and other local
forms of geographical and physical space, not to mention the body, are
literally disappearing. As Virilio himself puts it, "The world disappears
in war, and war as a phenomenon disappears from the eyes of the
world."[12]

In a related point of emphasis, Virilio maintains that our visual
capacities are themselves transformed by the war-machine insofar as
the "visual field" is reduced to the "technical sightline" of a military
device.[13] As perception is mediated by the logic of violence as speed, a new
vision of the world emerges. With the perfection of near-instantaneous
real-time speed of delivery, television is transformed into a "planetary
grand-scale optics" or "tele-surveillance," which fosters a preoccupation
with security and a kind of universal voyeurism.[14] Local space and time
disappear and are replaced by a single, global and virtual "real-time."
With the triumph of this sort of "sightless vision" and the arrival of an
"age of intensiveness," space is further compressed, and power
becomes even more total. Unlike Jean Baudrillard, who welcomes the
disappearance of politics into a trans-political age of the "intensity of
the instant," Virilio is harshly critical of this development as signaling
a totalizing proliferation of violence.[15]

Because of the rise of technology in its relation to the military-
industrial complex, Virilio argues that the logic of violence increasingly comes to dominate the very way we understand knowledge. This
claim is further developed by means of the identification of a shift from
strategy to logistics. By logistics, Virilio means the triumph of means
over intelligence, where "rationality is considered only in terms of its
efficiency, whatever the horizon."[16] Whereas violence begins with a
strategic conception of quantitative, calculative rationality designed to
maneuver and prepare for attacks in geographical space, it is transformed by means of the logic of speed into a logistical conception of
technological, instrumental rationality dedicated to management and
hyper-centralization.[17] With the triumph of effectiveness, Virilio again

claims that war and violence become increasingly total and omnipresent. The logic of violence tends toward what he calls Pure War. From the standpoint of logistical rationality, violence is no longer "acted out in repetition," but involves an ongoing state of "infinite preparation."[18] In such a situation of pure war, "all of us are already civilian soldiers" participating in "acts of war without war."[19]

Virilio suggests that this totalizing logic of war and violence is exemplified in the way states tend no longer to be interested merely in the outward colonization of other peoples—what he calls "exo-colonization." Rather, Virilio claims that nations are increasingly engaged in projects of "endo-colonization"—the "inward" colonization of one's own population by means of systematic underdevelopment and "pauperization" in the name of a more complete investment in the economy of war: "In the society of national security . . . the armed forces turn against their own population: on the one hand to exact the funds necessary for Pure War, the infinite development of weaponry . . .; and on the other to control society."[20] Echoing Michel Foucault's account of "surveillance societies" and Gilles Deleuze's discussion of "control societies," Virilio claims that logistical rationality justifies a strategy of policing and managerial control designed to condition people for more effective participation in the ever-expanding war-machine.

A Violent Peace?

The strength of Virilio's work consists in its incisive and penetrating analysis of the logic of contemporary war and the proliferation of violence even in what is claimed to be a state of peace. Most importantly, Virilio's readings of contemporary culture help one to appreciate the sense in which much discourse about peace is dangerously misguided because it is blinded by its own complicity in the logic of violence and the war-machine. This is precisely the same danger that lurks in the work of those who enlist Yoder in support of the kind of transformative social strategy mentioned above. In Virilio's terminology, this is to defend a logistical conception of peace that is bound to fail because it is thoroughly embedded in the very logic of violence. My reading of Yoder by way of Virilio is meant to suggest that Yoder's theology involves many of the same resources and interpretive moves that Virilio deploys in revealing the totalizing logic of Pure War and the war-machine.

Virilio's analysis of the war-machine can be read as an updated and more militarily sophisticated version of what Yoder calls Constantinianism. In other words, the tendencies Virilio identifies can be added to the list of the many neo-Constantinianisms that Yoder insisted on identifying as an unsettling reminder to those who like to claim that we have reached something called post-Christendom that allegedly provides a newfound opportunity for the nonviolent church to articulate its theology on equal ground with the now disestablished established church.[21] In short, Virilio articulates various tendencies of the logic of violence with which I think Yoder would agree. Yoder's resistance to the triumph of effectiveness, his refusal to read the peace of Christ in terms of the instrumentalist project of "putting handles on history in an attempt to move it in the right direction," is an attempt to call into question just the kind of policing of time that Virilio identifies as characteristic of the rise of logistics.

Indeed, Virilio's claim that "the will to organize time is a questioning of God" would serve nicely as a guiding hermeneutical principle for the interpretation of Yoder's theology as a whole.[22] At the same time, Yoder's interpretation of Constantinian violence also echoes Virilio's account of the aesthetics of disappearance, as he narrates the slide of the visible, embodied church into a preoccupation with the doctrine of the church's invisibility. On Yoder's reading, the church's complicity with violence is intimately linked to the disappearance of the visible church as an embodied politics of resistance. More recently, Yoder's interest in patience as an attempt to imagine a counter-epistemology of peace can be read against the background of an appreciation of the logic of violence as speed that Virilio so helpfully articulates.

Not only are these important features of Yoder's work illuminated and enhanced by this kind of positive engagement with Virilio. Even more important for the purposes of understanding Yoder's theology is the sense in which he is able to avoid certain weaknesses that have been associated with Virilio's work. Although Virilio is helpful in diagnosing the contemporary escalation of violence even in the absence of acts of war, he is noticeably less instructive in articulating the possible forms that resistance might take.

When he is pushed on the question of what it would mean to resist the kind of totalizing violence he outlines, Virilio tends to fall back on typically banal liberal clichés that appeal to education and better understanding. When asked "What strategies can we adopt to fight this exponential growth of destructive power?" Virilio answers: "Today, the target is to try to have an understanding of speed. Understand what's been happening for twenty-five years."[23] There is, of course, some truth to such an appeal for increased understanding, insofar as it can make us aware of our unacknowledged complicity with the war-machine. But if that is all there is to say on the matter, it remains a rather thin account of resistance. The significance of Yoder's work in this context is that it provides the kind of thick descriptions of counter-political and counter-epistemological practices that Virilio calls for but does not finally deliver.

The Territorial Lure of the Slow? A Critique of Virilio and a Yoderian Rejoinder

At the same time, I suggest that Yoder's theology is better suited to respond to criticisms that have been directed at Virilio's account of the contemporary merging of violence and technology. William Connolly has argued that Virilio's work is limited by its nearly single-minded preoccupation with speed and the crisis of the physical dimension. Connolly claims that Virilio's interpretation of the logic of speed is overdetermined by the military paradigm such that he fails to appreciate the possibility of other less-threatening "modalities and experiences of speed."[24] In particular, he suggests that Virilio undervalues the positive contribution speed might make in de-sanctifying closed and exclusionary identities.[25]

Connolly also maintains that Virilio's critical analysis of the transition from geopolitical space to the chrono-political merging of space-time reveals an underlying commitment to the centered, territorial "memory of the nation" as the place where political deliberation should occur. In other words, Virilio remains committed to a concentric model of identity as a closed and bounded site of power from which identity emerges as a possession to be secured and protected against external threats. Connolly argues that such a spatial orientation is equally part of the logic of violence. And yet Connolly does not offer these objections as a complete refutation of Virilio's analysis of the relationship between speed and violence. Rather, he calls for a more ambiguous appreciation of the logic of speed. Connolly writes,

> Speed can be dangerous. At a certain point of acceleration, it jeopardizes freedom and shortens the time in which to engage ecological issues. But the crawl of slow time contains injuries, dangers, and repressive tendencies too. It may be wise therefore

to explore speed as an ambiguous medium that contains some
positive possibilities. The positive possibilities are lost to those
who experience its effects only through nostalgia for a pristine
time governed by the compass of the centered nation, the security
of stable truth, the idea of nature as a purposive organism or a
set of timeless laws, and the stolidity of thick universals.[26]

While I think it is misleading to interpret Virilio as if he were
recommending a return to concentric and exclusionary identities of
possession and control, I am not concerned with adjudicating the debate
between Virilio and Connolly. What is important for the present discussion is to recognize that Yoder's theology provides just the kind of
ambiguous analysis of the relationship between violence and speed that
Connolly calls for Virilio to acknowledge. In short, the value of Yoder's
nonviolent theology is that it provides an appreciation of both the logic
of violence as speed and the violence of territoriality, which may justify
a more positive appreciation of the value of speed. In doing so, Yoder
is simultaneously critical of both the logic of violence as speed and the
aesthetics of disappearance that Virilio identifies, on the one hand, and
the equally violent logic of the bounded, territorial space of possessive
identity that Connolly worries about, on the other.

It will be helpful to outline some of the key resources that I take to
support such a reading of Yoder's work. Against the background of
Connolly's critique of Virilio, I begin with Yoder's discussion of the
counter-political nature of the church as the diasporic, scattered body
of Christ. From there, I will work backward to the question of violence
and speed that I began with, but this will now be approached from the
standpoint of Yoder's counter-epistemological notion of "patience as
method." Finally, it will be instructive to note how these two closely
interrelated moments in Yoder's nonviolent theology come together in
his understanding of the practice of witness.

The Scattered Body of Christ

Yoder's theology implies that the logic of violence manifests itself
in what Virilio calls an aesthetics of disappearance. This is why he
highlights the importance of the visible otherness of church as the body
of Christ. But this is not to recommend a static, concentric conception
of space of the kind that Connolly foists onto Virilio. Rather, Yoder's
ecclesiology is best read as an ongoing experiment in the possibility of
a nonviolent and nonconcentric organization of political space. One of

the most important aspects of Yoder's ecclesiology in this regard is his account of the diasporic, nonterritorial existence of the church. This, in turn, is best understood against the background of Yoder's claim that the church must cultivate a readiness for radical reformation that consistently rejects the essentially violent temptations toward closure, finality, and purity that haunt so much contemporary theology— including much theology that claims to be oriented toward peace. In other words, Yoder's reading of the scattered body of Christ is most importantly an attempt to articulate an ecclesiology that resists the Constantinian temptation to self-absolutization.

Yoder's commitment to a nonconcentric model of identity is reflected in his appreciation of the significance of Jewish diaspora existence. "Dispersion is mission."[27] Scattering is the grace of God. It is possible to remain Jewish in exile, not because Jewish identity is strong, unbending, and self-sustaining. Rather, it is because Judaism understands its peoplehood as a gift over which it is not finally in charge. Jewish identity is fluid in a way that allows it to flourish in many different social settings.[28] Because its life is gift, God is able to "renew the life of faith anywhere."[29] It is significant that Yoder uses the terminology of renewing. The continued survival of the people of God is crucially not understood in terms of preservation, but rather in terms of its receptivity to God's ongoing generosity. Jewish identity in exile is not to be secured by reproducing and protecting what has been left behind at home. Rather, it is continuously refashioned as it enters into and interacts with different social contexts. In doing so, Jewish identity itself undergoes significant and unpredictable changes, even while it remains in some ways the same.

On such a reading, the Jeremian call to "seek the peace of the city" names a way of engaging the world that simultaneously refuses both the universalist (chrono-political) temptation to privilege the language of the wider culture, and the isolationist (geopolitical) temptation to preserve and maintain the language of home in a kind of sectarian withdrawal. Diaspora Judaism neither fully renounces its past identity for unqualified citizenship in the new world, nor does it seek merely to preserve and maintain itself as a kind of static given. Both options presume a territorial conception of self-identity that defines itself over against otherness. The significance of the diasporic scattering of the body is that it allows identity to be understood as an ongoing negotiation with the other. Yoder suggests that in becoming resident aliens, Jewish diaspora existence represents a third alternative to the standard options of the universalist denial of the body and its existence in space and the isolationist preservation of it through policed boundaries.

Yoder's depiction of Jewish identity—and by extension his understanding of the church as the body of Christ—is thus similar to the nonconcentric model of identity and social existence that Connolly calls for.[30] The diasporic notion of a scattered body rejects the idea of a closed and bounded space existing within a series of outwardly expanding circles. Rather, identity is viewed as a negotiation of exchange, sometimes affirming, sometimes critical. It involves multiple networks of overlap and engagement with other cultural identities, each of which is itself interpreted as a potential gift in the hope that it participates somehow in the unpredictable and excessive economy of God. Because it renounces the temptation to understand its identity as a stable entity to be protected and preserved, one's social existence in space is thus "complicated and compromised by numerous crosscutting allegiances, connections, and modes of collaboration."[31]

Patience as Method

In addition to his nonviolent reconfiguration of political space, Yoder's theology equally involves the development of a nonviolent counter-epistemology. This is at least part of the meaning behind his oft-repeated declaration of the epistemological priority of the church to the world. In other words, the world names a series of violent habits of thought that are dedicated to security and insulation against risk. By contrast, Yoder's nonviolent epistemology does not attempt to secure or defend the truth of its distinctive claims against all comers. It is not an attempt to make Christianity necessary by developing arguments designed to make others "have to believe."[32] Rather, it assumes that truthfulness is an utterly contingent gift that can only be given and received and that it emerges at the site of vulnerable interchange with the other. Accordingly, it is fundamentally open-ended and radically concrete, refusing any self-legitimating appeal to theoretical abstraction. Among the most important aspects of such a nonviolent epistemology is Yoder's understanding of "patience as method."

Much contemporary critical theory locates the problem of epistemological violence in the existence of totalizing metanarratives. The possibility of a nonviolent epistemology is then said to involve an appreciation of micro-narrative particularity in which knowledges are given more fragmentary and ambiguous forms of expression. While Yoder is critical of the kind of violence associated with epistemologies of totalizing metanarrative singularity, his reconfiguration of knowledge moves beyond the tendency to focus on metanarrativity as such to emphasize the significance of speed of delivery. Epistemological violence is associated not only with the scope of narrative, but it is also located in the speed with which such narratives, whether macro or micro, unfold.

In other words, epistemological non-Constantinianism is not merely opposed to metanarrative but also to hypernarrative. The problem with much contemporary theology is that it features a preoccupation with the epistemological and rhetorical movement of speed. This can be seen in the current preference for developing sweeping historical narratives that are not subject to ongoing self-critical scrutiny the way Yoder's reading of non-Constantinianism is. In short, theology operates according to a violent logic of speed whenever it is unwilling to risk the possibility of ongoing, timeful "open conversation."

The value of Yoder's work is that it lingers. Not only is it important to appreciate his account of patience as an epistemological virtue in which the church cultivates a readiness for radical reformation as an alternative to manipulative and possessive modes of inquiry. Perhaps even more important is the sense in which Yoder's work *practices* patience. Yoder's theology proceeds patiently, entering vulnerably into the world of another, rather than employing an accelerated and possessive or logistical hermeneutics of mastery and control. This is also exemplified in the way he keeps coming back to and complicating his understanding of non-Constantinianism with various versions of neo-Constantinianism, as noted above. In addition to the vision of a non-Constantinian epistemology of peace that Yoder offers, patience is instructively exemplified in Yoder's own rhetorical practice in a way that distinguishes it from much contemporary theology and ethics.

Yoder patiently enters into the messy world of concrete social reality, refusing to outfit history with handles for easier, more efficient negotiation, while others remain captured by the temptation to master contingency in their deployment of fast-moving hypernarrative strategies. He refuses to short-circuit debate and genuine engagement by moving on too quickly. And it is because he appreciates the connection between violence and speed in this way that Yoder helps to envision the possibility of the church as a counter-political and counter-epistemological interruption of the logic of violence. The Constantinian logic of violence deploys speed as an evasion of risk, as an attempt to make theology necessary and secure. But Yoder argues that Christian theology fails when it tries to escape vulnerability, because the gospel message of peace is a gift given in Jesus Christ.

One can see such an attempt to practice patience exemplified in Yoder's life-long engagement with the just war tradition. What is particularly noteworthy about his numerous encounters with the just war tradition is the sense in which they embody a spirit of charitable receptivity to the voice of the other. He takes the possibility of a just war more seriously than many of his fellow pacifists. In fact, it might be suggested that he takes the just war tradition more seriously than many defenders of just war themselves. Yoder argues that christological pacifists have a stake in defending "the integrity of just-war thought" as a tradition "with teeth," and proceeds to do so by calling it to be more honest than it characteristically has been in articulating and observing the criteria for discriminating between just and unjust wars.[33] In particular, he calls contemporary defenders of just war to be more honest in recognizing the stringent limits and restraints the tradition imposes on warfare.[34]

Instead of suggesting that the just war tradition is essentially violent and that it therefore must be rejected *as such,* Yoder seeks charitably to engage the just war tradition on its own terms. He calls it to be clearer in articulating its general presumption against violence. In doing so, Yoder sets out to challenge two common and interrelated assumptions that inhibit debate about violence and nonviolence in the Christian tradition. First, he calls into question the assumption that the just war tradition is the majority view in the Christian tradition. Second, he challenges the idea that pacifism and just war are diametrically opposed stances.[35] Rather, he argues that the consistent embodiment of the just war tradition is a historical rarity, and that the majority stance is actually a realistic or blank-check endorsement of war in the name of national self-interest. When just war is thus properly situated alongside pacifism as a minority view, Yoder suggests that both pacifists and the defenders of the just war tradition have much to learn from a more serious engagement with one another.

To say that Yoder's engagement with the just war tradition exemplifies a stance of charitable receptivity to his dialogue partners is not to suggest that he is uncritical of the just war position. Indeed, he is far more critical than many other pacifist approaches, because his criticisms are more direct than the more common theoretical objections to the idea of just war in general. The value of Yoder's engagement with the just war tradition is that he strives to move beyond the general question of the rightness or wrongness of war as such and proceeds more deeply into the particularities of the debate, such as a discussion of the kinds of christological commitments involved in their various conceptions of charity or an examination of the kind of social formation the rival stances presume.

It is also noteworthy that Yoder often preferred to redirect the discussion to more specific questions, such as the possibility of Christian participation in police work.[36] Instead of claiming to produce a final adjudication of the debate between pacifists and just warriors, much of Yoder's work is dedicated to making that discussion more complicated by elaborating the subtle differences and varieties these stances have taken.[37] In all of these ways, he seeks to resist a logistical, totalizing, and concentric model of dialogue between pacifists and just warriors that is rooted in a logic of speed.

In Yoder's hands, pacifism and the just war tradition are not presented as two entirely distinct or concentric wholes. Rather, there are numerous strands of overlap and willingness to entertain the possibility of ongoing development and reformation in a way that cannot be predicted in advance. As Yoder himself puts it, "The exposition I have chosen is to let the panorama of diverse theories unfold progressively, from the dialogue already in progress, rather than proceeding 'foundationally' on the ground of what someone might claim as 'first principles.'"[38] Yoder's interest in defending the integrity of the just war tradition is part of a larger attempt to create conditions for productive dialogue and disagreement to take place. He worries that contemporary discussions too often short-circuit the possibility of genuine debate by oversimplifying and failing to engage the detailed complexity of rival stances.

But it is important to recognize that this way of understanding dialogical engagement grows out of Yoder's attempt to articulate a nonviolent reconfiguration of knowledge. While he aims to make the just war tradition vulnerable to a pacifist interpretation of the Christian tradition, Yoder's work is equally an attempt to make Christian pacifism vulnerable to a just war understanding. This does not occur at the cost of critical engagement. Rather, Yoder seeks to show that such a discussion need not be an all-or-nothing affair. He denies the temptation to throw out the just war tradition as such in the way that pacifists too often do. Yoder's engagement with the just war tradition differs strikingly from other pacifist critics of just war who, in making their criticism too complete and thorough, embody the violence I have called methodological Constantinianism.

Accordingly, one of Yoder's main contributions is his attempt to cultivate the patience required to keep the debate alive. He does this from the standpoint that unapologetically defends a particular strand of the Christian pacifist tradition. But he also does so in a way that attempts to take seriously the alternative of a just war as a genuine option in the Christian tradition. Whether defenders of the just war tradition respond in kind by treating such an understanding of Christian pacifism as a genuine option is something he cannot guarantee. It can only be hoped that a gift offered in a spirit of vulnerability is received and exchanged as a counter-gift in return.

The Practice of Witness

Yoder's joint emphasis on the diasporic, scattered body of Christ and his understanding of patience as method are brought together in his account of the missionary character of the church, and in particular the practice of witness. In short, the category of witness captures both the assumption that the church is called to be *for* the nations, and the recognition that it must remain nonviolent in being so oriented. Witness is rooted in the confession of the lordship of Christ, and the conviction that the model of lordship Christ embodies is the rule of the lamb. Yoder claims that "to confess that Jesus Christ is Lord makes it inconceivable that there should be any realm where his writ would not run. That authority, however, is not coercive but nonviolent; it cannot be imposed, only offered."[39]

Because Christians confess that Jesus is lord of the whole cosmos, the church is called to share the gospel message as good news for the world. But because this good news involves a breaking of the cycle of violence that includes the renunciation of logistical effectiveness and possessive sovereignty, it can only be offered as a gift whose reception cannot be guaranteed or enforced. A non-Constantinian understanding of witness does not begin with a theory of universal validation through which the truth of the gospel message can *then* be justified to all people. Yoder maintains that this is just another manifestation of the

Constantinian preoccupation with effectiveness in attempting to make history come out right. He is thus calling into question the sense in which the category of witness itself tends to be understood in terms of the violent logic of speed. Yoder's genealogical analysis of Constantinianism suggests that such an apologetic conception of witness is only intelligible against the background of the presumption that humans are responsible for controlling the world. However, witness looks different from the standpoint of the non-Constantinian church's *hope* that God is in control of history.

To say that witness is gift is to say that the gospel message is offered in the absence of any additional handles designed to guarantee its reception. The test of witness is not simply whether or not it is received in fact, but whether it is received *as gift*. The gift of good news is to be received "as it is" or "in its own right" and not by means of an additional vehicle or medium that might guarantee its successful passage. Because the gospel message is that of a peace that rejects the primacy of effectiveness, the message itself is the only available medium. Accordingly, Yoder claims that "the challenge to the faith community should not be to dilute or filter or translate its witness, so that the 'public' community can handle it without believing, but to so purify and clarify and exemplify it that the world can perceive it to be good news without having to learn a foreign language."[40] Although Yoder emphasizes that the good news turns on being received by the listener, this is not to suggest that it is preoccupied with what people want to hear.[41] Such an assumption would suggest that there is a sense in which the gift is known prior to its being received in such a way that it equally ceases to be a genuine gift.[42] Rather than identifying underlying conditions or developing new strategies for the effective deliverance of the truth, the church is called to embody its otherness in a way that makes intelligible the truth of Christ for the world. To emphasize the missionary existence of the peace church is to suggest that it lives, not as instrument, but as example. The task of the church is thus not to Christianize the world, but to *be* the church. As Yoder himself puts it, the primary meaning of witness is "the functional necessity of just being there with a particular identity."[43] Witness thus names a way of life characteristic of the body of Christ, a scattered body whose existence is nonterritorial and nonconcentric. In so being, the church is called to provide a concrete example of good news to and for the world. The good news is that of an alternative way of life that is not rooted in the violent impulse toward self-preservation, but rather in the nonviolent and vulnerable receptivity of the other as gift.

This interpretation of Yoder's political and epistemological reconfigurations of peace echoes key aspects of Virilio's work. Like Virilio, Yoder rejects an outlook of split-second responsiveness and technical effectiveness that ultimately turns on the desire to secure power. But at the same time, this is not a complete refusal of movement that might justify an attitude of closure. Yoder's account of the church and its modes of knowledge is an attempt to develop a conception of timefulness that resists both the absolute priority of speed and its ultimate overcoming.

A pacifist outlook is constantly moving, sometimes radically, but only because it involves the patience to hear all the relevant sides of the conversation. It is crucial to recognize that the standard alternatives of a static exclusivism that silences the voice of the other and a hyperaccelerated tolerance that allows a space for the other to talk without hearing what it has to say are equally implicated in a logic of violence as speed. The great significance of Yoder's work lies in its ability to demonstrate that no such approach is capable of receiving the gracious gift of God in Jesus Christ that is peace itself.

—8—

The Agony of Truth: Martyrdom, Violence, and Christian Ways of Knowing

It is hard to resist the temptation to see truth as a kind of settlement, as an agreement of some sort. We like to see truth as something arrived at—the terminus of a journey or the endpoint of a conversation. As David Bentley Hart puts it, "What is called truth is usually a consensus wrested from diversity amid a war of persuasions."[1] By this, I take it that Hart means to highlight the common assumption that truth names a point at which things finally come together—a kind of last word, where we reach a state of comforting, harmonious unity, a sense of closure in which differences have been overcome once and for all. In doing so, we assume that truth names what Rowan Williams has called a "total perspective."[2] In a similar vein, we like to speak of truth as a possession, as something grasped, and, when grasped, something we have a certain mastery over. We speak as if truth is something we can handle, or perhaps something others are unable to handle. In doing so, we imply that truth belongs to an economy of ownership and production, sometimes even of credit and debt.

Let us group this collection of impulses together under the heading of standard epistemology. Theologically speaking, it might be said that these descriptions go some way toward spelling out what is meant in the Christian tradition by the notoriously difficult term "world." What follows, then, is a series of gestures toward a counter-epistemology that arises from the church's confession that Christ is the truth. Here truth will appear to be unsettled rather than settled. It will bear traces of what, following Stanley Cavell, we might call a "rationality of disagreement."[3] It arises from an excessive economy of gift, and thus it exists as a seemingly unnecessary and unwarranted donation. As such, the truth of Christ involves a kind of ongoing contestation and thus cannot but be inherently conflictual when set beside the world's desire for harmonies of closure. In short, if truth is understood by way of an analogy to the truth of Christ, then it should be understood to name an essentially agonizing and agonistic reality.

For these reasons, it is necessary to imagine an alternative to conceptions of knowledge that arise from the assumption that faith and freedom are to be pitted against one another as a kind of basic antinomy.[4] The main weakness of any such approach is that it seeks to violently guarantee or secure knowledge in some fixed source or ground, whether such a ground is conceived in terms of knowing subjects or objects known. To see this, however, it is necessary to appreciate that questions of knowledge and the university are intimately bound up with substantive ethical and political matters. Standard epistemology, by contrast, is inherently procedural. It approaches knowledge as a matter of form that is said to be neutral with regard to content. So it tends to be blind to its own involvement in aspects of political formation.

Because I am interested in exploring the truth of Christ, I begin with an examination of how Christian conceptions of knowledge are entwined with questions of peace and violence. The guiding question that animates this discussion, then, is "What sorts of knowledge are appropriate to the Christian confession of the peace of Christ?" What follows is an attempt to provide a few gestures toward a more peaceable—which is to say more Christian—conception of knowledge. I interpret Christianity as a counter-epistemology that crucially involves an epistemology of peace. Among other things, such a view features no basic opposition of faith and freedom. Rather, it requires a radical transformation of the standard notions faith and freedom, and the idea of the university, as they are taken up into and thus redefined by the body of Christ.

But I am not so much interested in the concepts of faith and freedom as such, let alone with a conception of knowledge in general or the idea of the university. Rather, I draw attention to the epistemological significance of martyrdom. I am interested in exploring how the practice of Christian martyrdom is significant for a Christian conception knowledge and truth. Following Hart, I assume that "theology must, because of what its particular story is, have the form of martyrdom, witness, a peaceful offer that has already suffered rejection and must be prepared to suffer rejection as a consequence."[5] One of the defining characteristics of the Christian tradition is the assumption that it is the martyr who most meaningfully has a claim to know the truth of Christ.

Contemporary Christian debates concerning the idea of the university and the kinds of knowledge it enacts seem to take place in the absence of any meaningful appreciation of the epistemological significance of Christian martyrdom. So what might knowledge look like amongst a people for whom martyrdom is a meaningful reality? What if truth is spoken from the mouths of those, like Saint Apollonia, whose teeth were knocked out and jaws cut in an attempt to silence her voice in favor of those who would worship other gods?[6] What if truth is illuminated by the flames that consume those who sing out songs of praise and thanksgiving while they are being burned at the stake?[7] What if truth best captured by those whose desire for friendship with God leads them to pray "O, how happy I would be were the Lord to call me as a witness to his truth—what greater honor could come my way from God"?[8] What if truth is written onto the tortured bodies of those who have disappeared "as part of the imaginative drama of a certain state project"?[9] In short, what if "the word of God will be sealed with blood and defended with the cross"?[10]

Martyrdom and Instrumentality

Before turning to sketch out a vision of knowledge that seeks to answer these questions, it will be instructive to examine more closely how we typically speak of martyrdom, and in particular, how we tend to link martyrdom with the question of truth. I want to identify three closely related claims that collectively define what we might call the standard conception of martyrdom. Perhaps the most common approach to martyrdom is to describe the martyr as one who died *for* or *because of* her or his beliefs. The martyr is then defined as one whose death is a consequence of a particular belief or set of beliefs she or he happens to hold. Or rather, the martyr dies because of an unwillingness to renounce certain beliefs even under threat of death. Martyrdom is thus understood to be a possibility that might arise when one is committed to the truth of a belief whose value is taken to override the value of one's life itself. As Brad Gregory puts it, in what is otherwise one of the most interesting and illuminating accounts of the phenomenon of martyrdom in the sixteenth century, "Contested teachings such as papal authority, believers' baptism, and justification by faith alone already separated Christians from one another. Martyrs demonstrated their willingness to die *for* these beliefs, proclaiming that commitment to the truth outweighed the prolongation of their lives."[11]

Second, and building on the theme of unwillingness to flinch in the face of death, martyrdom is often understood as a way of conquering or controlling the threat of death. The martyr is understood as one who defeats death by refusing to let death have the last word. In other words, the value of martyrdom is that it demonstrates that death no longer has power over us. Reflecting such a position, Carole Straw has suggested that Christian martyrdom is based on a "feeling of control over death and torture."[12]

Third, and returning to the question of truth, martyrdom is often spoken of as evidence or confirmation of the truth of a particular belief. The stories of martyrs are often invoked in the service of a larger apologetic project, which points to the willingness of people to die for their beliefs as constituting at least a partial justification for the truth of those beliefs. At their worst, it seems that this is how the story of martyrs often function. Indeed, it might be argued that the very idea of the martyrology was created for this sort of apologetic purpose of securing the truth of the Christian faith.

It is instructive to note that each of these three common approaches reads martyrdom in a strikingly instrumentalist fashion. They paint a picture of martyrdom as a more or less technological concept. They imply, in other words, that martyrdom names a kind of mechanistic process whereby the martyr is understood and justified by some end result that he brings into being, some change that she effects. With respect to questions of knowledge, these descriptions of martyrdom suggest a kind of two-stage process: first we come to hold a particular belief that then leads us to act in various ways. In such cases, the belief held is somehow taken to be meaningful or true in and of itself, and martyrdom is understood to be a merely contingent outcome that might follow from holding that belief, depending on what circumstances and political contexts one happens to find oneself in.

Martyrdom and Truth

Against such approaches, I want to paint a manifestly non-instrumental picture of martyrdom. In particular, I shall argue that instrumentalist conceptions of martyrdom radically distort the very meaning of martyrdom itself. Martyrdom names an approach to knowledge and a way of life more generally which assumes that the truth of Christ cannot somehow be secured, but is rather a gift received and lived out in vulnerable yet hopeful giving in return. On such a reading, the martyr is not one who dies *for* or *because of* her beliefs. Rather, the death of the martyr is in some meaningful way the very expression of belief itself. Martyrdom does not arise out of a feeling of control over death. Rather, it is but an expression of a way of life that gives up the assumption of being in control.

Martyrdom is not a phenomenon that can be understood by appealing to instrumental notions of cause and effect. Rather, it is a practice that involves the renunciation of an overriding preoccupation with effectiveness. Accordingly, the martyr is not to be invoked as evidence of the truth of a particular belief. Rather, martyrdom is a practice that constitutes and makes intelligible a certain kind of knowledge. Following Michel Foucault, I seek to explore how martyrdom "engender[s] new domains of knowledge that not only bring new objects, new concepts, and new techniques to light, but also gives rise to totally new forms of subjects and subjects of knowledge."[13] In short, martyrdom is a practice that contributes to the constitution of a people whose lives and deaths require us to think of truth in some strikingly different ways.

It is worth emphasizing at this point that such an epistemological reading of martyrdom does away with much of the apparatus of contemporary epistemology—propositional truth-claims, justificatory structures, and the like. It is less concerned with what subjects might know or what objects might be known, and more with matters of style or performance—a certain *way* of knowing. It is not invested in the enterprise of identifying key beliefs and the actions they might imply, but assumes that to know is to engage in the work of the body. Accordingly, it sees knowledge neither as a purely theoretical event that admits of practical application nor as an exercise of the mind that has certain implications for the body. Rather, it approaches knowledge as an embodied social performance or practice. Epistemology is read as a profoundly moral and political enterprise.

I am suggesting that martyrdom is not a product or result of what Christians claim to know. Rather, martyrdom names a distinctly Christian way of knowing, a way of knowing that is characteristic of the body of Christ, and in particular, a way of knowing nonviolently, a nonviolent body of knowledge. Drawing on Hart once again, we might speak of the "style of the martyr's expenditure, which is made in the hope of a return that it is powerless of itself to effect, but which is also made by a soul committed to the grace of an infinite God who can always give souls to one another in the dimension of peace, in the shared scope of his infinite beauty. That such a gift can truly be given can be demonstrated only by ceaseless giving."[14]

Let me offer just a few brief observations in support of these claims. First, it is important to notice that the witness of the martyr does not turn on the ability to make truth fully present in a way that suggests truth is something we have some sort of direct access to or control over. For example, the martyrdom of Saint Apollonia turns crucially on the sense in which her voice has been silenced. Indeed, it might be suggested that the significance of Apollonia's martyrdom is that it displays a witness to truth that somehow happens precisely because of the silence of her voice and not in spite of it. The witness of Apollonia, who has been violently robbed of the power to speak, is that of a speechless voice. The truth she embodies is reflected as much, if not more, in those moments after she has been silenced than in the threatening words her captors sought to erase.

In Apollonnia's story, silence is not given the last word. Hers is a voice that cannot be silenced even as it is prevented from speaking, but that of a witness that cannot be reduced to or captured by those possessions known as words. This suggests that the truth of Christ is not merely a belief uttered or expressed or otherwise made present by us. Rather, it is a performance enacted in and through which truth is given as an offering or gratuitous gesture. This has everything to do with the question of agency. To identify truth with the voice of silence implies that it is not something we are fully able to possess. This contrasts starkly with the usual ways in which we think of ourselves as epistemic agents whose knowledge turns on a voice that articulates beliefs and thereby makes them present and thus grounds them in some sort of settlement.

In a related sense, it is important to appreciate the sense in which the martyr only exists as martyr in a way that is vulnerably dependent on the being of others. In other words, martyrdom is not something that we can bring about. Despite the temptation to invoke voluntaristic notions of willingness and unwillingness in the contemporary portrayals of martyrdom noted above, it is crucial to recognize that one cannot choose to become a martyr. Rather, the notion of self-directed choice is the very antithesis of the logic of martyrdom. As Gregory puts it, "The martyrs' agency depended upon relinquishing control, their strength upon a naked admission of their utter impotence and total dependence on God."[15] This is partly reflected in "martyr" being a title given by others to honor those whose lives and deaths are said to witness the truth of Christ.

Martyrdom, in other words, is a work of memory. And significantly, the very practice of naming martyrs is a contested one. The naming of martyrs is the work of the church, and this is by no means an easy and straightforward task. It is an ongoing hermeneutical exercise that requires a constant need for examination and interpretation. Martyrdom is a meaningful description only insofar as it is subject to ongoing interpretation and negotiation. The figure of the martyr is under constant interrogation, not only by those who bring about their deaths but also by those who would honor them. The very designation of martyrdom is a fragile and tenuous one, existing as it does in a kind of suspension between the twin extremes of suicide and victimhood.

But the point I am making here is that it is out of this very suspense that we can see the interruption of the violent world of mastery, possession, and control by a nonviolent offering of a radically different way of being and knowing called peace. Christian knowledge is characterized by a profound sense of otherness. The "otherness of the church" in this respect has everything to do with its attitude toward the other, its vulnerability to the stranger and even the enemy.[16] And it is this stance of vulnerability, this refusal to seize control of one's life, that is best captured in the Christian practice of martyrdom.

The Agony of Truth

In an attempt to sharpen some of these all-too-vague gestures and to lay bare the conversation partners lying behind the above reading of martyrdom and epistemology, it will be instructive to draw attention to some key moments in the work of Michel Foucault, Gillian Rose, and John Howard Yoder. My suggestion that martyrdom constitutes a counter-epistemology in which truth is seen as an agonistic reality owes much to Foucault's attempt to move from a conception of the subject as foundation to an account of the "self-as-sacrifice." In his essay "Truth and Juridical Forms," Foucault opens with the recognition that "[t]wo or three centuries ago Western philosophy postulated, explicitly or implicitly, the subject as foundation, as the central core of all knowledge, as that in which and on the basis of which freedom revealed itself and truth could blossom."[17] Against the background of such a claim, Foucault sets out to construct a critical "genealogy of the modern subject" that identifies and unsettles the particular forms of violence reflected in this conception of the subject as foundation.[18] Closely related to this is Foucault's critique of the notion that truth is grounded in origins, that it is rooted in originary "seeds of knowledge."[19]

Foucault claims that the modern idea of the subject as foundation is but one more attempt to ground truth in a kind of original source and thus to secure or seize truth by means of a violent will to power. Furthermore, Foucault maintains that this sort of violence is particularly powerful because it is masked by the appearance of the freedom of the subject. In an attempt to provide an alternative to this temptation to the power of settlement, Foucault develops a reading in which both truth and the self are redefined as agonistic notions, as involving a sense of struggle, or a kind of ongoing contestation.

One of the main elements in this sense of agonistic dispossession of both self and truth is Foucault's reading of Christian practices of martyrdom. It is worth quoting Foucault at length on this:

> The revelation of the truth about oneself . . . cannot be dissociated from the obligation to renounce oneself. We have to sacrifice the self in order to discover the truth about ourselves, and we have to discover the truth about ourselves in order to sacrifice ourselves. Truth and sacrifice, the truth about ourselves and the sacrifice of ourselves, are deeply and closely connected. And we have to understand this sacrifice not only as a radical change in the way of life but as a consequence of a formula like this: you will become the subject of the manifestation of truth when and only when you disappear or you destroy yourself as a real body or a real existence.[20]

Elsewhere, Foucault suggests that truthful speech (*parrhēsia*) involves a sense of risk, in which the self is put into a situation of significant vulnerability. As Foucault himself puts it, "Someone is said to use *parrhēsia* and merits consideration as a *parrhēsiastēs* only if there is a risk or danger for him in telling the truth."[21] In short,

Foucault helps us see that a world in which martyrdom is a meaningful reality sees truth, not as a stable possession that we might be able to capture fully, but as an agonistic sense of struggle in which the notion of the self as an agent of truth is put in question. Conversely, he suggests that where truth is understood agonistically, we should expect that martyrdom will occur at least in part because the self is not understood as a self-enclosed entity that is to be preserved at all costs.

As instructive as I find Foucault's reading of the self-as-sacrifice, it is also necessary to emphasize that this does not entail the complete erasure of the self. The notion of sacrifice implied in my reading of martyrdom is not that of a "purified" or "one-way sacrifice."[22] It does not call for a kind of total surrender to the other. It is at this point that the work of Gillian Rose is helpful. She critiques the position she calls the "new ethics," which she takes to be represented most straightforwardly by the work of Levinas and Derrida. In particular, Rose objects to their attempt to define "the ethical" in terms of a conception of the purified otherness of the Other and the kind of one-way sacrificial orientation it elicits. Rose suggests that such a view covertly participates in exactly the kind of violence it seeks to avoid. As Rose herself puts it,

> *New ethics* would *transcend* the autonomy of the subject by commanding that I substitute myself for "the Other" (heteronomy) or by commending attention to "the Other." Yet it is the inveterate but occluded *immanence* of one subject to itself and to other *subjects* that needs further elaboration. Simply to command me to sacrifice myself, or to commend that I pay attention to others makes me intolerant, naïve and miserable. . . . [T]he immanence of the self-relation of "the Other" to my own self-relation will always be disowned.[23]

Put differently, Rose worries that new ethics equally participates in a violent vision of truth as ownership. It retains an underlying stance of mastery, of being in control, in the sense that the logic of self-sacrifice continues to presume the power of the self to give itself up. By contrast, she argues that a genuinely nonviolent account of truth as dispossession or gift requires, not a total giving of the self to the Other, but an ongoing agonistic exchange of giving and receiving—of generous receptivity or receptive generosity—that exists only when we refuse to settle the difference between self and other.[24]

Rose suggests that truth is to be understood precisely in terms of the categories of ambiguity, ambivalence, and the anxiety of the self, and not in terms of a dualism that forces us to choose between complete self-presence and the total obliteration of the self. Genuine knowledge involves an appreciation of its own fragility and the necessary riskiness of its endeavors. Truth is agonizingly difficult. It is an agonistic work of engagement. Or as Rose herself puts it, "Certainty does not empower, it subjugates—for only thinking which has the ability to tolerate uncertainty is powerful, that is, non-violent."[25]

Equally important to Rose's critique of the new ethics is its tendency to essentialize or hypostatize violence. The nonviolent thinking referred to in the above quote from Rose is to be differentiated from what she refers to as a "peace beyond time."[26] In other words, Rose's appeal to peace is not an attempt to invoke a reality that is somehow purified of violence. This is the approach she takes to be characteristic of the new ethicist. For Rose, peace is neither a possession we can wield nor a wholly emptied dispossession or pure sacrifice. Rather, peace names a sense of struggle that exists against the background of a recognition that we are always already implicated in some form of violence. To quote from Rose yet again:

> Instead of the monolithic, violent "coherence" of "logic" and "politics," contrasted with the articulated peaceable "coherence" of Talmudic casuistry, with its perfect jurisprudence of general and particular, this evident inversion [of peace] would be opened to an exposition that can acknowledge that it *does not know in advance* whether such institutions are violent or peaceful, for it is able to find out—by reconstructing the changing relation between universal, particular, and singular. This is experience—the struggle to recognize: to know, and still to misknow, and yet to grow.[27]

Peace is itself an agonistic reality. It does not name a settled territory that we can fully embody or own. It is not something we own as a first instance called knowledge, which then informs our actions. Rather, it is a gift that might be given through us only when we no longer seek violently to control it. In the language of this essay, it is the work of the martyr.

All that I find helpful in Foucault and Rose about these matters of truth and agonism, of self and dispossession, of peace and violence, I find reflected in the work of John Howard Yoder. And so I close with the significance of Yoder's work as an attempt to spell out this vision of a nonviolent body of knowledge constituted and made intelligible by practices of martyrdom. In particular, I note Yoder's emphasis on truth and peace as witness, which is of course just another name for the martyr. Much of this is captured in Yoder's understanding of the set of temptations he grouped together under the label of Constantinianism. It is crucial to appreciate that the question of Constantinianism and non-Constantinianism names a form of epistemological inquiry and is not merely a question of political organization.

Yoder's account of the Constantinianization of the church names a sense in which the church seeks to assume a stance of control or self-legitimation. Instead of embodied discipleship in practices of giving and receiving God's gift of peace in Jesus Christ, Yoder helps us see a church that has increasingly turned to a series of self-legitimating strategies designed to ensure its ongoing survival. Theology thus becomes preoccupied with the organization and policing of time, with settlement and order, or what Yoder calls the attempt to move history in the right direction. Such an approach involves a denial of God, or at least signals an unwillingness to receive God's unpredictable future gifts.

Yoder's narration of the non-Constantinian church, by contrast, attempts to tell a nonviolent counter-epistemology. It names the kind of knowledge that is made possible because of the lives and deaths of the martyrs. The knowledge of martyrs it is not preoccupied with epistemic justification but is shaped by the epistemological virtues of patience and hope. It is an agonistic mode of knowledge that proceeds in fragments and ad hoc alliances, not the development of large-scale totalities. This knowledge resists closure, refusing the lie of the total perspective and the search for a purified idiom of speech, recognizing that language about God is not finally limited to our current vocabularies.

Finally, Yoder's counter-epistemology recognizes that theological knowledge is not a matter of disembodied beliefs, the truth of which needs to be secured through abstract rational analysis. Rather, the church resists the assimilation of knowledge and violence because it recognizes that Christian convictions are not possessions. In doing so, it operates as an embodied way of knowing, rooted in charitable practices of giving and receiving and especially in ongoing receptivity to life as a gift from God. The faith of the church becomes unintelligible when it is expressed in abstraction from a life of disciplined imitation of Christ. The church does not develop and seek to sustain a stable, settled body of knowledge but engages in an agonizing and ongoing conversational exchange of difference that is truthful only when it proceeds in the absence of external guarantees. It cultivates a readiness for radical reformation and an appreciation of the sense in which it is always already involved in some form of failure.

Conclusion: An Unsettled Truth

In conclusion, I return to the question of faith, freedom, and the idea of the university. I suggested at the outset that the conception of agonistic, nonviolent inquiry opens the possibility of moving beyond the standard impasse of faith and freedom. It sees faith neither as a rival source of knowledge by which to secure the necessity of truth nor as a threat to reason, but rather as a contingent and thus inherently vulnerable gift that makes possible a new way of understanding knowledge. Similarly, it understands freedom neither as a procedural hedge that guarantees us protection against the unfreedoms imposed in the name of truth nor as a threat to truth, but rather as the expression of the fragility and vulnerability of human reason.

From the perspective of the contemporary university, with its preoccupation with technical efficiency and explanatory power—or, failing that, its concern for the edification of the subject—this view cannot but seem odd and almost entirely out of place. But that is to say that the truth of Christ will be different from other ways of knowing. There is an otherness to Christian ways of knowing that has everything to do with its orientation toward the other. What, then, of the university and other institutions that claim to be dedicated to the pursuit of truth? I confess that I am tempted to say that it should be a place where we are free to receive the gift of martyrs, and in so being, a place that is faithful to the truthful witness that they embody.

But at the same time, Christians are a diasporic people who know that they can be at home anywhere. So perhaps what is most important is that Christians embody faithful practices of knowledge—to see the theological virtues of faith, hope, and charity as epistemological virtues—so that they can operate anywhere precisely because they do not feel the need to control knowledge by fixing it in some settled somewhere called the university.

Dislocating Identity

—9—

Christian Pacifism as Friendship with God: MacIntyre, Mennonites, and the Genealogical Tradition

"To begin is impossible." Or so begins one recent account of the possibility of a postmodern ethics.[1] To put it a little less cutely, there are no pure starting points, no foundational or necessary origins of inquiry. All beginnings are contingent and provisional, constituting at most one aspect of a larger conversation already under way. But we have to begin somewhere. So let me begin by suggesting that the primary question for Anabaptists with respect to postmodernity should not so much be whether we should accept or reject it—whatever "it" is, and whoever "we" are—but rather, what does it means to live in the midst of it.[2]

For the purposes of exploring how Anabaptist-Mennonite theology might be understood within the network of diverse and often competing influences that go under the name "postmodernism," two strands are particularly worthy of attention. The first is the version of Thomistic Aristotelianism articulated by Alasdair MacIntyre as a response to the failure of the Enlightenment project of providing an independent and unified foundation for ethics. The second is the Nietzschean Genealogical tradition, embodied in the work of Michel Foucault and Jacques Derrida, which MacIntyre takes to be his most significant rival. The discussion that follows sets out to explore the recent state of Mennonite theology by bringing it into conversation with MacIntyre and the Genealogical tradition as represented by Derrida. I undertake such a discussion in order to

147

shed new light on the common Mennonite concern with Christian pacifism. By approaching the question of Christian pacifism against the
background of a reading of the debate between MacIntyre and the
Genealogical tradition on the politics of friendship, I hope to gesture
toward some new conversation partners that a Mennonite discussion
about peace would benefit from engaging.

MacIntyre: The Politics of the Common Good or Charity as Friendship with God?

When, in *After Virtue,* he sought to overcome the excessively
abstract character of modern moral philosophy by developing an
account of the virtues, MacIntyre turned to Aristotle's discussion of
friendship in order to clarify his understanding of how ethics is located
in the concrete political context of the *polis*. In contrast to the ethics of
modern liberalism, which he takes to be based on the notion of individual autonomy and the general principle of freedom derived from it,
MacIntyre argues that Aristotelian friendship suggests an alternative
conception of ethics rooted in the "shared recognition of and pursuit
of the good."[3] More specifically, he claims that the Aristotelian account
of the *polis* is best understood in terms of an "interrelated
network of small groups of friends," which involves the "sharing of all
in the common project of creating and sustaining the life of the city."[4]

Such an understanding of friendship, MacIntyre maintains, exists
in sharp contrast to the characteristically modern notion of friendship,
which is not only essentially private but is also primarily the name of
an "emotional state" rather than a form of political organization.[5] In
an Aristotelian account of friendship, by contrast, no conceptual space
sustains a meaningful distinction between public and private.
Friendship for MacIntyre, as for Aristotle, is thus a fundamentally
political notion. It names the kinds of relationships that are dedicated
to the common pursuit of the goods recognized as being most central
to the collective life of the *polis*.

While many of these same themes are continued and further
developed in MacIntyre's more recent work, it is noteworthy that his
emphasis on the ethical-political significance of friendship appears to
have diminished. At the same time, he has made the transition from the
straightforwardly Aristotelian standpoint defended in *After Virtue* to
the Thomistic Aristotelian tradition he claims to represent in *Whose
Justice? Which Rationality?* and *Three Rival Versions of Moral Enquiry*.[6]

Although he does not abandon his claim that a proper understanding of the virtues presupposes a substantive conception of the common good, he no longer tends to develop this in terms of friendship. Rather, MacIntyre now tends to speak in terms of a more formal account of justice and the good itself.

In looking at the larger narrative that MacIntyre's work constitutes, it appears that his emphasis on friendship actually becomes weaker as his embrace of Aquinas becomes stronger and more thorough. This is odd, because in Aquinas's appropriation of Aristotelianism, the ethical significance of friendship was never abandoned or weakened. On the contrary, friendship actually appears to become even more central in Aquinas than it is for Aristotle. For Aquinas, friendship functions as the "form of the virtues," describing the relationship between humans and God whereby God claims us as friends.[7] Thus, MacIntyre's appropriation of Aquinas in order to supplement and complete his earlier understanding of Aristotelianism actually appears to run in a direction opposite that of Aquinas himself, as least as far as the question of friendship is concerned.

In order to understand what is at stake in MacIntyre's apparent divergence from Aquinas on this matter, it will be instructive to look more closely at Aquinas's theological transformation of Aristotelian friendship into charity as friendship with God. Aquinas accepts the general structure of Aristotle's account of friendship, and in particular his account of the friend as another self in which self-knowledge is subordinated to one's knowledge of others through friendship. As Aristotle himself puts it, "As then when we wish to see our own face, we do so by looking in a mirror, in the same way when we wish to know ourselves we can obtain that knowledge by looking at our friend. For the friend is, as we assert, a second self."[8] While he accepts Aristotle's description of the friend as another self, Aquinas significantly transforms Aristotelian friendship. In particular, he does so by situating it primarily in the context of friendship with God, a possibility that Aristotle explicitly denied on the grounds that there is not sufficient equality between humans and gods, and thus no possibility for a meaningful relationship to develop between them.[9]

Aquinas develops a conception of friendship in which it is God who is one's other self. It is through friendship with God that we come to know ourselves best. And it is only against the background of God's first claiming us as friends that we are enabled to embark on the process of training and habituation into the life of the virtues. In order to overcome the suggestion that there is too great a distance between Creator and creature to speak meaningfully of friendship, Aquinas claims that such a relationship is to be christologically mediated by participation in sacramental practices within the church.[10] The possibility of having such a relationship with God is not, for Aquinas, an abstract or conceptual achievement, let alone a personal, interiorized experience of some sort. Rather, it is concretely embodied and materially disciplined by developing the particular kind of character that can only be achieved by the imitation of Christ through the habitual practice of sacraments such as baptism and the Eucharist. For Aquinas, then, no self-understanding exists prior to a relationship in which God claims us as friends. Indeed, the "self" does not exist at all prior to the participation that God makes possible—first, by the incarnation of God in Christ, and second, by the continued presence of Christ in the sacramental practices of the church.

Not only does Aquinas's account of friendship thus theologically radicalize Aristotle's understanding of the friend as another self, but it also appears to call into question the strong notion of a unified and stable autonomous individual. Insofar as it makes selfhood and moral identity inseparable from one's relationships with other selves, and in particular with God, Aquinas's account of friendship might be read as suggesting an account of the self that is at least structurally a mix of disparate sources. Such a self is notably contingent, at least insofar as it is dependent on a divine initiation of friendship. Yet in spite of MacIntyre's questions regarding the Enlightenment notion of the autonomous individual considered in abstraction from all social context, he nevertheless continues to emphasize the unity and well-integrated character of the self to a greater degree than Aquinas's understanding of friendship in terms of interrelated other selves seems to permit.

That MacIntyre can even attempt to provide an account the self in abstraction from a discussion of the possibility of friendship with God seems to call into question his alleged Thomistic Aristotelianism. For Aquinas, the very notion of selfhood is unintelligible apart from an ecclesial and sacramental participation with God through the imitation of Christ. It is thus odd that when MacIntyre turns to develop a critique of the Genealogical tradition, it is not based on the hopeful possibility of friendship with God, but rather on the claim that "the individual human being is a *unity* in which the directedness of the different aspects of his spiritual and social existence have to be ordered hierarchically into a unified mode of life."[11] While MacIntyre initially turns to friendship in order to stress the concrete political interrelationships of a community of selves (in the plural), he apparently abandons the notion of friendship in favor of an emphasis on the unified self (in the singular) in order to combat what he takes to be the destabilizing and ultimately destructive forces of the Genealogical account of difference.

Derrida, Difference and the Politics of Friendship

This apparent tension with respect to MacIntyre's claim to represent the tradition of Thomistic Aristotelianism is worthy of examination in its own right. But it becomes even more interesting to reflect on this apparent shift because the Genealogical conception of difference has itself recently come to be more explicitly articulated in terms of a discussion of the politics of friendship. There are several suggestive hints in this direction in Nietzsche himself.[12] These are in turn further developed in Foucault's later work, in which friendship names an aesthetic practice of collective self-creation offered as an alternative to the politics of identity based on the "exclusion of the other."[13] But the most extensive discussion of friendship within the Genealogical tradition is to be found in the recent work of Jacques Derrida. In an attempt to make more explicit the politics implied by his understanding of deconstruction, Derrida seeks to develop a "democratic" politics of friendship. In doing so, he sets out to provide an alternative both to the standard understanding of democracy and to what he calls the canonical reading of friendship. Such a politics claims to "free a certain interpretation of *equality* by removing it from the phallogocentric schema of *fraternity*" that he takes to be central to the traditional understanding of friendship, including Aristotle's account of the friend as another self.[14]

In other words, Derrida is attempting to rethink the notion of friendship without the bonds imposed by presence and proximity and thus to be respectful of the possibility of "infinite difference" within friendship.[15] Derrida himself puts it in the form of a question: "Is it possible to think and to implement democracy, that which would keep the old name 'democracy,' while uprooting from it all these figures of friendship (philosophical and religious) which prescribe fraternity, the family and the androcentric religious group?"[16]

Derrida's recent turn to the notion of friendship is thus offered as an extension of the general concern to develop an account of alterity that seeks to take seriously the place or "voice" of the "other."[17] Stated briefly, Derrida claims that the traditional understanding of friendship is based on a "logic of opposition" characteristic of the kind of "metaphysical" or logocentric thinking that he has been attempting to deconstruct throughout his career. At the same time, however, he claims that it is beset with contradictions and ruptures that turn that logic back against itself, such that it is unable to sustain even its most basic sets of contrasts. In particular, he claims that the traditional idea of friendship is based on a conception of unity and similarity that is opposed to difference and otherness, so that the friend is someone who is ideally similar to oneself.[18] Although he does not deny altogether that some conception of similarity properly belongs to the notion of friendship, Derrida approaches the discussion from the other end, emphasizing the radical alterity of the friend. He focuses primarily on the otherness aspect of Aristotle's other self thesis, claiming that the friend is irreducibly other, that the otherness of the friend is "absolutely originary."[19]

Derrida's attempt to rethink friendship in support of an expression of a new form of radical democratic politics is best understood in terms of this emphasis on the friend as both self and other. In short, Derrida describes the politics of friendship as one that enables a recognition of the otherness and irreducible singularity of the other: "The grace of friendship leaves the other, lets it be, gives it what it has and what it already is."[20] Even here, however, he cautions that the "grace of friendship" does not exist in the absence of conflict and discord.[21] Derridean friendship thus names a basic tension between unity and difference.[22] Although he does not want to go so far as to deny the very possibility of friendship, Derrida emphasizes that such relationships are necessarily unstable.

Friendship is constituted both by a kind of sharing and by a gap of irreducible otherness, such that there is a sense of antagonism or conflict, of *aporia* or *polemos,* which lies "at the very heart of friendship itself."[23] Yet this is not to suggest that he wishes to mark a point of absolute rupture between the self and the other as friend. On the contrary, his discussion of friendship is designed to challenge the very distinction between self and other. In Derrida's hands, the friend is in part constitutive of the "self" to whom she is "other." As Derrida himself puts it, "The voice of the other friend, of the other as friend . . . is the condition of my own-proper-being."[24]

Accordingly, as with the Thomistic Aristotelian notion of the other self with which MacIntyre began but has increasingly left behind,

Derrida takes the notion of friendship to suggest a kind of interdependence of selves. Such a notion challenges the idea of a strongly unified and stable subject. But he does so in a much more agonistic manner, arguing that there is a more radical and pervasive sense of difference in the otherness involved in various aspects of friendship. In doing so, he makes conflict and struggle constitutive of friendship itself.

Perhaps even more significant about Derrida's discussion of friendship in regard to a debate with MacIntyre is that he appears to reintroduce God into the Genealogical tradition. Whereas the Genealogical tradition is commonly assumed to have begun with Nietzsche's pronouncement of the death of God, some have suggested that Derrida's recent work amounts to a sort of rebirth of the theological.[25] Building on his deconstruction of the so-called "metaphysical tradition," Derrida rejects the "onto-theological" notion of God as a supreme being.[26] But he nevertheless claims to be interested in the possibility of reconceiving the notion of God without the logocentrism and oppositional logic on which, he claims, it has traditionally been based. In short, Derrida describes such a non-ontological conception of God as a transcendent alterity, a wholly and infinite other.[27] "'Every other (one) is God,' or 'God is every (bit) other.' . . . In one case God is defined as infinitely other, as wholly other, every bit other. In the other case it is declared that every other one, each of the others, is God inasmuch as he or she is, *like* God, wholly other."[28]

In attempting to free God from the ontological tendency to categorize and identify, Derrida suggests that a relationship with God is most fully achieved at death. In other words, God meets us in the context of a "gift of death," which is at the same time an irreducibly singular and ultimately individual experience and yet one in which one is confronted by the gaze of the absolute other which is God.[29] Thus, the possibility of finally achieving friendship is, for Derrida, endlessly deferred, and the politics of friendship consists in living in the midst of this inherently unstable situation.

To sum up the discussion thus far, both MacIntyre and the Genealogists attempt to develop a politics that provides an alternative to the liberalism of Enlightenment modernity. But MacIntyre argues that an account of the unity of the self directed toward the good is ultimately required in order to prevent the slide into the unconstrained conflict between competing wills to power that he takes to be the result of the Genealogical emphasis on rupture and difference. In order to do so, however, he has increasingly distanced himself from his earlier appeal to the notion of friendship. But from the perspective of Genealogists such as Derrida, it appears that MacIntyre has not broken sufficiently with the universalist and objectivist assumptions of Enlightenment rationalism.

Derrida has come to pay significant attention to the very notion of friendship that MacIntyre has apparently left behind. This marks a paradoxical inversion of the positions through which the original debate was staged. MacIntyre presents himself as representative of the Thomistic Aristotelian tradition yet appears to move increasingly away from a discussion of friendship and in particular the theological question of friendship with God. The Genealogists, on the other hand, are treating the topic of friendship with increasing seriousness, and Derrida is even teasing us with the possibility of a conception of theological friendship. As a way of further examining the significance of this exchange, I follow Derrida's linkage of friendship to the problem of violence in order to explore the relationship between the theme of friendship and the question of what means to embody a politics of Christian pacifism.

Milbank, Charity, and the Ontology of Peace

Among the many possible ways of reading the debate between MacIntyre and the Genealogists, none is more suggestive for the question of Christian pacifism than that of John Milbank. In short, Milbank argues that behind their many significant differences lies a more fundamental similarity in that they both presume what he calls an "ontology of violence."[30] Though MacIntyre wants to avoid the irrational conflict he takes to be characteristic of the Genealogical tradition, he claims that this cannot be settled by standards imposed from the outside. Accordingly, he develops a Thomistic Aristotelian version of dialectical rationality among competing traditions of inquiry, one aspect of which involves his account of unified selves noted above.

MacIntyre suggests that such selves are involved in the ongoing task of continuously narrating and re-narrating such conflicts over time. But Milbank argues that such an account of dialectically constrained rational conflict between competing traditions ends up simply reproducing the problem of interminable conflict that MacIntyre is trying to overcome. He argues that it remains implicated in an understanding of the world that takes such violence or "agonistic difference" to be ontologically basic.[31] In a similar way, he claims that the Genealogical tradition, including Derrida's recent gestures toward the possibility of friendship with God, is also rooted in just such an account of originary violence insofar as it continues to presuppose a Nietzschean conception of the will to power. As Milbank himself puts it,

> Antique thought and politics assumes some naturally given ele-
> ment of chaotic conflict which must be tamed by the stability
> and self-identity of reason. Modern thought and politics (most
> clearly articulated by Nietzsche) assumes that there is *only* this
> chaos. . . . If one tries, like MacIntyre, to oppose antique
> thought to modern thought, then the attempt will fail because
> antique thought—as Plato already saw in *The Sophist*—is
> deconstructible into 'modern' thought: a cosmos including both
> chaos and reason implies an ultimate principle, the 'difference'
> between the two, which is *more* than reason, and enshrines
> permanent conflict.[32]

As an alternative to both MacIntyre's Thomistic Aristotelianism and Derrida's version of the Genealogical tradition, Milbank argues that Christianity admits of no recognition of original violence. Rather, he claims that the Christian tradition is to be understood as the expression of a counter-ontology of peace. He suggests that Christianity "conceives differences as analogically related, rather than equivocally at variance."[33] In developing such general claims, he seeks to theologically deconstruct any approach that assumes the necessity of violence. In place of original violence, he offers an "analogical coding of peace." Such a vision of peace is said to deny the opposition and reduction of difference to self-identity. By putting it this way, Milbank means to suggest that a counter-ontology of peace also involves a counter-politics of "the peaceful transmission of difference" or "differences in a continuous harmony."[34]

It is important to note that Milbank's account of the Christian ontology of peace highlights the significance of charity as friendship with God. As Milbank himself puts it, "Charity is originally the gratuitous, creative positing of difference, and the offering to others of a space of freedom, which is existence."[35] In other words, charity names the gracious self-giving of God in friendship such that violence and difference do not have to be given the final word. Indeed, Milbank claims that theology must refuse to give violence the last word or the first. To do so would be to obscure the hopeful possibility embodied in Christian practices such as forgiveness that are oriented to peace.[36]

On Milbank's reading, both MacIntyre and Derrida presume a vision of original violence whereby peace, to the extent that it is meaningful at all, is understood to be a secondary response of sorts to a violence that precedes it. But Milbank claims that this involves a systematic perversion of Christian theology, and especially its account of creation *ex nihilo*. According to Milbank, Christian theology is at least in part defined by the assumption that peace is original and violence is understood to be a secondary phenomenon.

Christian Pacifism and Friendship with God

It might be objected that Milbank is mistaken about certain important details in his treatment of MacIntyre and the Genealogists. Still, the important question from the standpoint of Mennonite theology is how he provides such a powerful account of ontological peace rooted in theological charity without finally embracing a pacifist politics of nonviolence. For as Milbank himself notes, "In no sense does *Theology and Social Theory* recommend 'pacifism,' and the formal specification of truth as peaceful relation cannot be applied as a criterion authorizing non-resistance."[37] Rather, he argues that in certain circumstances, such as "when a person commits an evil act,"[38] the need for "some measures of coercion" is justified, and that while "such action may not be 'peaceable,'" it "can still be 'redeemed' by retrospective acceptance, and so contribute to the final goal of peace."[39] In such cases, Milbank suggests, violence can actually be "beneficial," such that the "good motives of those resorting to it are recognized and recuperated by the defaulter coming to his senses."[40] Without further clarification, however, such a claim sounds all too reminiscent of the conception of instrumental reason that his polemic against secular reason is designed to deconstruct. At the very least, let me suggest that Milbank is obliged to spell out more concretely his understanding of the nature of such beneficial violence and the justification used to support it.

In one important sense, however, Milbank's argument is instructive even in the face of what I take to be significant shortcomings. It is notable that his rejection of Christian pacifism is not rooted in the standard appeal to political realism, namely, that pacifism is politically naive in underestimating the widespread power of violence. Rather, by building on both MacIntyre and the Genealogical tradition, Milbank helps us get beyond the temptation to employ the simple Enlightenment dualism of real and ideal. Instead, I suggest that Milbank's failure to embody a politics of Christian pacifism must be approached in terms of an examination of the specifically theological reasons that push him toward such a position.

In particular, although Milbank is basically correct in attempting to develop an ontology of peace in connection with a conception of charity as friendship with God, his account is at its weakest in depicting the God who claims us as friends. Specifically, Milbank's theology remains insufficiently christological to the extent that it fails to pay adequate attention to the life, death, and resurrection of Jesus. In his attempt to counter the ontology of violence that he takes to lie behind both MacIntyre and the Genealogists with an ontology of peaceful, harmonious difference, Milbank appears to overemphasize the creative and aesthetically expansive power of God the creator at the cost of neglecting the suffering power of the crucified God. As David Toole suggests, Milbank's mistake, finally, "is to stress the incarnation of the logos as the decisive moment and not to stress even more that the logos incarnate passed through the cross."[41]

In fairness to Milbank, to claim that his theology is insufficiently christological is admittedly somewhat of an overstatement. On the contrary, it might be suggested that the two chapters on Christology in *The Word Made Strange* capture some of the most important aspects of his overall constructive position.[42] Accordingly, it would be more accurate and helpful to explore certain specific respects in which his Christology remains inadequate. In particular, Milbank's Christology is problematic to the extent that it appears to relativize the significance of the identity and character of Jesus.[43] As Milbank himself puts it, the identity of Jesus "does not actually relate to his 'character,' but rather to his universal significance for which his particularity stands, almost, as a mere cipher."[44]

Instead of focusing on the concrete unfolding of Jesus' life in the particular acts of forgiveness and healing that he performed, Milbank's Christology is based on the "logic" of "non-identical repetition," which he claims can be derived from the event of *poesis,* or the church's aesthetic exercise of ascribing the name "Jesus" to that significant figure in the Christian story. And despite his emphasis on the aesthetic practices of the church, it appears that Milbank also relativizes the people of God, in the fundamentally related sense of both Israel and the body of Christian disciples. Furthermore, these joint relativizations are closely related to the sense in which his project appears to be devoted to the Constantinian task of developing a civilizational religion.

Milbank is driven by the need to replace the secularism of modern liberal nation-state in all its grand scale.[45] Despite his gestures toward the development of a counter-polis in the final chapter of *Theology and Social Theory*, one gets the sense that he wants the church to simply supplant the world rather than embodying a concrete alternative in the midst of it. Put differently, for all his emphasis on developing an alternative to the world, it appears that there is no category of witness in Milbank's theology. And I am suggesting that all of this is closely related to his lack of attention to the concrete details of Jesus' life, death, and resurrection.

Conversely, Mennonite discussions of Christology tend to be strongest on the question of the particulars of the story of Jesus, which are at the same time a way of defining the peculiar shape of the people of God. For example, Mennonites read the Gospels—and at their better moments, the Bible as a whole—as the inauguration of a radically new community rooted in the specific form of life exemplified by Jesus. This includes the practice of economic sharing that is the Lord's Supper, and the habitual training of our collective bodies as sites of resistance that need not be shaped by the sword.

But Milbank also emphasizes the sense in which theology concerns the formation of a counter-politics. This is why it is instructive to compare his work with a typically Mennonite perspective. According to Milbank, "[t]he gospels can be read, *not* as the story of Jesus, but as the (re)foundation of a new city, a new kind of community, Israel-become-the-Church."[46] If such an emphasis on politics is no more than an opposition to the privatization of theology whereby Christianity has become primarily a matter of individual salvation, then this is a welcome, and in fact necessary, point of emphasis. But where such a claim becomes problematic is the implied disjunction reflected in the very grammar of the position, namely that the Gospels are *either* about the formation of a new politics *or* the story of Jesus.

While Milbank is clearly not making the strong Troeltschian claim that "the preaching of Jesus and the creation of the Christian church were not due in any sense to the impulse of a social movement,"[47] he does seem to suggest that with respect to the political question of the church as a counter-community, we are better off looking elsewhere than the story of Jesus. He turns instead to the category of aesthetics, and in particular to his account of non-identical repetition and the related conception of the harmonious resolution of difference that he derives from the logic of creation and the interrelationship between the persons of the Trinity. And while Mennonite theology could certainly benefit from a more substantial discussion of creation and Trinitarian themes, it does not follow, as Milbank's work seems to imply, that such a "radically orthodox"[48] stance means that one must give up the more typically Mennonite claim that the Gospels are the story of the (re)foundation of a new community *precisely because* they tell the story of Jesus.

Only on the basis of a robust Trinitarianism is such a claim possible in the first place. It is because of Jesus' divinity that the church is to be seen as the embodied foretaste of the kingdom of God. At any rate, the particular shape of such a new Christian counter-community will look very different, depending on whether or not it is rooted in the concrete display of the character of Jesus. Or at least that is what we appear to get in the case of Mennonite theology vis-à-vis Milbank.

Milbank's account of non-identical repetition is helpful, however, in that it avoids reification and a correlative representational account of the imitation of Christ in terms of objective mirroring of a static and external reality. Accordingly, it might be objected on Milbank's behalf that his account of the "name of Jesus" is simply an attempt to avoid the tendency toward a reified account of the identity of Jesus and the patterns of discipleship that might be identified as a characteristic weakness of Mennonite theology. While this objection is certainly justified in some cases, it is important to recognize that such a representational account of disciplined imitation it is not a necessary characteristic of Mennonite theology as such. In fact, it might be suggested that there are specific resources within Mennonite ecclesiology that guard against such an interpretation. Practices such as communal discernment, the ongoing task of negotiating and renegotiating the life of the community, can be ways of resisting the assumption that we need to develop some fixed, once-for-all pattern of discipleship that is based on some final account of the identity of Jesus.

I suspect this discernment is closely related to John Howard Yoder's characteristic reminder that we are to resist the Constantinian temptation that assumes it is up to us to guarantee that history will come out right. Yet in order to avoid these temptations, it does not follow that we must give up concrete appeals to the identity and character of Jesus altogether. Rather, the church's hermeneutic practice of reading and performing the scriptures seems precisely to require some particular account of the concrete character of Jesus, even if such an account is never taken to be absolutely final in and of itself. To develop a reified Christology in this latter sense is not only to treat Jesus in abstraction from the other two persons of the Trinity but also to treat the Bible as a depository of facts that are entirely intelligible apart from their instantiation in the life of the church. It would be unfair to suggest that Mennonite claims regarding the nonviolent character of Jesus are necessarily guilty of these problems, precisely because they are most significantly made in terms of the actual performance of embodied ecclesial practices of nonviolence.

In objecting to Milbank's aesthetic turn to christological *poesis*, I am not arguing against the appeal to aesthetics as such. On the contrary, I am calling into question the sense in which his understanding of non-identical repetition appears to be based on a lingering dichotomy between the aesthetic and the more concretely real. At the same time, Mennonite accounts of discipleship sometimes privilege the latter while retaining the same dichotomy of the available options. But I want to suggest that it is more appropriate to understand Mennonite theology as rendering the assumption that one must choose between aesthetics and concrete reality fundamentally unintelligible.

This approach is exactly what the appeal to friendship with God is designed to do. For the life of discipleship is not simply an attempt to repeat or copy the life of Jesus. Rather, friendship with God names that relationship whereby we are called by God to participate in God's very life through the aesthetic and embodied performance of the practices of the church. Moreover, while Milbank is correct to recognize that the body of Christ is a profoundly political body, his tendency to develop this position in terms of a preference for aesthetics over against the concrete reality of the character of Jesus leads him to underestimate the possibility of a nonviolent politics characteristic of Christian pacifism.

Mennonite theology, by contrast, is best understood as an attempt to understand cross and resurrection as a combination of an aesthetic conception of discipleship as non-identical repetition with an account of the concrete display of Jesus' life in nonviolent acts of forgiveness and reconciliation. In other words, even though it has not traditionally been developed in those terms, a proper understanding of friendship with God is just another name for the traditional Mennonite understanding of discipleship. Yoder, summarizing the Schleitheim Confession, wrote:

The foundation of the call for nonresistance is unity with Jesus. You could of course say "unity with Christ," but the Christ it is talking about is not some cosmic figure, and not some present mystical guide alone, but the continuation in our experience, because we are to be an undivided body. We are to be a part of what he is, and he is what he was.[49]

Conclusion

Let me summarize the main points of my argument by bringing the various strands of the foregoing discussion together. By approaching the debate between MacIntyre and the Genealogists in terms of the question of friendship with God, I am suggesting that MacIntyre's defense of Thomistic Aristotelianism is at its weakest when it comes to articulating Aquinas's theological transformation of Aristotle. When set beside the Derrida's version of the Nietzschean Genealogical tradition, there is evidence of desire for security, a will to overcome contingency, that appears to animate MacIntyre's emphasis on the unity of the self.

I have argued that a more thoroughgoing appreciation of Aquinas on friendship with God provides resources for rethinking such a strong conception of the unified self. The recent work of Milbank, however, provides a decisive challenge to both MacIntyre and Derrida. In particular, he suggests that a properly theological understanding of creation can account for contingency and the structural instability of the human subject that stops short of a Genealogical account of the will to power and the corresponding ontology of violence. Derrida's apparent theological turn to friendship with God continues to accord too great a role to the agonistic narrative of conflict and violence. At the same time, there is no need to abandon the notion of friendship as a network of interrelated selves, as MacIntyre has done, in order to mount a response to the Genealogical conception of originary violence.

And yet Milbank's own conclusions regarding pacifism can be called into question by a conception of discipleship that refuses to understand the (re)foundation of a new Christian counter-community in terms of the distinction between aesthetics and concrete reality. In other words, even Milbank's radically theological attempt to develop a counter-politics based on the ontology of peace is theologically deficient in that it lacks the kind of concrete specification that would be provided by a more adequate account of the person of Jesus Christ.

Taken together, it appears that despite various protests to the contrary, MacIntyre, Derrida, and Milbank all proceed in an overly theoretical and speculative manner. That is, they tend to speak in terms of abstract notions such as charity and friendship in general, rather than of the particular friend Jesus, "the concrete universal through whom we have perfect charity represented to us."[50] In the same way that it helps to identify the problems associated with the lure of theory, such an understanding of Christian pacifism as friendship with God allows us to avoid such distorting conceptual dualisms as public and private, ideal and real, christocentrism and theocentrism, and self and other that have dominated recent discussions of Christian pacifism. Instead, it places the emphasis where it really matters, namely, on the kind of politics embodied by the church, the very body of Christ.

For all of these reasons, I think that a Mennonite account of Christian pacifism construed in terms of friendship with God is peculiarly suited to illuminate, and in turn be illuminated by, the debate between MacIntyre and the Genealogists on the politics of friendship with which this discussion began. At the heart of MacIntyre's project lies the question "Aristotle or Nietzsche?" And judging by Derrida's recent work on friendship, this same question is in many ways central to the Genealogical tradition as well. It might equally be central to Mennonite questions about peace—but only if it is supplemented with yet another question that one can imagine being asked with appropriately stubborn insistence by John Howard Yoder: "But what about Jesus?"

—10—

Curing the Body of Christ: Memory, Identity, and Alzheimer's Disease by Way of Two Mennonite Grandmothers

For those of us who inhabit bureaucratic and technologically driven cultures often referred to as "late capitalism," many of the more important aspects of identity are reflected in concerns belonging to the field known as bioethics or medical ethics. We turn to the medical ethicist when we face questions concerning the right to exercise control over our own lives or the lives of our loved ones. This often happens in situations where what is lacking is the very capacity to exercise any such meaningful form of control. And yet, if the figure of the medical ethicist serves as a sort of stock character representing certain dominant cultural forms, it does so as one who is notoriously uninterested in questions of culture and identity.

The field of medical ethics, especially as it is practiced in pluralistic social orders, typically exists in abstraction from substantive discussions about the good life. The work of the medical ethicist is essentially procedural, and because of this, it is almost necessarily abstract, as it seeks to provide a means for guiding difficult choices that confront anonymous beings. The medical ethicist thus serves as an emblematic image of a conception of culture and identity that is premised on the possibility of suspending notions of culture and identity for the purpose of negotiating something known as the domain of the ethical. Carl Elliott, an astute commentator on the state of contemporary medical ethics, thus warns: "Constrained by the demand for immediately useful answers, clinical ethics (at its worst, at any rate) comes dangerously close to being a purely technical enterprise carried out in isolation from any kind of deep reflection about the examined life, the way lives ought to be lived and the way they ought to end."[1]

This chapter offers some general theological reflections on this confusing state of affairs, serving as a kind of theological exploration of what Elliott calls the "examined life." It does so by weaving together three themes: (1) body of Christ (i.e., the church); (2) Eucharist or communion, commonly understood as the act which makes the church, and (3) questions of memory and identity, set against the background of the challenge of Alzheimer's disease. All three of these themes come together in Luke's account of the Lord's Supper in Luke 22:19, where Jesus says: "This is my body which is given for you. Do this in remembrance of me." In *Remembering Whose We Are,* a penetrating set of theological reflections on the challenge of Alzheimer's disease, David Keck suggests that "the central act of the Christian community is an act of remembering."[2] By participating in communion, we are incorporated into and thus morally formed and in fact constituted by the church's shared memory of Christ's life, death, and resurrection.

I have titled this chapter "Curing the Body of Christ." I want to begin by commenting briefly on the reasons for this choice of words. Discussions in medical ethics often turn upon a basic distinction between *cure* and *care*. It is assumed that these reflect rival options for understanding the ends of medicine, such that one must decide whether medicine is primarily about curing a disease or caring for a patient in some broader way. But taking a closer look at the meaning of cure suggests that this might be a false dichotomy. For the Latin word *curare,* from which we get the English "to cure," actually means "to care for." Accordingly, one might argue that curing and caring for amount to the same thing historically. Only very recently, with the advent of modern technological medicine, did curing come to be understood primarily as medical treatment of specific illnesses considered in and of themselves. In its original setting, medicine did not name a specific realm or sphere of activities that was intelligible in and of itself. The health of the physical body was understood to be intimately bound up with a more general account of the good life as such. The ambiguity between cure and care might thus serve as a way of identifying some of the limits of contemporary medicine and medical ethics as they are more commonly understood.

At the same time, curing can also refer to an act of preservation, as in curing pork or fish. And I mean to allude to this aspect of its meaning as well. In speaking of curing the body of Christ, I mean that we ought not to lose sight of the role the church might play as a key dialogue partner in approaching questions of medical ethics. All too often the church is missing from discussions of medical ethics, whether Christian or otherwise. But we ought to resist the assumption, convenient as it may be, that the church is concerned merely for one part of the person, namely the soul, so that the body is given up to the domain of some other institution, such as the hospital or the state.[3] For the church, at least as Paul understands it, does not carve up the person into discrete realms. This implies that for Christians no such thing as the domain of "the ethical" can be set alongside other interests and concerns. Christian ethics is not limited to the negotiation of interests and concerns, of decisions and choices, but names an embodied way of life.

To preserve a meaningful role for the church in debates about medical ethics, however, will involve a significant critique of the ethos of preservation. Among other things, this is because the church names a body, a people, who claim that life is a gift, not a possession. The vision of a good human life, according to the Christian tradition, is perverted if it is approached from the perspective of a logic of owner-ship and control. Indeed, it is just such a logic that Christians have called sinful. It is what the radical reformers called "world" and what John Howard Yoder called Constantinianism.

Christians are a people who ought not to be preoccupied with protecting an abstraction called "life" for its own sake. They ought not to live in such a way that they reflect an overriding need to produce mechanisms designed to secure their ongoing survival. Christian identity is not adequately captured by spatial metaphors. It does not inhabit a territory whose boundaries are in need of constant policing. Rather, it is a gift received and shared and will thus lead to an identity-transforming blurring of the lines we characteristically draw between the self and its various others. Preserving the role of the church in discussions of medical ethics thus serves to counter the sense in which our participation in those fields we designate as "the medical" seem to call out a survivalist lust for preservation.

To capture all this from a somewhat different angle, a Christian approach to medical ethics turns upon a particular understanding of the relationship between memory and the body—which I shall call "embodied memory." Such an understanding of memory is perhaps best summed up negatively. The account of memory that I will be sketching is not based on a basic distinction between mind and body. I speak of memory not as a purely cognitive act but as equally involving the work of the body. In addition, this conception of memory is not in the first instance something that belongs to individuals. Rather, memory is at least in part the exercise of the entire community. But this is not to endorse a communitarian conception of memory that simply casts the net of belonging ever wider. Such an approach claims appropriately that memory does not belong to individuals, but contends illegitimately that it is owned by some larger body. It makes the mistake of understanding the church to be an instance of community.

The conception of embodied memory that I speak of assumes that the church determines what we mean by community and not the other way around. On such a view, the notion of memory is only tenuously captured by the metaphor of belonging, for the kind of belonging practiced by the church names a series of practices designed to school us out of a desire for belonging. Difficult and counterintuitive as it may be, this means that our memories are not to be thought of as possessions that we own in some fashion or another. Let me try to develop these overly general and schematic claims more substantively by reflecting on what I have learned from my two grandmothers.

Ethics, Identity, and Memory

My paternal grandmother, Grandma Huebner, I knew simply as Grandma. Ethics for Grandma rested crucially on the notion of memory. As my father relates, in his book, *Church as Parable: Whatever Happened to Ethics?*, "my parents would seldom confront us with specific prohibitions. Instead they would remind us of our identity. 'Remember who *we* are!' or 'Remember who *you* are!' were the phrases often repeated by my mother as we walked through the door for an evening out with the 'young people.'"[4] Yet in appealing to memory in this way, Grandma was not appealing to memory as a category of moral psychology that has significance in and of itself. Rather, her reminders to remember who you are presupposed that identity had already been determined by the existence of a particular shared history.

Moreover, she recognized that such identity is not something that can be claimed as one's own possession.

You, whoever it is you are, do not create your own identity. You do not get to write your own narratives, but rather, you are helped by others to discover which narratives you are already a part of. In other words, who you are is dependent on your history and not vice versa. Thus, moral education is dependent on the telling of stories. Again, as my father relates:

> I was constantly reminded that we did not do certain kinds of things. These reminders often came with a story to illustrate. It was these multiple stories that defined the composite "we." Sometimes they would be from the Bible, sometimes from our Mennonite history and, on occasion, they would be from my parents' personal history. Yet, even as I separate them out in this way, I am aware that they are told in a way that brought aspects of each other together into one story. The personal stories were most interesting for us as children because it felt like they were most immediately ours. Included were heroic events of how my father as a child with his parents had stood up for their convictions in the face of death threats during the Russian Revolution. Some of my relatives were even killed, yet they remained faithful.[5]

By being provided with such a set of interrelated stories, while at the same time being taught how to live them out by concretely embodying them in specific social practices, my father was given an identity to which he was then expected to appeal in cases of moral judgment. These stories, stories in which my father was not even an active participant, determined his character and thus provided him and his sisters with resources for moral reasoning. That is what it meant for my Grandma to tell her children to "remember who you are." She was reminding her children that character precedes moral deliberation.

Finally, it is important to note that my Grandma recognized that these stories were not the universal stories of a common morality that is available to all rational persons simply in virtue of their being rational agents. They did not belong to everyone. Rather, they were situated within a particular social context, namely the context of the Mennonite church. They were stories that identified her and her community as different, stories that set them apart from the world. Quoting from my father yet again:

An important moral category for my mother was the low German word *aundasch*, which literally means 'different.' It functioned as a moral term for her because whenever she saw someone outside the community do something we should never do, she would call it *aundasch*. She seemed to know implicitly that just as their actions flowed from their historical narratives, ours had a different narrative. Because the narratives were different, so were the actions. She was not critical of their story. It just was not our story, hence could not be used to justify our actions. It made no sense for us to act on the basis of someone else's identity. She knew that acts come not in isolated and disconnected episodes but they arise out of religious and cultural identities. Our story was the story of Jesus and the church. We must be the kind of people capable of "putting on" that story.[6]

All of which is to say that the church must be a key participant in any meaningfully Christian account of the moral life. It is the church that provides us with the stories that train our memories so that we can remember truthfully.

To summarize, what lessons am I suggesting that we can learn from my Grandma Huebner about Christian ethics? First, moral education is based on the formation of character through the telling and retelling of stories. Second, moral rationality is thus subordinate to character and the stories that constitute it. Third, these stories are primarily the stories of the church, and as such, they set us as Christians apart from the world. Finally, and most importantly, all of this hinges crucially on memory. Thus, it is remembering who we are that constitutes the primary ethical task for Christians—or at least, so my Grandma taught her children and her grandchildren in turn.

Moral Identity and the Erosion of Memory: The Challenge of Alzheimer's Disease

At this point, however, I want to turn to my maternal grandmother, Grandma Hildebrand, whom I grew up calling Oma. I suggest that Oma constitutes an objection to the conception of Christian ethics that I have just finished describing by means of Grandma. And this is not because Oma substantially disagreed with anything that Grandma represents about ethics. In some ways, you can get this from many a Mennonite grandmother.

Rather, Oma might be taken to constitute an objection to this understanding of ethics because Oma suffered from Alzheimer's disease. And Alzheimer's disease, as is well known, is a disease that erodes a person's ability to remember. Accordingly, it might be suggested that if memory is so crucial to Christian ethics, then the Alzheimer's patient who can no longer remember must somehow be placed outside the realm of the ethical. The reality of Alzheimer's disease thus appears to call into question the very conception of Christian ethics that I developed by way of a reading of Grandma.

What is perhaps so tragic about the story of Oma is that she was always a person who was extremely proud of her ability to remember. When she was a teenager, she committed to memory a poem of over 200 lines. And she was undoubtedly the most dedicated storyteller I have ever met. I'm sure I have heard at least a couple of hundred times the story of how she, as a young girl on her way from the Ukraine to Canada with her family, was forced to stay behind in Germany to recover from an eye disease, unsure of whether she would ever see her parents again. Now it is up to me to more actively participate in the telling and retelling of these stories.

Oma used to devour books and magazines in her spare time, one after another—mostly theological books and Mennonite newspapers. Even after she was stricken with Alzheimer's disease, she would still read tirelessly. Indeed, she would often spend her whole day reading. Only now she would read the same page of the *Mennonite Reporter* over and over again, each new time for the very first time, all day long, and likely never make it to the end of the page. It used to hurt me profoundly to watch her get stuck in such a seemingly futile and endless cycle, like a skipping record that has lost its capacity to make music. So I would occasionally turn the page for her, just to make it seem like she was making some kind of progress.

But by far the most painful of all the new experiences that her memory loss brought about was when my grandfather, or Opa, died. We were all gathered in the funeral home as a family. She recognized that the whole family was there, but noticed that Opa was not. "Where's Dad?" she asked. And nobody really knew what to say. Well, actually they all knew very well what to say, but none of them wanted to be the one to have to tell her. So they took turns reminding her that he had died, and that we were at the funeral home. Or they held her hand, just to be materially present, as she looked toward the coffin, only to jolt away in horror upon recognizing who was in it. She had to be confronted over and over again with the death of her husband, often by turning around and seeing him, as if for the first time, lying there in the coffin. To the extent that it is meaningful to conjure up images of hell, I'm inclined to think it must be something very much like that.

But in spite of all of this, what I find so interesting about Alzheimer's disease is that, for a while at least, she still could still remember, at least in a partial way and once you got her going. She could still recite her 200-line poem. She tried to teach it to me, but I could never seem to get past about line 20. And she could even be taught new poems, if they were relatively simple and repeated often enough. She could still tell me the stories of her childhood move to Canada, just like she always did, as long as I was able to fill in some of the blanks.

When my parents were planning a trip to the Ukraine to visit the area where Oma and my other grandparents had come from, they asked Oma to draw them a map of her village so that they could see if they could find out where her house had been. It wasn't the most accurately detailed map in the world. It had been more than seventy years, and she was only 11 years old when they left. But they were able to use it to take them right to the house, and the old pear tree was still there in the same place, just as she had drawn it. So it is not that the memories themselves are gone. Rather, what she was losing was the ability to place herself in those narratives. Although she was still able to remember the stories, for the most part, she was having a more and more difficult time recognizing her own role in those stories.

This way of understanding the loss that is characteristic of Alzheimer's has been nicely described by Michael Ignatieff in his haunting novel, *Scar Tissue*. A key moment in the story occurs when the narrator, in discussing his mother's struggle with memory loss, comes to the following conclusion:

> I suspected that the breakdown in her memory was a symptom of a larger disruption in her ability to create and sustain a coherent image of herself over time. It dawned on me that her condition offered me an unrepeatable opportunity to observe the relation between selfhood and memory. I began to think of my mother as a philosophical problem. My mistake had been to suppose that a memory image could subsist apart from an image of the self, that memories could persist apart from the act of speaking or thinking about them from a certain standpoint.

> It was this junction between past and present that she was los-
> ing. She was wondering who the "I" was in her own sentences.
> She was wondering whether these memories of a blue beer mug
> in a warm suburban garden were really her own. Because they
> no longer seemed to be her own, she began to throw them
> away.[7]

In many ways, this describes the struggle of my Oma to a tee.

Along somewhat similar lines, David Keck suggests that Alzheimer's disease is best understood in terms of "deconstructing narratives," which ultimately lead, in the case of end-stage Alzheimer's, to a kind of "post-linguistic terror."[8] It is a loss of the ability to make linguistic sense of one's environment, and consequently, a loss of one's very place in that environment, since this kind of negotiation of one's surroundings, one's engagement with the world, is itself a linguistic skill. It is like "being reborn every minute—being perpetually thrown into an unfamiliar world with no memories and no capacity to organize the bewildering array of strange sensory data that confronts you."[9] In other words, it is the gradual destruction of the ability to claim our stories as our own, and thus the deterioration of the capacity to maintain an understanding of oneself as a narrative unity. According to Keck, end-stage Alzheimer's presents three ethical and theological difficulties:

> First, as cognitively functioning people, we have personal expe-
> riences which shed only partial light on what this kind of
> dementia might be like. Second, the very idea of a person going
> through such an experience is an idea we shun like the person
> itself. King Lear's speech, "Pray, do not mock me / I am a very
> foolish fond old man," while an example of someone suffering
> mental derangement, still retains power, dignity, and beauty.
> We can be drawn to the king in ways we are unlikely to be
> drawn to an Alzheimer's patient. And third, the complete lin-
> guistic breakdown which is end-stage dementia means the end
> of all possibilities of meaning and continuity. An incoherent
> babbling narrator whose words seem to come out randomly is
> not a narrator, and many may well wonder if this person is still
> a person at all.[10]

Rethinking Identity: Memory and the Given Body

Although I am not convinced that it presents insurmountable problems, it is worth considering the extent to which Alzheimer's disease presents an interesting challenge to any conception of Christian ethics that emphasizes character formation and identity. Indeed, I think Alzheimer's disease and Amyotrophic Lateral Sclerosis (i.e., Lou Gehrig's disease) present some of the most interesting of the so-called medical conditions for philosophical and theological reflection. Think of how tempting it might be to suggest that it is somehow more appropriate that a great mind like Stephen Hawking is stricken with ALS than Alzheimer's. As bad as it is—and it is bad—at least he can continue his cosmological speculation on the nature and origins of the universe. Would it then be better if Lou Gehrig, such a great athlete, had suffered from Alzheimer's? Could you still hit a baseball in the early stages of Alzheimer's disease? Could you retain the ability to pick up the spin of a curveball, make the appropriate adjustments, and still have time to swing the bat and make contact with the ball? I do not pretend to have the answer to these questions. But I think it is questions such as these that provide fruitful grounds for further reflection.

But what is the specific challenge that Alzheimer's presents for Christian ethics? Remember that the understanding of Christian ethics I have been discussing sees ethics as a skill, just like hitting a baseball. If the first moral task for Christians is to remember who we are, then the Alzheimer's patient seems to present a special challenge. But why is this? Is it because the she can no longer remember who she is, or because she no longer has a self (a "who she is") to remember?

The point I am getting at is that ethics and identity ought not to be understood as two separate questions. If narrative is a more determinative reality than character, and if you lose your ability to remember those narratives, or at least to recognize your own place in them, then it would seem to follow that Alzheimer's disease represents the very destruction of the character of its victims. And if, as I have suggested, ethics is largely a character-based enterprise, then it would appear that Alzheimer's patients must be left out of the realm of the ethical altogether. But does all of this really follow? I do not think it does. And for the remainder of this discussion, I will try to explain why.

Alzheimer's disease might represent a kind of critique of our modern fetishism of the notion of the disengaged autonomous individual. The reason Alzheimer's disease appears so destructive in contemporary industrialized capitalistic societies such as ours, I suspect, is that memory has come to be seen as the exclusive property of individuals understood as self-sufficient entities. At the very most, we might consider sharing our memories with our therapists, only to be encouraged to turn around and leave many of them behind. But if memories belong to autonomous individuals, then Alzheimer's cannot but initiate a process of destruction in which the very personhood of its victims is at stake. In a world in which we are schooled into a life of therapeutic forgetfulness, Alzheimer's is not so much a disease as it is a fitting conclusion to life.

But the church is not the world. And so long as the church is called to be the church, I suspect that the description of Alzheimer's exists, not so much as a disease, but rather as a judgment of unfaithfulness, much like the stories of the Old Testament. So how might the church provide an alternative to all of this? How does the church constitute an alternative to the abandonment of its victims to a lonely wasting away in personal care homes? It is worth noting that the phenomenon of the personal care home is itself the product of modern industrial capitalist societies such as ours, because I suspect it is tempting to forget. Time is a scarce resource. And so long as our parents and grandparents have done good retirement planning, it just makes good economic sense to have them spend the last years of their life at the personal care home. But our question is whether it makes any theological sense. So what difference does it make for the church to be the church with respect to the question of Alzheimer's?

In the church we are called to be materially present to one another. But what I want us to consider is that this is at the very same time to be memorially present to each other as well. The church is not merely a context in which we share our bodies with one another. It is a context in which we provide each other with memories as well. I am not introducing a sharp dualism between mind and matter here. In fact, I am not introducing any kind of dualism, sharp or otherwise. Rather, I am trying to think about an understanding of what might be called embodied memory.

If memory is detached from the concrete practices and embodied habits that define the church as a particular kind of community, a body, then we abandon victims of Alzheimer's disease to a long and painful process of solitary destruction. But if memory can be understood as a skill that is shared and schooled in the context of the entire community, then Alzheimer's need not represent a kind of permanent excommunication from the church. Notice, however, that I am not trying to come up with a way to describe Alzheimer's in such a way that its victims can be seen as retaining the capacity to remember. I am not trying to take the sting away from Alzheimer's disease. I am only trying to look at it in the larger context of the church.

I am suggesting that Alzheimer's redirects our attention to the importance of remembering *for* each other. The issue of memorial agency is crucial at this point. I am not trying to provide a way for us to claim that Alzheimer's patients do, in fact, remember, because I think that much of what is problematic is the very idea of remembering as something that is done by individuals, whether they are Alzheimer's patients or not. It is not autonomous individuals who remember. Rather, memory is a function of the entire community, the body of Christ.

We Mennonites have always believed in the notion of the hermeneutical community. We have assumed that the very activity of reading the Bible presupposes a process of previous initiation and training into the practices of a particular community. And it is similar with respect to memory. We know that the Lord's Supper is to be understood as a practice that trains the church to remember truthfully and thereby constitutes us as part of the body of Christ such that we have become the very memory of God. It is the practice of communion that constitutes and disciplines the memory of the church.

As Christians, we cannot remember truthfully unless and until we have been initiated into the life of the church through practices such as baptism and communion. The memory of the church only exists insofar as it has been trained by the grammar of cross and resurrection. Memory cannot be divorced from the context of the church in which we embody this kind of disciplined memory for one another, just as the incarnation is the embodiment of God's own memory among us.

It might be helpful to think about all of this in terms of the notion of friendship. According to St. Thomas Aquinas, the theological and ethical significance of friendship is best understood in terms of the idea of the friend as another self. Aquinas argued that we come to know ourselves, not by some sort of introspective awareness, but by looking at our friends. In other words, no such thing as the self exists in abstraction from friendship with others and ultimately with God. In a similar way, I am suggesting that no such thing as memory exists without friends who provide us with an embodied context of shared memory. Accordingly, I agree with Keck when he suggests that even better than the idea of remembering who you are, we are to understand the first task of Christian ethics as remembering *whose* you are.

Which brings us right back to Grandma. I suspect that my Grandma would disagree with none of this, even though she would likely ask why it is necessary to talk about Thomas Aquinas in order to understand what she was saying. Although she repeated to her children "Remember who you are" rather than "Remember whose you are," she knew full well that memory is not something that belongs to individuals. Rather, she knew that memory only exists in a context of the given body of Christ. She knew, in other words, that memory is a gift that is shared with others. She knew that it is only possible to remember who you are in the first place in the context of the church, which provides you with such a memory. And she knew that this memory must be disciplined by the practice of communion, in light of cross and resurrection. And for these very reasons, I think it is fair to say that Oma remembers all of this too. Only now I am explicitly reminded that she only remembers it to the extent that I and others are there to help remember it for her. But that is, after all, as it should have been all along.

—11—

Image, Identity, and Diaspora: The Ethics of Visual Culture in Charles Taylor and Atom Egoyan

Much recent work in ethics can be seen as an attempt to come to grips with the ethical ambiguity of the alleged triumph of the visual in contemporary culture. In particular, some of the most interesting and fruitful ethical reflection surrounds questions related to the interplay of image and identity. Ever since Plato, and probably even before, it has been taken for granted that moral identity is somehow essentially bound up with the negotiation of images. And yet it is tempting to claim that the relationship between image and identity has emerged only recently, somewhere on this side of the technological revolution. Moreover, such an assumption is often accompanied by the worry that we have, like Dr. Frankenstein, created a monster that threatens to overwhelm and destroy us.

But such claims are just a bit too comfortingly simple to be true. This all-too-familiar form of hyper-paranoia is one of the distinctive products of the media industry itself, and is in many ways one of its primary sources of nourishment. Just as recent critics of globalization have suggested concerning the ability of capitalism to regenerate itself, visual culture is self-generating in that it incorporates and indeed thrives on its own critique.[1] Accordingly, it appears that the relationship between image and identity is somehow necessarily ambiguous. It is not possible to be simply for or against visual culture.

This sense of the ambiguity of the visual is best captured by what W. J. T. Mitchell calls the "'postmodern' paradox of the pictorial turn." According to Mitchell, "on the one hand, it seems overwhelmingly obvious that the era of video and cybernetic technology, the age of electronic reproduction, has developed new forms of visual simulation and illusionism with unprecedented powers. On the other hand, the fear of the image, the anxiety that the 'power of images' may finally destroy their creators and manipulators, is as old as image-making itself. Idolatry, iconoclasm, iconophilia, and fetishism are not uniquely 'postmodern' phenomena. What is specific to our moment is exactly this paradox."[2] In other words, the proliferation of images continues and their grip over identity appears to tighten despite—or rather precisely because of—the growing sense of panic about their potentially destructive effects.

This chapter is an attempt to contribute to and further complicate this picture by placing side by side two very different accounts of the relationship between image and identity. The first is the movement that has come to be known as ethical anti-theory. It characteristically begins with the rejection of a representational construal of ethical knowledge and the moral life in general that is based on a model of the internal picturing of external reality. For example, anti-theorists such as Charles Taylor, Bernard Williams, and John McDowell have argued that the enterprise of ethical theory presupposes a general dualism between mind and world, or subject and object, and that this creates a kind of detachment or alienation of the self from certain crucial projects and attachments that are at least partially definitive of one's identity. Accordingly, the project of anti-theory is an attempt to strengthen and secure a conception of selfhood and identity against the threats imposed by this particular construal of the visual.

The second approach to the relationship between image and identity is drawn from the films of Atom Egoyan. I find Egoyan's work to be among the more astute and penetrating interpretations of the many-layered complexities of visual culture. In particular, Egoyan draws attention to the dangers involved in the attempt to safeguard identity over against images. The films of Egoyan are thus dedicated to an exploration of precisely the task undertaken by the anti-theoretical project associated with Taylor. One of the more important threads one can see weaving its way throughout Egoyan's work is the interplay between notions of image, identity, and diaspora. While Egoyan happily grants that identity is at least in part constituted by the projection of images, he also warns of the potential dangers of fetishization or reification through which such images can become "exoticized" in an attempt to secure a return home from exile. Building on such a description, I develop an interpretation of the role of images in Egoyan's films, focusing especially on *Exotica* and *Calendar*. I offer such a reading in an attempt to move beyond the limited discussion of image and identity offered by ethical anti-theorists.

Identity Beyond Image: Charles Taylor's Retrieval of the Self

One of the central features of Taylor's philosophy is his rejection of what he calls the "epistemological tradition." By this, Taylor means to refer to a conception of knowledge that rests on a basic distinction between "inner" epistemic capacities and "outer" reality.[3] In addition, he claims that this model of knowledge as representation includes three closely connected theses about the nature of the human agent. First, it presumes a conception of the "subject as ideally disengaged." It sees the self as fundamentally independent of external reality, whether natural or social.[4] Second, Taylor claims that the epistemological tradition depends on a "punctual view of the self." According to such a view, the self is seen as a disengaged subject that is able to treat its representations instrumentally, in an attempt to gain advantage for itself and others.[5] The third thesis, which Taylor identifies as the social consequence of the first two, involves an "atomistic construal of society." This is to name the assumption that society is best understood as a collection or composite of individual purposes.[6]

Taylor argues that such a perception-based representational construal of knowledge creates a sense of alienation between the self-as-moral-agent and its various identity-constituting projects and attachments. In other words, the epistemological gap between external reality and internal representations is accompanied by a kind of moral gap. On such a view, the self is caught between external and objective reasons for action, on the one hand, and motivations, which are taken to be internal and subjective, on the other. Taylor and other anti-theorists identify this moral gap as one the primary defining characteristic of the enterprise of ethical theory, whether in its Kantian or utilitarian guises.

According to the anti-theorists, ethical theorists assume that ethical reasons, seeking to be universal and objective, demand impartiality. And yet they maintain that the actual motivations of moral agents are more likely to reflect concerns that are partial and particular—emotions such as love and affection and social relationships such as friendship.

It is suggested that ethical reasons require us to assume an "external" stance. They place us in an imaginary space that would exist in abstraction from any background context that might be central to one's self-understanding. Motives such as love and friendship, by contrast, depend on precisely that background context that is denied a place in the theoretical construal of reasons for action.

Taylor argues that this background context is at least partially constitutive identity. It is an essential characteristic of who we are. Accordingly, Taylor claims that the project of ethical theory induces a sense of ongoing vacillation between the self-as-object and self-as-subject. Moreover, he argues that this vacillation ultimately becomes debilitating in the sense that it produces a schizophrenic sense of disharmony in one's very sense of self.[7] Taylor's project is an attempt to rescue the self from this internally alienating, schizophrenic state of affairs. In doing so, he sets out to deny the parallel gaps between subject and object, and motives and reasons. In their place, Taylor accords a much more significant role for the various constitutive "sources" or "goods" that make up one's identity. In short, Taylor's ethics is based on an attempt to identify certain background "sources of the self." He calls for a rethinking of ethics as an attempt to cultivate richer languages that allow us to become as articulate about these sources as possible.

In developing this alternative, Taylor argues for the need to shift our central metaphors—from representation to participation or engagement, or from picturing to dealing. The so-called epistemological tradition and the related enterprise of moral theory see ideas or mental states as *picturing* a reality from which they are fundamentally distinguished.

By contrast, Taylor suggests that we should understand our knowledge of the world as grounded in our *dealings* with it.[8] Reality should not be spoken of as something out there. This gives the impression that we are on the outside looking in. Rather, Taylor attempts to develop what might be called a participational construal of reality. He speaks of reality as something with which we are actively engaged in everyday life. This is meant to rule out the theoretical tendency toward objectification noted above. As Taylor himself puts it, "We can't turn the background against which we think into an object for us. The task of reason has to be conceived quite differently: as that of *articulating* the background, 'disclosing' what it involves. This may open the way to detaching ourselves from or altering part of what has constituted it—may, indeed, make such alteration irresistible; but only through our unquestioning reliance on the rest."[9]

Yet despite this alleged shift from a kind of Kantian preoccupation with ethical theory and its preoccupation with images, it appears that a residual commitment to characteristically Kantian themes survives in Taylor. In particular, he remains committed to the pursuit of subjective sovereignty designed to safeguard the stability of the subject by securing identity over against difference.[10] Although he develops it in terms of background goods rather than self-prescribed universal moral laws, Taylor remains preoccupied with the Kantian pursuit of guarantees for the integrity and stability of the self. I suggest that this quest for the supremely stable self is just as central to the enterprise of ethical theory as the representational conception of vision Taylor so helpfully identifies.

This association with theory is perhaps most clearly exemplified in the predominant metaphors of strength that govern Taylor's ethics. Indeed, the very heart of Taylor's position hinges on a contrast between what he calls strong and weak evaluation. He argues that the dominant contemporary understanding of the self, the self as it is construed according to the enterprise of ethical theory, is best described as a kind of "weak evaluator." This is to identify a conception of the self for whom self-reflection and self-evaluation is based on merely de facto second-order desires that she or he just happens to hold. Over against such a view, Taylor paints a picture of the self as a "strong evaluator." This names a vision of the self that is solidly rooted in firmly held constitutive goods. Moreover, these self-defining goods are said to provide the self with strong sources for its high standards.[11] As Taylor himself puts it, "the most reliable moral view is not one that would be grounded quite outside our intuitions but one that is grounded on our *strongest* intuitions, where these have successfully met the challenge of proposed transitions away from them."[12]

For and Against Images: Atom Egoyan on Identity and/as Pathology

The above suggestion that Taylor's account of strong evaluation betrays a problematic sense of dependence on the sovereign subject of Kantian moral philosophy becomes even more striking when it is contrasted with the very different account of the relationship between image and identity reflected in the films of Atom Egoyan. Egoyan's vision of the self presents a stark contrast to Taylor's preoccupation with strength and security in the name of overcoming an alienated sense of self-identity. Indeed, Egoyan suggests that alienation is often the product of just this kind of preoccupation with securing identity. And what makes Egoyan's work all the more relevant to the present discussion is that he develops it by offering an alternative account of the complexities of visual culture.

Egoyan's films might be approached as an attempt to draw attention to a related ethical danger that is also rooted in a conception of the visual. Such a danger, it might be suggested, arrives as if through the back door of Taylor's account of the relationship between image and identity. Taylor is concerned with the way an overemphasis on the visual can induce a sense of detachment from one's identity-constituting background goods. For Taylor, the problem with images is that they tend to serve as a substitute for a substantive conception of identity and selfhood. But Egoyan's concern might be said to run in exactly the opposite direction. He is worried that images invite a kind of pathological overemphasis on identity. His films are designed to explore a kind of perverse preoccupation with identity that can be equally damaging to one's sense of self.

Although too much is often made of their relationship, it might be helpful to approach Egoyan's work by locating it against the background of David Cronenberg, whose films are also rooted in the ambiguities of visual culture. In particular, one might see Egoyan's work as an attempt to extend and further develop the theme of image as virus presented so starkly by Cronenberg in *Videodrome*. Building on his earlier treatment of themes concerning the intersection of sexuality, addiction, identity, disease, and alienation in such low-budget bodycentric horror films as *Shivers* and *Rabid*, Cronenberg's work takes a decidedly McLuhanesque turn in *Videodrome* by investigating the merging of identity and technology, or the technologization of the self. *Shivers* tells a story of psycho-sexual transformation resulting from an infestation of infectious parasites, the result of a scientific experiment gone disastrously wrong—two favorite Cronenberg tropes. With *Videodrome*, Cronenberg turns to a more in-depth examination of technology itself, and in particular the notion of media as a parasitic extension of the body. In short, *Videodrome* can be read as a prolonged parody of the same broadly Cartesian linkage of identity as representation that Taylor also attacks. In Cronenberg's case, the dualism of mind and body or subject and object is subverted by displaying the transformation and eventual overcoming of the "real" by its various "representations."[13]

A more recent film, *eXistenZ*, suggests that virtual reality is never merely a game but is a very real way of life. In an admittedly paradoxical manner, Cronenberg's films explore the sense in which this Cartesian conception of identity and its ultimate overcoming by media can be seen as the twin first principles underlying the Hollywood aesthetic. In other words, the allegedly anti-Cartesian technologization of the body that Cronenberg recounts somehow presupposes and continues to support a Cartesian worldview. Even if its ultimate goal is a kind of post-Cartesian blending of media and reality, the Hollywood aesthetic actually generates a self-perpetuating process in which it is endlessly transformed and sustained by an ongoing strategy of combining and dividing them. Its paradigmatic happy ending allows just enough of an opening for the "real" to escape and circle back to an apparently genuine level of purity, only to be recatechized by technological processes yet again. It is just such a conception of Hollywood aesthetic sensibilities that *Videodrome* and other Cronenberg films are set over against.

Yet it would be a mistake to conclude that the primary message of *Videodrome* is anti-technological. Rather, Cronenberg attempts to convey a much more ambiguous outlook concerning technology and media. As Cronenberg himself puts it, "There is as much positive and exciting about it as there is dangerous and negative."[14] At this point the work of Egoyan becomes relevant. Egoyan's films can be read as an attempt to capture the essential ambiguity of technology and visual culture in a way that that extends and nuances the work of Cronenberg. Just as Cronenberg explores the kinds of problems that result from a fetishization of televisual media, so Egoyan is preoccupied with the role of the spectator and the controlling power of images.

Egoyan's emphasis on the technologically mediated character of contemporary communication is even more extreme than that of Cronenberg. But his exploration of these problems involves much more subtlety and richness. He is at his best in capturing the extent to which media has become an ineliminable part of the texture of the everyday while preserving a very real sense of dramatic suspense. Such an approach comes as a welcome contrast to the kind of literalism and metaphorical directness demanded by the fantastic approach characteristic of Cronenberg's preferred genre of the horror film.

Egoyan's work has been described as an attempt at exploring the sense in which "all people are fighting for their own identities, but the currency with which they're fighting is the projected images they're receiving or trying to make."[15] This tension is perhaps most compellingly entertained in *Exotica*, a film that might be described as Egoyan's most thematically complete work. We are introduced early on to these twin themes of spectatorship and control. The film opens with a scene at an airport in which Thomas, an exotic pet shop owner, is being watched by two customs officials working to perfect the techniques of surveillance and suspicion. Throughout the rest of the film, we watch as Thomas's calculated attempts to procure a particular image of himself slowly unravel.

At the same time, Francis, a tax auditor who is sent to investigate Thomas on suspicion of smuggling contraband eggs for sale in his store, experiences his own struggles with identity. Through a series of flash-backs and some old home video footage, we learn that Francis's daughter has been killed tragically and that his wife has also recently left him. In an attempt to find an emotional replacement for them, he frequents a local strip club called Exotica to see Christina, an exotic dancer with a schoolgirl act, who not only physically resembles his daughter but also happens to be her former babysitter. By interweaving these ritualistic visits to Christina with the video images of his lost daughter, Egoyan suggests that Francis's ultimately failed reification of the schoolgirl stripper is directly related to his fetishization of the video images of his daughter. In doing so, he suggests that the struggle for control over one's sense of self can all too easily assume the stance of the pornographic gaze just to the extent that it involves an obsessive exploitation of images. As Egoyan himself puts it, "One of the really dangerous things about recorded evidence of our behavior is that it can become exoticized as well. An image can seem to be completely fixed when in fact it is some-thing that can be psychologically manipulated. Our photographic indus-tries have led us to believe that there's nothing more natural than wanting to make a record of people we love; in fact our need to document is very complex."[16] *Exotica* is Egoyan's attempt to document this complexity by means of an examination of the way the triumph of image over identity has itself become a form of pathological addiction.

Egoyan's take on these struggles over image and identity is even further deepened by an emphasis on the theme of exile or diaspora in his films. Indeed, it is possible to see Egoyan's work as a kind of post-colonialist corrective to the rather traditional (at least by now) Sartrean struggle for individual authenticity in the midst of existential alienation adopted by Cronenberg, and which is in many ways Taylor's preoccupation as well. While this sense of cultural displacement is suggested by the dominant metaphor of the exotic in *Exotica,* it is most fully developed in *Calendar,* a film set in Egoyan's ancestral homeland of Armenia. The film revolves around two main characters, whose names we never learn and whose identities are thus hidden to a certain extent: a photographer and his wife. Eventually, we learn that they are both Canadians of Armenian descent and that they are visiting Armenia on an extended photo-shoot.

The photographer wants to take pictures of ancient churches for a calendar project he is involved in. In this, the couple are accompanied by a local driver, who insists on playing the unwelcome additional role of tour guide. In one sense, the story line could hardly be more straight-forward and simple. Partly because he is more attached to his camera and the images he creates with it than he is to her, the photographer's wife leaves him for the driver in what is also clearly a choice to return from exile, to come back home to Armenia. But what makes the film work in a way that compliments and deepens some of his earlier work is its reflection on the relationship between the themes of image and exile by presenting the camera itself as an additional character in the film.

We eventually learn that we are watching all of this, not as it takes place in present time, as it originally appears to the viewer, but rather from the standpoint of some time in the future, once the photographer has returned, alone, back to Toronto. This is first introduced by a flashback technique that serves to parallel and accentuate film's central preoccupation with geopolitical displacement and the struggle for reorientation. There is a sudden interruption of what we have been watching by the accelerated rewinding of those images, indicating that we are suspended somewhere between past and present. Video footage is thus woven into the film itself in a way that reflects the extent to which video image has become integrated with the "selective process of memory."[17]

The couple's competing interpretations of the breakup of their relationship are directly related to the creation of images they have made of themselves and others around them. She thinks she has undertaken a triumphant return to the homeland. And he thinks that she has merely succumbed to a reified and ultimately artificial conception of Armenia, not least by the images she has projected onto the driver. And he thinks he has managed heroically to resist this temptation by returning back to Toronto to finish the calendar project.

But perhaps the main point of the film is that he is equally implicated in this misguided attempt to secure a return home in the face of exile. For as the film moves on, we realize that he has become a prisoner to his own created images, both photographic and video. We see this as we watch him entertain a parade of unsuccessful foreign dates who increasingly resemble his former wife. In one sense, these women serve as a failed substitute for Armenia, suggesting that he has perhaps not so easily been able to leave it behind after all. But even more significantly, they may serve as embodiments of his drive to secure a way home by a series of technologically mediated surrogates. It is not the women themselves but the images of Armenia they represent that he is attracted to. And yet it is this desire to exert a kind of control over his own sense of Armenian identity that ends up eroding this very identity itself. The film ends while yet another one of his dates speaks on the phone in a foreign language to another lover. In the background, the photographer writes a letter to his ex-wife (notice the shift in medium), explaining that he has been reduced to "watching while the two of you leave me and disappear into a landscape that I am about to photograph."[18]

Conclusion: Identity without Guarantees

Like Cronenberg, Egoyan is not so much interested in pinning all the world's problems on technology as he is in exploring its fundamentally ambiguous character. One way he tries to achieve this is through the introduction of the camera itself as a central character in all of his films, as I noted above. In doing so, he means to highlight the way it is fraught with the same kinds of tensions and ambiguities as are all his other characters.[19] Although its participation in the overall scheme of things can be genuinely welcomed to a certain extent, Egoyan suggests that a technologically driven and image-oriented culture such as ours often has a destructive sense of pathology lurking just around the corner. Or as Ron Burnett summarizes Egoyan's films, "Any over-investment in the image needs to be problematized if only to examine the image's capacity to simultaneously entice and undermine, to provide meaning and pull it away."[20] The more his characters assume the spectatorial stance of trying to seize upon images and exercise control over them, the more they experience a significant loss of identity.[21]

I think this lesson needs to be more fully appreciated by anti-theorists like Taylor. Accordingly, by juxtaposing Egoyan's films with Taylor's critique of an excessively theoretical conception of ethics, I hope to have at least gestured in the direction of a broader conception of ethical anti-theory that includes greater critical attention to the kind of pornographic stance that trades in the exoticization and control of images.

Taylor and his fellow anti-theorists may be correct to warn against the sense in which reflection-as-representation can create a sense of detachment from one's sense of self.

But Egoyan suggests that a related set of dangers can arise when one is too preoccupied with securing identity, as the anti-theorists often seem to be. It is thus important to maintain a sense of ongoing interplay between the themes of image, identity, and diaspora. Taken together, Egoyan's films might be seen as suggesting that diaspora is the natural condition of visual culture. His is a world in which technology and the proliferation of images have created a sense of proximity that simultaneously makes us citizens of everywhere and yet unable to call any one place home.[22] One of the great merits of Egoyan's work is that it does not present diaspora as a static and merely negative state of loss, against which we must secure a passage back home.

For Egoyan, diaspora names a way of being in the world. It involves an appreciation of the ongoing negotiation of identity through images coupled with the recognition that there are no final guarantees to which we might appeal in an attempt to protect a sense of self-identity. To over-invest in particular self-images is one of the great temptations that appears to be inherent in contemporary visual culture. In light of this background, Egoyan helps to identify the problems in any attempt to solidify identity over against difference, as Taylor does. His films succeed by virtue of their ability to provide a healthy dose of vulnerability in a way that might be said to counter the overpopulation in Taylor's work of metaphors of strength and security. But equally important is that he does not altogether abandon identity to the marketplace of competing images. It *is* important to strive for authenticity about one's identity, as Taylor suggests. But in doing so, one of the most important lessons to learn is that identity often dissolves at just those points where we most strongly try to safeguard it.

—12—

Between Victory and Victimhood: Reflections on Martyrdom, Culture, and Identity

The first form of rulers in the world were the 'tyrants,' the last will be the 'martyrs.' . . . Between a tyrant and a martyr there is of course an enormous difference, although they both have one thing in common: the power to compel. The tyrant, himself ambitious to dominate, compels people through his power; the martyr, himself unconditionally obedient to God, compels others through his suffering. The tyrant dies and his rule is over; the martyr dies and his rule begins.

—Søren Kierkegaard

The martyr does not want to die, but by accepting his or her death manages to socialize it, puts on a public show and converts it to a sign, places it at the emancipatory service of others and thus salvages some value from it.

—Terry Eagleton

On February 23, in the year 250, Pionius, a well-known leader of the church in Smyrna, was captured by Roman officials. They acted under the command of the emperor Decius, who headed up one of the most severe campaigns of early Christian persecution. This date also happened to be the anniversary of the martyrdom of Polycarp, scorned as an "atheist" by his Roman adversaries and threatened with being torn apart by wild beasts before being "bound like a noble ram chosen for an oblation from a great flock" and ultimately put to death by fire and the sword.[1] Pionius is referred to as an "apostolic" figure, and was respected for his exemplary displays of virtue and his oratory skills. He is acknowledged as one whose "mind [was] ever fixed on the almighty God and on Jesus Christ our Lord the mediator between God and man."[2] And this got him into trouble with the Roman officials. "The Martyrdom of Pionius" records the following exchange:

> "Surely you are aware," said [Polemon] the verger, "of the emperor's edict commanding us to sacrifice to the gods."
> "We are aware," said Pionius, "of the commandments of God ordering us to worship him alone."
> Polemon said: "Come then to the market-place; there you will change your minds."[3]

But after being presented with an opportunity to experience the "good life" of the market-place, Pionius responds, "I too agree that life is good, but the life that we long for is better; and so too of light, that one *true light*. All these things are indeed good, and we do not run from them as though we are eager to die or because we hate God's works. Rather, we despise these things which ensnare us because of the superiority of those other great goods."[4]

Pionius's unflinchingly repetitive, almost taunting declarations of his convictions in response to the Roman threats were not enough to save his life, however. Indeed, it would be misleading to suggest that Pionius viewed life itself as something to be preserved. For what makes Pionius's words intelligible is not an abstraction called life so much as a certain *way* of life. His claims are not directed to the end of life in general, but rather to the one in whose death a new and utterly different kind of life is made known. Pionius's words and actions point to a way of a life that does not resort to violence in order to stave off death.

For Pionius and his companions, death is not an ultimate threat or a final frontier that needs to be overcome and tamed, though they also make it equally clear that neither is it something they actively desire. Rather, in Christ both life and death as they are commonly understood are thoroughly reconceived and reordered. And such a different understanding could not but appear completely irrational and nonsensical to the "cultured" Roman world, a world that prided itself on the strength of its knowledge and power.[5] Pionius's claims are repeatedly met with laughter and "loud guffaws."[6] This sense of radical difference is brought to a head when, after a series of lengthy exchanges with his captors and the crowds, Pionius is given one final opportunity to come to his senses and reconsider his refusal to offer sacrifices to the gods:

> As Pionius was silent, hanging in torture, he was asked: "Will you sacrifice?"
>
> "No," he answered.
>
> Once more he was tortured by his fingernails and the question was put: "Change your mind. Why have you lost your senses?"
>
> "I have not lost my senses," he answered; "rather I am afraid of the living God."
>
> The proconsul said: "Many others have offered sacrifice, and they are now alive and of sound mind."
>
> "I will not sacrifice," was the answer.
>
> The proconsul said: "Under questioning reflect within yourself and change your mind."
>
> "No," he answered.
>
> "Why do you rush towards death?" he was asked.
>
> "I am not rushing towards death, he answered, "but towards life."[7]

At this point, there is apparently nothing left to say, so Quintillian, the proconsul, formally reads the sentence brought against Pionius: "Whereas Pionius has admitted that he is a Christian, we hereby sentence him to be burnt alive."[8]

Finally, or perhaps not so finally, "the flames were just beginning to rise as he pronounced his last Amen with a joyful countenance and said: 'Lord, receive my soul.' Then peacefully and painlessly as though belching he breathed his last and gave his soul in trust to the Father, who has promised to protect all blood and every spirit that has been unjustly condemned."[9]

Martyrdom, Culture, and Identity

It might seem odd to begin an essay on contemporary culture with an account of early Christian martyrdom. For it is often assumed that the very idea of culture is a relatively recent invention. Culture is commonly seen as a concept whose genealogy can be traced back to the Enlightenment distinction between nature and culture, between that which is found and fixed, and that which is made and variable. From there it is said to have reached a kind of high point—or low point, depending on your social status—in the nineteenth century, when it was associated with a sense of aesthetic transcendence reflected in artistic, musical, and literary achievements. By the beginning of the twenty-first century, however, culture has become popular, ordinary, and ubiquitous—often significant in its political potential for those excluded from previous conceptions of high culture. Everything from geography and gender to garbage and graffiti is understood to be invested with cultural significance.[10] All of this no doubt seems a long way away from third-century Smyrna. But I suggest that recent debates concerning the question of culture could benefit from greater attention to the stories of martyrs like Pionius and Polycarp.

The aim of this chapter is to argue that a theological account of martyrdom is peculiarly situated so as to contribute to contemporary cultural theory in some interesting and potentially illuminating ways. In what might be called the standard approach, theories of culture are deployed in the service of reading early Christian texts and institutions. And while my interpretation of martyrdom no doubt relies on some elements of such an approach, I want equally to put the matter the other way around, exploring how certain theological convictions and practices might inform recent debates about culture.

The standard approach too often assumes that culture is a theologically neutral category that can be applied to any phenomena under investigation, whether martyrs or martinis. But as the British Marxist literary and cultural theorist Terry Eagleton has recently suggested, "If there is a history and a politics concealed in the word 'culture,' there is also a theology."[11] Building on Eagleton, I am interested in examining some theological assumptions implicit in contemporary questions about culture, and—here turning Eagleton around—exploring what sorts of insights about culture might be gleaned by looking at Christian theology.

But perhaps the connection between culture and the theology of martyrdom is even more explicit than Eagleton's way of putting it allows. In a recent reading of martyrdom, Elizabeth Castelli has argued that the martyrological tradition of memorializing the lives and deaths of the martyrs functioned as a way of "producing culture."[12] As Castelli puts it, the "Memory work done by early Christians on the historical experience of persecution and martyrdom was a form of culture making, whereby Christian identity was indelibly marked by the collective memory of the religious suffering of others."[13] More specifically, she claims that this work of collective memory is marked by a disposition toward a kind of cultural stasis and solidity, that martyrdom functions as a way of fixing identity, such that cultural practices become static and absolutized.[14] In other words, she argues that the cultivation of the memory of martyrs functions to produce a totalizing cultural politics of exclusion that "generates its own self-authorizing claims to a privileged status in relation to truth and public authority."[15]

Castelli is no doubt correct to warn against these dangers, and tragically, there is too much truth to Castelli's reading. And yet I worry that she overstates the tendency of martyrdom to encourage concentric, static, and essentially violent images of culture and identity. In so doing, she obscures the radical potential of the martyr as a figure of resistance to precisely these sorts of cultural formations. I am interested in exploring martyrdom as a critical practice that interrupts and explodes the logic of security and the controlled mastery of the self. The memory of this sort of martyrdom functions, albeit fragmentarily and episodically, to generate a new and radically different image of identity that is not driven by the desire to insulate itself against risk. The memory of martyrdom is thus at once a gracious and dangerous memory, in that it frees us from the temptation to ground our identities in solidified cultural practices. To put it this way is not to suggest that martyrdom is somehow against culture, though Castelli's line of reasoning sometimes seems to suggest just such a conclusion. Rather, I shall offer a reading of martyrdom as a cultural logic that defies the drive to fix and master, and thus points beyond a culture of preservation and security.

Culture and Struggle, or the Difficulty of Martyrdom

In an attempt to clarify what is at stake here, let me approach this in terms of the theme of struggle. Castelli's reading of martyrdom must be situated against the background of contemporary cultural studies, which reads culture agonistically, as a field of contestation and difference. In other words, Castelli argues that martyrdom can be understood as a form of cultural production because it constitutes a particularly stark sense of conflict. As Castelli herself puts it, "Martyrdom has to do foundationally with competing ideas about the character and legitimacy of different systems of power."[16] In the context of early Christianity, she claims that "competing narratives of identity and status were being negotiated in the penal system, using the body of the condemned as the field of contest."[17] And yet this is not merely a historical claim regarding the conflict between Christians and Romans.

The distinctive twist that marks Castelli's contribution is in the way she links her account of the struggles of early Christianity with an interpretation of the growing prominence of the figure of the martyr in contemporary popular culture. She notes that the martyr has recently become a hot commodity in the North American culture industry. The market for martyrs is growing in rap music, comic book martyrologies, teen-oriented versions of the classic martyrs stories, biographies of contemporary martyrs, the raging debate over the suicide bomber, and increasing academic and literary interest in the topic.[18] She suggests that this current popularity of the martyr is a manifestation of the kinds of battles over identity commonly referred to as the culture wars. Indeed, she concludes her argument with a examination of the way evangelical Protestantism has recently come to combine the notion of martyrdom with the rhetoric of the culture wars in its increasingly vigorous attempts to stake a claim to a distinctively Christian identity in a secular world.

Castelli focuses on the strange phenomenon of the martyr cult associated with Cassie Bernall, who was killed for allegedly confessing her commitment to Christ to the two young gunmen at Columbine High School. By bringing these apparently disparate readings together, Castelli claims that the notions of culture and martyrdom are linked by the common themes of struggle and identitarian conflict. More specifically, she suggests that while they may arise out of a sense of struggle, it is even more significant to appreciate how they respond to such a contest of differences. Castelli's interpretation turns on the assumption that martyrdom and culture jointly name an attempt to overcome struggle, to achieve stability and solidity in the midst of flux. They are both motivated by an urge to eradicate difficulty and difference, to move toward settlement in the midst of some sort of conflict over identity.

Castelli rightly identifies the sense in which both martyrdom and culture are marked by the presence of difference and contestation, and she offers many suggestive observations along the way. But I think her account of martyrdom suffers in the end from being insufficiently complicated. While she stresses the significance of struggle, her analysis is weakened in that she does not provide an adequately nuanced picture of what struggle looks like or consists in. She tends to speak of conflict and struggle *as such*, rather than exploring the different possible forms culture wars might take. In this regard, it is instructive to contrast her interpretation of martyrdom with the appearance of the martyr in the work of the radical cultural theorists, Michael Hardt and Antonio Negri. Against the background of a discussion of the struggle to resist the dominant global politico-military complex they refer to as "Empire," Hardt and Negri identify two opposing images of the figure of the martyr:

> The one form, which is exemplified by the suicide bomber, poses martyrdom as a response of destruction, including self-destruction, to an act of injustice. The other form of martyrdom, however, is completely different. In this form, the martyr does not seek destruction but is rather struck down by the violence of the powerful. Martyrdom in this form is really a kind of *testimony*—testimony not so much to the injustices of power but to the possibility of a new world, an alternative not only to that specific destructive power but to every power as such. . . . This martyrdom is really an act of love; a constituent act aimed at the future and against the sovereignty of the present.[19]

In the most general sense, it is instructive to note that Hardt and Negri do not speak of martyrdom in the singular, as if the martyr is a relatively straightforward and unambiguous, almost static figure, as Castelli's discussion often seems to imply. Rather, they emphasize differing conceptions of martyrdom, suggesting a kind of contestation internal to the concept of martyrdom itself. They recognize different ways of reading the figure of the martyr and that claims to martyrdom function at many different levels, whereas Castelli tends to take the identification of the martyr at face value. In other words, Hardt and Negri appreciate that martyrdom is an essentially contestable or difficult concept. To draw upon the language of Gillian Rose, they suggest that the practice of naming a martyr is a form of work and involves an assumption of political risk. It requires complex and in many ways ongoing forms of negotiation, what might be called the labor of judgment.[20] This is why the concept of martyrdom inescapably involves the delicate task of discriminating between genuine and false martyrs, a task that must in many ways necessarily remain unfinished.

These differences are further reflected in the way Castelli reads martyrdom with an eye to the present, whereas Hardt and Negri offer an account of martyrdom that is oriented toward the future, emphasizing the radical potential of the martyr. Castelli tends to situate the struggles of the martyr in the context of some given social order or another. She sees the martyr as one who is engaged in a contest between rival conceptions of power, both of which are still located within some larger cultural context, such as the battle between liberals and conservatives in the recent North American culture wars, which her discussion of evangelical Protestantism calls to mind. By contrast, Hardt and Negri evoke an image of martyrdom that involves the exploding or overturning of given social orders and their corresponding forms of power, and points the way to new conceptions of culture and identity. They paint a picture of the martyr as one who inaugurates a radically new order and thus gestures toward a culture beyond the standard options of power and control. To return to the above example, Hardt and Negri's second kind of martyr could not be understood in terms of a struggle between liberals and conservatives. Rather, the struggle here is against a conception of culture in which the options of liberal and conservative frame the available range of alternatives. This type of martyr may serve to herald a hitherto unknown and unrepresentable cultural logic.

Martyrdom, Eschatology, and Identity

Put in theological terms, and thus moving beyond Hardt and Negri, this is to suggest that martyrdom is an essentially eschatological notion. It is only against the background of an understanding of the coming kingdom of God that that the martyrdoms of Pionius and Polycarp become intelligible. Without such images as the triumph of the lamb and the heavenly banquet, along with the theological virtues of faith, hope, and charity that give them a kind of material display, their deaths are reduced to a crude occurrence of meaningless suffering, or at most a form of masochism, and their witness becomes essentially narcissistic. In other words, martyrdom involves an appreciation of the eschatological interruption of history and its dialectic of victory and victimhood. The martyr thus performs a kind of uncoupling whereby the world as we know it is stripped of its apparent givenness and strange new possibilities emerge. Or in the words of Paul, "If anyone is in Christ, there is a new creation: everything old has passed away; see, everything has become new!" (2 Cor 5:17).[21]

Castelli provides a reading of martyrdom stripped of its eschatological remainder and thus deprived of its revolutionary potential. She situates the martyr in the midst of a contest over scarce cultural resources and thus obscures the sense in which the story of the martyr might reveal radically new cultural possibilities. Accordingly, it might be suggested that her depictions of the martyr retain too many echoes of Hardt and Negri's suicide bomber, who sets out to destroy and triumph over rival conceptions of identity. But what if the martyr is at home in an understanding of culture that sees power, not as a zero-sum game of triumph and loss, but rather as an expression of excessive charity and uncontainable goodness? What if difference is not read as a form of simple opposition and brute conflict but as a gracious intrusion of otherness into the world of the same?

Whereas Castelli reads martyrdom as involving a kind of struggle or contest *over* identity, I am suggesting that martyrdom constitutes a rethinking of identity as itself involving an element of struggle and contestation, or at least what might be interpreted as such. For in the context of eschatological expectation, what initially appears as struggle can become transformed into a wild and unpredictable exchange of gifts. Such a conception of martyrdom marks a shift from an understanding of difference as a form of domination and destruction where one side triumphs over another, to a conception of difference as an ongoing exercise of gift giving and receiving.[22] Here the very ideas of culture and identity are thoroughly redefined. They can no longer be captured with metaphors of solidity and do not name any sort of familiar and fixable territory called the self that is to be protected and secured against the threats of the other. Rather, martyrs inhabit a world in which otherness and difference are internal to the very ideas of culture and identity themselves. And yet they simultaneously exist in our world—a world that does not like to have its lust for power called into question. So it is not surprising that their lives often end as they do. That their existence as martyrs is subject to our memory means that their very testimony is often subject to distortion.

Too often the memory of martyrs is invoked in an attempt to seize identity, to fix it and to exercise a form of mastery over it, much as Castelli's interpretation suggests. But from a theological perspective, such an approach can only be understood as a perversion, a kind of false martyrdom. For in terms of the notion of martyrdom I have been describing, identity is not understood as a thing to be seized but rather as a gift that can only be properly received in the absence of a drive to control. Likewise, the memory of this sort of martyr presumes a people for whom culture is not a kind of settlement made to contain and guarantee their ongoing survival, but rather a charitable interplay of differences.

Of Heroes, Victims, and Martyrs

To summarize the discussion so far, I have suggested that Castelli helpfully identifies a connection between martyrdom and culture and that she appropriately draws attention to the interrelationship among the themes of identity, difference, and struggle. But her conversation ends just where things might start to get really interesting, namely, the question of what sort of struggle is involved here, or of what difference looks like more specifically. The struggle of martyrdom need not be interpreted as a simple question of triumph and loss. It might be understood as a form of gift-exchange. In other words, the very existence of the martyr is a testimony to a vision of life as gift, and not as a given that needs to be protected and secured. And here the options of triumph and loss are no longer adequate to name a meaningful range of alternatives. In order to develop these claims, I turn to Rowan Williams, who contrasts the image of the martyr with that of two other figures who strike a significant presence in the contemporary cultural landscape, the hero and the victim. What I find particularly helpful is Williams's suggestion that the significance of martyrdom is located in its potential to gesture beyond the interminably violent dance of victory and victimhood.

Williams argues that contemporary culture is marked by an apparent inversion of the positions of the hero and the victim. According to the standard interpretation, the predecessor culture—often referred to in terms of the labels of modernity or colonialism—can be defined by the image of the hero. In a heroic culture, identity is understood according to the category of conquest. To be is to be victorious, to exercise power over, to overcome whatever challenges might stand in one's way. It is to inhabit a position of sovereignty, to vanquish one's opponents—in short, to dominate.

But in an apparent twist of fate worthy of Hollywood screenwriters, it now appears that no character dominates the recent cultural stage more than that of the victim, the very subject of domination. From talk show television to international tribunals, we are repeatedly presented with the message that to be is to be victimized, to suffer under the hands of some form of power or another. It has become customary to define oneself in terms of that by which we are afflicted, whether illness or anguish, overt physical abuse or subtle psychological manipulation. Identity is thus no longer understood as an expression of sovereignty but as an experience of subjugation. Accordingly, Williams suggests that contemporary culture is marked by the triumph of an image of "self-as-victim."[23] Whereas power used to reside in the hands of the powerful, it is now said to be wielded by the powerless.

It is customary to read such a development as a story of liberation, a flight from captivity, and even a contemporary analogue to the story of Exodus. But perhaps such a reading remains a bit too close to the surface. What if it is just too romantic and sentimental to be true? And what if it misses the point of the story of Exodus? It might be more truthful to speak of a certain "pose of victimhood" whereby the position of the victim is exploited as a way of gaining access to positions of moral authority and political power. Such a response no doubt risks being misunderstood as a reactionary hedge designed to conserve the position of the status quo. But this would be precisely the wrong conclusion to draw. It is the new logic of victimhood that functions all too often as a form of preservation and survival against the uncomfortable threats of the new. It is not so much the liberation of the voice of the victim her- or himself that is at stake here, but the possibility that the face of the victim is but a new expression of the same old mechanisms of power. As the Slovenian cultural theorist Slavoj Zizek observes, "The ideology of victimization penetrates intellectual and political life even to the extent that in order for your work to have any ethical authority you must be able to present and legitimate yourself as in some sense victimized. . . . [W]e are potential victims and the fundamental right becomes the right, as Homhi Bhaba puts it, to narrate; the right to tell your story; to formulate the specific narrative of your suffering. This is the most authentic gesture you can make."[24]

Culture consists in the power to rewrite the stories of our past. The self is nothing but the ability to seize hold of one's own voice. Identity is constituted by narrative, and the only story that counts is that which is told from a first-person perspective. To quote Zizek again, "Ultimate authenticity is based on the idea that only the person who is immediately affected by circumstances can tell the true story about his or her suffering."[25] The only problem with such an assumption, as both Zizek and Williams point out, is that such stories are self-confirming and entirely invulnerable to critique. We can make them into whatever we want, or at least nobody has the right to call my experiences of suffering into question. So the position of the victim circles right back to the conception of power exemplified by the hero.

According to the reigning paradigm of contemporary cultural studies, then, the victim has been relieved from a life of suffering and subjugation at the hands of the victor and achieved a sense of justice. But Williams argues that this alleged shifting of the balance of power from hero to victim is not so much of a shift at all. The victim has simply become the new face of the hero. What is instructive about Williams' reading of contemporary culture, in other words, is his claim that the victim and the hero are simply two sides of the same coin. The culture of victimhood simply reproduces the same logic of power as that of victory, namely a competition for security and control. Put differently, the hero and the victim are both expressions of a desire to escape difficulty. They both reflect what Williams elsewhere describes as an attempt to "imagine an environment without friction."[26] The hero seeks to overcome such friction in a kind of final utopian triumph, while the victim equally lives a frictionless existence precisely because of a resignation to suffering and loss. In both cases, what is missing is an ability to put the self into question, such that the notions of culture and identity remain fundamentally closed and fixed entities.

The figure of the martyr, by contrast, suggests the emergence of an entirely different model of culture and identity. Whereas the hero and the victim both name forms of social control, martyrdom implies a conception of life lived out of control. This is at least partially reflected in the fact that one cannot designate oneself a martyr. Rather, to have one's identity narrated in terms of a story of martyrdom essentially involves the existence of others with whom one's life is inextricably bound up. The martyr is a figure whose very identity is constituted by the memory of others. Martyrdom thus points to a conception of culture that is not reduced to a conflict between self and other, but rather one in which self and other are interpenetrably interwoven. Among other things, martyrdom is thus the expression of a message of hope in which we are saved from the temptation to place our hope in ourselves, to confuse salvation with survival. To turn once again to Williams, this is to suggest that martyrdom is essentially

> about something other than *heroism*. It has to do with freedom from the imperatives of violence—a freedom, in this instance, that carries the most dramatic cost imaginable. It is not the drama that matters, however, it is the freedom that is important. If we focus on the drama, if we long for the opportunity of heroism, we are in thrall to another kind of violence because we are seeking a secure and morally impregnable place for the self to be. We want to be *victims*, to enter a world where there

are clear divisions between the forces of darkness and the forces of light. We want, in fact, to get back to that clear frontier between insiders and outsiders which is so comprehensively unsettled by the trial of Jesus in the Gospels.[27]

An Uncomfortable Hope

In conclusion, let me return to Castelli's observation about the increasing presence of the martyr in contemporary popular culture. In light of the foregoing discussion, it might be suggested that what is commonly referred to as the martyr is really an example of the hero or victim. What passes for martyrdom bears closer resemblance to the mirror-image logics of victory and victimhood. But let us linger a little longer on the question of the martyr in contemporary culture. For I do not seek to defend an overly sentimental and nostalgic reading of martyrdom that privileges the ancient martyrs as somehow necessarily more genuine than contemporary examples. Perhaps the seeming popularity of martyrdom should tip us off to the fact that something strange and interesting is going on with respect to the question of martyrdom and culture, or at least something worthy of deeper cultural and theological reflection.

In a world of violence, let me suggest that we should find ourselves in the strange position of expecting that genuine martyrdom be simultaneously widespread and rare. Where a people whose lives are grounded—or rather ungrounded—in the peace of Christ are confronted by the many forms of violence characteristic of what the early Christians called the world, it is almost inevitable that death will occur. And yet, precisely as a people of peace, we do not consider ourselves to be immune from violence, but we recognize that we too are always already implicated in some form of violence or another. And we should feel this ambiguity, this tension between affirmation and self-critique, reflected in the stories of Pionius and Polycarp. But just because of this, we should be wary of too quickly appointing ourselves as the gatekeepers of martyrdom, or of too casually identifying someone as a martyr. Both of these temptations reveal a lust for uncomplicated territorial control that the difficult logic of martyrdom ought to warn us against. But neither should we therefore be inclined to deny the possibility of genuine martyrdom. For that would be to resign ourselves to the present and to assume that the way things are is the way things have to be. At least those of us whose identity is marked by a confession of our belief in a strange and surprising God ought to remain haunted by the way martyrs are able to unsettle us, even as we claim to have a grasp on them.

Epilogue:
A Sermonic Exploration

—13—

Putting Ourselves in Question: The Triumphal Entry and the Renunciation of Triumphalism

Scripture Texts: Psalms 118:1-2, 19-29;
Mark 11:1-11; Philippians 2:5-11

What is striking about many biblical texts is the recurrent theme of unexpectedness, of strangeness, of mystery. The psalmist tells us that "the stone that the builders rejected has become the chief cornerstone" (118:22). The wisdom of God is rooted in that which flows against the stream. It consists of that which has been dismissed by those who are normally considered to be wise. It flies in the face of received opinions and disturbs what we refer to as common sense. The story of Jesus' triumphal entry into Jerusalem is destabilizing at its very core, for its central image of Jesus, the one who has been proclaimed king, riding into town on a lowly donkey is a rejection of the usual mechanisms of kingship.

The triumphal entry involves the renunciation of triumphalism. This theme is echoed, perhaps even intensified, by Paul. In this letter to the Philippians, Paul writes that the lordship of Christ is not that of one who rules by domination and might. It does not resemble what he elsewhere calls "the powers." Rather, we are reminded that Jesus emptied himself, became humble, and took the form of a servant. Unlike other rulers, Jesus does not rule by forceful imposition. He rules, not by wielding power, but as a servant. To model our lives after Jesus, as Paul calls us to do, is thus to have our lives radically changed. It is far more than just being given a second chance. It is to be remade, as we are inscribed into a fundamentally different *kind* of life. To confess that Jesus Christ is Lord, as Paul calls us to do, is to have our lives transformed on the basis of a redefined model of lordship. To confess that Jesus is the master is to begin to participate in a way of life that renounces mastery. It is to embark on the hard journey of learning how to give up the temptation to be in control.

What is noteworthy about each of above texts is that they repeat a pattern that is fundamentally disruptive. Each involves a way of putting ourselves in question. They disturb many of our central convictions and upset the exceedingly comfortable character of our lives. They challenge the assumptions we hold dear and unsettle the boundaries and territorial schemes of order that we erect to protect ourselves and to exclude those others whom we deem threatening. All of which is to say that they are profoundly mysterious in the sense that they transcend what it is that we can grasp with our knowledge. Paul tells us to have among us the mind of Jesus Christ. This is to remind us that we will not be saved by the contents of our own minds. The story of Jesus Christ is not something that we could possibly come up with on our own. Rather, our minds are in need of transformation. He calls us to have our minds renewed so that they might be seen as participating in the mind of Jesus Christ.

Not only does this include the redefinition of what counts as knowledge, but it challenges the assumption that knowledge involves always having something to say. To say that the mind of Christ, the wisdom of God, is mysterious is to say that there are some matters that are not up to us to settle and determine. There are some things whose business it is not ours to resolve. Or rather, the business of settling things is finally not up to us. Our task is not to make everything come out right. It is not to make everything turn out as we think it ought to be. Rather, it is to have our "oughts" rethought. One of Paul's central messages is the reminder that life is a gift. As such, it comes unexpectedly, undeservedly, and unnecessarily. Moreover, its very nature as gift means that it is canceled out when it is turned into something we possess and exercise control over. We are called to live a life of gift-exchange with others, which means that we are called to become vulnerable to one another. And so the temptation to settle is itself unsettled.

During the season of Holy Week, we come to the climax of the

Christian year. It is a time when we celebrate and are confronted with what it means to participate in the life, death, and resurrection of Christ. Those who prepare by participating in the Lenten exercise of giving up things in which we falsely place our hopes are taught even more directly to rethink much of what we have come to hold dear. Indeed, this is a time when time itself is redefined. "This is the day that the Lord has made; let us rejoice and be glad in it." Or rather, let us learn what it means to be truly glad. For the day of the Lord is unlike other days. And the kind of gladness and rejoicing it requires differs from conventional conceptions of rejoicing. It forces us to take long and unsettling look at those things that typically make us happy.

The triumphal entry involves the renunciation of triumphalism. This means that happiness and rejoicing do not involve the sorts of things we might typically associate with victory and triumph—things like power, fame, honor, self-satisfaction, and comfort. Each of these names a way of celebrating and fastening our hopes to that which is the same, that with which we are familiar—most notably ourselves. But the day of the Lord names an alternative way of life, a way of life that is open to otherness, to strangeness, and to that which we name as different. It was, after all, because Jesus was so completely strange, so entirely other, that he was put to death on the cross. And to speak of his resurrection is to come to recognize a way of life whereby the other is not treated as a threat to be done away with.

To enter Holy Week is to be introduced to and redefined by what we might call God's time. God's time is a time that cannot easily be reconciled with other ways of understanding time. The passage of time is often read as a defensive exercise in self-justification. History is narrated as a way of declaring our self-importance. This happens most clearly when we read all prior history as somehow leading up to us—the source of hope, the bearers of progress, the cutting edge. We hear this when we hear it said that we are standing at the edge of history. This is surely one of the most clichéd and overused sayings of all time. It is perhaps especially, and most disturbingly common in times of war. But that is why it is all the more important to revisit it, to unsettle it, and find new—or perhaps old—meaning in it. What does it mean to speak of history in this way, and who are the "we" placed at its edge?

Often, to say that we are standing at the edge of history is to embark on an exercise in self-legitimation. It is an attempt to articulate a scheme in which we might be said to save ourselves, or at least to place our hope in ourselves. And yet such an attempt cannot but be exposed from the perspective of the mysterious mind of Christ as a dangerous exercise in self-deception. The "we" that is named in such a claim are those who see themselves as the bearers of power. To utter such a "we" is to identify with those whose legitimacy is called into question by the redefinition of lordship involved in the confession of the lordship of Christ.

And yet there is a sense in which it is true that we are standing at the edge of history. It is not that history has come to an end and reached its terminus at a place where we happen to find ourselves standing. Nor is this to suggest that on the other side of the edge there is something altogether beyond history. The influential Christian ethicist Reinhold Niebuhr famously located the cross outside of history. But to locate the cross outside of history as Niebuhr does is a convenient way to make Jesus irrelevant so that he does not interfere with what we think needs to be done. It allows us to claim that Jesus is not a political figure, thereby paving the way for us to be more realistic about the necessity of war from time to time. It is yet another way of insulating us against the possibility of serious self-critique. It is to refuse the possibility of putting ourselves in question. It is a way of making us invulnerable —even, perhaps especially, to ourselves.

If there is a truth to the claim that we are standing at the edge of history, it is that history—as read from the perspective of Holy Week—is radically redefined. To live in a time that is defined by the life, death, and resurrection of Christ is to inhabit a time that is profoundly untimely when measured from the perspective of other ways of understanding time. It is not primarily about progress, but it involves the recognition that we have more often than not fallen short of the model we were called by Paul to imitate. It does not involve exclusions, the setting of boundaries, and the policing of territories. Rather, it calls us to be vulnerable to one another, to love even our enemies. It is not an exercise in self-legitimation, a way of securing power, but an ongoing practice of dispossession and the renunciation of our lust for power. It helps us to recognize that history is not necessarily to be associated with the triumph of the good guys, or at least those whose "goodness" consists in the fact that we find them on "our side." Most importantly, God's time is not moved by violence. Rather, it is moved by God through those whose lives may be said to participate in the model of

Christ that Paul identifies—servants, the humble, those who empty themselves, those who count others better than themselves, those whose lives are lived as gifts to be given, not as possessions to be controlled.

As central as these disruptive emphases may be, it is important to acknowledge that this is a difficult message to hear. It is not that we fail to hear it altogether. The point is too obvious to be entirely overlooked. But it is nevertheless difficult to hear it well. There is a tension between recognizing the call to have ourselves put in question and the temptation to miss the full meaning of the words we hear. It might be suggested that it is an attempt to point to this very struggle that is the main task of the biblical texts I have been examining. It seems that a recognition of the difficulty involved in hearing the message well is built into the passages themselves. Let us return to the psalmist again. Having been told that the wisdom of God is built upon that which others have rejected, that God's wisdom flows against the stream of common sense, we read the following words: "Save us, we beseech you, O Lord! O Lord, we beseech you, give us success!" (118:25). As I read it, the juxtaposition of these two lines is meant to be jarring. It is designed to seem contra-dictory. For the preoccupation with our success is the very thing God's wisdom is calling into question. It is from our deep longing for salvation that God promises to save us.

This is of course even further intensified in the story of the triumphal entry, which is meant to capture a similar tension. As Jesus is riding into Jerusalem on a humble donkey, the people place their robes on the ground, exalting him, and thereby treating him like the very king he refuses to be. We want so badly to be glorified ourselves that we fail to see the glory of the one who refused to be glorified. We want so badly to be victorious that we fail to see the triumph of the one who renounced triumphalism. Jesus is not the kind of king who arrives in gold-plated carriages and walks on red carpets. He is not protected and kept safe by the company of gun-toting security guards. Rather, he is proclaimed as king, as messiah, because he exposed the lie of such a conception of kingship. He was the kind of king who dared to tread on the rough ground of ordinary existence. He was, after all, born in a stable. He does not come to be protected from the messiness of life.

Jesus does not sidestep ugliness. Rather, he comes to embrace it. As the British theologian Herbert McCabe has noted, Jesus did not belong to a "nice clean world" of honest and respectable people. His are not the kind of people who work hard, who repay their debts on time, who preserve order. In other words, Jesus does not belong to the kind of people who make up the North American middle class. Rather, his genealogy places him squarely in a "family of murderers, cheats, cowards, adulterers, and liars." In other words, he belonged to *us,* to those same people who make up the North American middle class. And yet he came to that part of us we have become masters at denying. He came to us in a way that refused to bypass the vulgar nature of our existence. He came to make our very ordinary lives holy and to find in ordinariness a certain kind of holiness. He came to transform the ordinary. That is the mystery of God's wisdom. And it is because he dared to come to us in this way, a way that was so thoroughly like us that it seemed utterly foreign, completely strange, entirely other, that he met the kind of end he did. That is the scandal of the cross.[1]

Part of the difficulty in being able to hear well the unsettling biblical message is that we have a tendency to make it all too familiar. We have learned to read the Bible in a way that removes the mystery. We have become masters at domesticating the disturbing messages of the biblical story. Rowan Williams puts it this way: "We brush aside rumors of the cross and stick with the God we can do business with. This God is pleased with our bustle, our willingness to make him an absorbing, even an expensive hobby. He is pleased that we treat our worship as something isolated and special, pleased by our religious professionalism. He is delighted that we so successfully manage the conditions under which he may be approached, saying 'yes' to this one, 'no' to that one, and 'possibly, if you do the following things' to another."[2] In other words, we almost habitually re-narrate the biblical story in ways that we are able safely to manage. And in so doing, we fail to see that the heart of the message is that we are called to a way of life that passes beyond management. We are called out of the safe-making schemes we invent in order to save ourselves, and into a life of gift-giving and receiving, a way of life whereby we are made vulnerable to one another.

All of this is but a way of exploring the topic of sin, which names a refusal to allow ourselves to be put in question. Sin names our habit of domesticating God, of refusing to recognize the otherness of God. Sin names a way of life that allows no space for the mystery of God's wisdom. It names a preoccupation with management and control. Put differently, the logic of sin is reflected in the will to save ourselves. And more often than not, it is rooted in good intentions. We are often misled in our thinking about sin by a tendency to be preoccupied with big sins, on those sins we find easy to identify. But even more important than a focus on the big sins is the capacity to recognize the ordinariness of sin, the banality of evil, as Hannah Arendt put it.

In order to come to a meaningful understanding of sin, we are perhaps better off looking at those everyday sins that arise from our good intentions. Augustine, in one of the most famous accounts of sin, claimed that sin is to be understood as something that is parasitic on the good. What he meant by this is that sin is grounded in an attempt to do the good. Sin has its origins in the very thing that is taken to overcome it. It can even be rooted in Christ, or at least what passes for Christ. It can be found in the way we use Christ as a means to manage the world, to set up boundaries, and to exclude others. Sin arises when we turn the unsettling messages of the Bible into comforting messages of self-consolation.

The church is supposed to be a space where sin can be discussed. It is supposed to be a place where we can be honest with one another, where we can be vulnerable to one another, and in so doing, become open to the possibility of forgiveness. But the great failure of the church is that it often ceases to be such a place. On the contrary, it tends to be a place where we come seeking confirmation. It is a place where we come to justify and legitimate ourselves rather than to put ourselves in question. Flannery O'Connor once spoke of the American South as a place that was not so much Christ-centered as Christ-haunted. In doing so, she pointed to what both Augustine and the Bible identify as the central tension captured by the language of sin. I think she also instructively captured what it might mean for the church to be the church. As Paul reminds us, the church is to be a place where we learn to model our lives in Christ. It is a place that is Christ-centered. And yet as such, it is a place that does not rest easy in Christ. It is not merely centered in Christ, but it is also haunted by Christ. Indeed, it might be suggested that the root of sin consists in our unwillingness to be haunted by Christ.

To allow ourselves to be haunted by Christ is ultimately an expression of hope. The emphasis on unsettling, on disruption, on hauntings, and the ongoing temptation to a life of sinfulness might seem to demolish our hope. But nothing could be further from the truth. These biblical texts are profoundly hopeful. Even as we pass through the darkness of the cross in times such as Holy Week, we find ourselves in the most hopeful of times. In the cross, hope is redefined. Our hope is that we have been given a hope that consists in something other than ourselves.

Our hope involves the possibility of putting ourselves in question. Our hope is grounded in a way of life that is triumphant precisely because it renounces triumphalism. It is in losing our hope that we may find it. This is the day that the Lord has made; let us rejoice and be glad in it. Amen.

Notes

Introduction

1. David Bentley Hart, *The Beauty of the Infinite: The Aesthetics of Christian Truth* (Grand Rapids: Eerdmans, 2003), 19.

2. John Howard Yoder, *The Politics of Jesus: Vicit Agnus Noster*, 2d ed. (Grand Rapids: Eerdmans, 1994), 237.

3. John Howard Yoder, *The Royal Priesthood: Essays Ecclesiological and Ecumenical*, ed. Michael G. Cartwright (Grand Rapids: Eerdmans, 1994), 129.

4. Yoder, *Politics of Jesus*, 239.

Chapter 1
A Precarious People: The Ambiguity of Mennonite Identity

1. Stanley Cavell, "The Availability of Wittgenstein's Later Philosophy," in *Must We Mean What We Say?* (New York: Cambridge University Press, 1976), 61.

Chapter 2
Radical Orthodoxy, Radical Reformation: What Might Mennonites and Milbank Learn from Each Other?

1. John Milbank, "Violence: Double Passivity," in *Being Reconciled: Ontology and Pardon* (London: Routledge, 2003), 38.

2. Graham Ward, "Radical Orthodoxy and/as Cultural Politics," in *Radical Orthodoxy? A Catholic Enquiry*, ed. Laurence Paul Hemming (Aldershot: Ashgate, 2000), 103.

3. John Milbank, *Theology and Social Theory: Beyond Secular Reason* (Oxford: Blackwell, 1990), 6.

4. See, e.g., John Howard Yoder, "Why Ecclesiology Is Social Ethics," in *Royal Priesthood*, 109.

5. John Milbank, "Can Morality Be Christian?" in *The Word Made Strange: Theology, Language, Culture* (London: Blackwell, 1997), 224-25.

6. Ibid., 231.

7. Milbank, *Theology and Social Theory*, 411.

8. Milbank, "The Programme of Radical Orthodoxy," in *Radical Orthodoxy? A Catholic Enquiry*, 36.

9. See John Milbank and Catharine Pickstock, *Truth in Aquinas* (London: Routledge, 2001), 19-59.

10. Catharine Pickstock, "Radical Orthodoxy and the Mediations of Time," in *Radical Orthodoxy? A Catholic Enquiry*, 63.

11. Catharine Pickstock, *After Writing: On the Liturgical Consummation of Philosophy* (London: Blackwell, 1998), 62-64.

12. Yoder, *Priestly Kingdom*, 5.

13. Stanley Hauerwas, *With the Grain of the Universe: The Church's Witness and Natural Theology* (Grand Rapids: Brazos Press, 2001). The Yoder passage is from "Armaments and Eschatology" *Studies in Christian Ethics* 1:1 (1988): 58. See also Yoder, *Politics of Jesus*, 246; and, programmatically, "To Serve Our God and to Rule the World," in *Royal Priesthood*, 128-40.

14. I have developed this argument at greater length with respect to the work of J. Denny Weaver in a review essay of his *Anabaptist Theology in the Face of Postmodernity: A Proposal for the Third Millennium* in *Preservings: Journal of the Steinbach Historical Society* 18 (June 2001): 145-48.

15. Milbank, *Theology and Social Theory*, 347 (Milbank's emphasis).

16. Milbank, *The Word Made Strange*, 1. I thank Peter Dula for drawing the significance of this to my attention.

17. Yoder, "To Serve Our God and to Rule the World," 139.

18. John Milbank, "The Name of Jesus," in *The Word Made Strange*, 155.

19. Milbank, *Theology and Social Theory*, 418 (emphasis added).

20. John Milbank, "'Postmodern Critical Augustinianism': A Short *Summa* in Forty-Two Responses to Unasked Questions," *Modern Theology* 7:3 (1991): 229.

21. Milbank, "Violence: Double Passivity," 38.

Chapter 3
Mennonites and Narrative Theology: The Case of John Howard Yoder

1. Published as Harold S. Bender, "The Anabaptist Vision," *Mennonite Quarterly Review*, 18 (1944): 67-88.

2. See, e.g., J. Denny Weaver, "Narrative Theology in an Anabaptist-Mennonite Context," *Conrad Grebel Review*, 12:2 (1994): 171-88; and Scott Holland, "How Do Stories Save Us? Two Contemporary Theological Responses," *Conrad Grebel Review*, 12:2 (1994): 131-53. See also Duane K. Friesen, "A Critical Analysis of Narrative Ethics," in *The Church as Theological Community*, ed. Harry Huebner (Winnipeg, MB: CMBC Publications, 1990), 223-46.

3. A note on Hauerwas is in order at this point, since it is primarily by means of an appeal to his work that Yoder has been regarded as a proponent of narrative theology. First, it is significant to note that Hauerwas neither refers to himself or Yoder as a narrative theologian or ethicist. That identification is made or implied by the various Mennonite theologians mentioned above (n. 2), presumably on the combined basis of Hauerwas's appeal to the category of narrative in certain cases and his heavy reliance on Yoder. But I think that it is problematic to refer to Hauerwas as a narrative theologian for precisely the same reasons that I will outline below with respect to Yoder. Furthermore, even if it were appropriate to count Hauerwas as a narrative theologian, it does not follow that this, together with his appeal to Yoder, justifies the conclusion that Yoder is a narrative theologian. Such a move clearly does not follow logically. Compare with the obviously false, yet formally identical statement: "Jones is a baseball player, and Jones attributes his skill at baseball to Mozart; thus Mozart is a baseball player." Of course, it remains possible that appeals to Yoder's work might be helpful in constructing a Mennonite account of narrative theology, and even to use Hauerwas as an instructive example. But that is a different matter than the identification of Yoder himself with the narrative theology movement. It is this latter claim that I am calling into question in this essay.

4. For matters of clarification, it is perhaps appropriate to add a note on the once-popular distinction between the "Yale" and "Chicago" schools of narrative theology at this point, especially since this typology has been introduced into the broader Anabaptist discussion by Scott Holland. See Holland, "How Do Stories Save Us? Two Contemporary Theological Responses." While it is true that there are people associated with both Yale and Chicago who emphasize the category of narrative, most notably Hans Frei and Paul Ricoeur, the differences between Yale and Chicago are perhaps more significant than the apparent similarities that might justify a typology that interprets them both as versions of narrative theology. What is particularly problematic about the Yale vs. Chicago typology is that there is no larger, more generic category called narrative theology (without qualification) of which Yale and Chicago constitute two distinct species. Moreover, whereas those associated with Yale make narrative the primary category, it appears that narrative has a secondary role at Chicago, insofar as it is understood in terms of imaginative constructions rooted in human subjectivity. Thus, it might be argued that the Chicago school is not really a version of *narrative* theology at all, but rather a version of liberal humanism that emphasizes the category of narrative for certain purposes. In the context of the Mennonite discussion, it is instructive to note that Holland's defense of the Chicago school appears

to rely less on the category of narrative and more on "universal human needs" ("How Do Stories Save Us?," 140), "deepened self-consciousness" (141), ways of "being-in-the-world" (143), the "more primordial" experience of mysticism (144), and the general category of "otherness" (147-48). In other words, although Holland does stress the importance of narrative, its status remains subservient to a more general category of something like collective human experience. Thus, it remains unclear whether Holland has really offered the account of how stories save us that he claims to have provided. It often sounds like it is not so much stories that save us but rather that we save ourselves. If I am forced to put it in those terms, the account of narrative theology that I will be considering in the following discussion is broadly of the Yale variety. A better approach, however, is to avoid the terminology altogether and to question the value of the typology itself. The selection of narrative theologians that I consider here has less to do with their belonging to a particular school than with its being constructive in my judgment to compare them with Mennonite theology in general and the work of Yoder in particular.

5. This objection has been stated most pointedly by Holland. However, in light of the problems identified in Holland's appropriation of the Yale vs. Chicago typology (see above, n. 4), I think it is more accurate to see his defense of "public theology" as an alternative to narrative theology. For an argument that more explicitly defends public theology as an alternative to narrative theology, see Friesen, "A Critical Analysis of Narrative Ethics"; and Alain Epp Weaver, "Options in Postmodern Mennonite Theology" *Conrad Grebel Review* 11:1 (1993): 63-76.

6. Hans Frei, *The Eclipse of Biblical Narrative: A Study in Eighteenth and Nineteenth Century Hermeneutics* (New Haven: Yale University Press, 1974), 1-3, 130. On the question of the gap between narrative and reality, see pp. 4-5.

7. For Frei's own account of his relationship to New Criticism, see Frei, "The 'Literal Reading' of Biblical Narrative in the Christian Tradition: Does It Stretch or Will It Break?" in *Theology and Narrative: Selected Essays*, ed. George Hunsinger and William C. Placher (Oxford: Oxford University Press, 1993), 140-43.

8. See, e.g., Gerard Loughlin, *Telling God's Story: Bible, Church, and Narrative Theology* (Cambridge: Cambridge University Press, 1996), 82-86.

9. Frei, "The 'Literal Reading' of Biblical Narrative," 147. It is primarily to this essay that defenders of Frei point as signaling a shift toward a greater role for the church in his account of biblical hermeneutics.

10. See William C. Placher, *Unapologetic Theology: A Christian Voice in a Pluralistic Conversation* (Louisville: Westminster/John Knox Press,

1989), 24-38, 123-37; and Ronald Thiemann, *Revelation and Theology: The Gospel as Narrated Promise* (Notre Dame: University of Notre Dame Press, 1984), 43-46. Experience and natural reason are also the options that provide the negative foil for Lindbeck, although he does not put it in precisely those terms. See George Lindbeck, *The Nature of Doctrine: Religion and Theology in a Postliberal Age* (Philadelphia: Westminster Press, 1984), 16-19, 32-41, 63-69.

11. Among Quine's vast body of work, narrative theologians tend to focus on "Two Dogmas of Empiricism," in *From a Logical Point of View: Logico-Philosophical Essays*, 2d. ed. (New York: Harper & Row, 1961), 20-46; and W. V. O. Quine and J. S. Ullian, *The Web of Belief* (New York: Random House, 1970).

12. Thiemann, *Revelation and Theology*, 74.

13. Ibid., 75-76. See also Lindbeck, *The Nature of Doctrine*, 64.

14. Thiemann, *Revelation and Theology*, 75.

15. See, e.g., ibid., 75 (emphasis added).

16. See, e.g., Lindbeck, *The Nature of Doctrine*, 33: "Like a culture or language, [religion] is a communal phenomenon that shapes the subjectivities of individuals rather than being primarily a manifestation of those subjectivities."

17. See Loughlin, *Telling God's Story*, 36, n. 21.

18. Ibid., 49.

19. Ibid., 49-51.

20. Ibid., 84-86. Loughlin is referring here to George Lindbeck, "The Story-Shaped Church: Critical Exegesis and Theological Interpretation," in *Scriptural Authority and Narrative Interpretation*, ed. Garrett Green (Philadelphia: Fortress Press, 1987), 161-78.

21. Hans Frei, "Theological Reflections on the Accounts of Jesus' Death and Resurrection," in *Theology and Narrative*, 63.

22. Michael Root, "The Narrative Structure of Soteriology," in *Why Narrative? Readings in Narrative Theology*, ed. Stanley Hauerwas and L. Gregory Jones (Grand Rapids: Eerdmans, 1989), 270-71. See also David F. Ford, "System, Story, Performance: A Proposal About the Role of Narrative in Christian Systematic Theology," in *Why Narrative?* 191-215, esp. 193-94. See also Stanley Hauerwas and David Burrell, "From System to Story: An Alternative Pattern for Rationality in Ethics," in *Truthfulness and Tragedy* (Notre Dame: University of Notre Dame Press, 1977), 27-34. Frei has also drawn attention to the intimate connection between narrative and identity in terms of the identity of Jesus. See Hans Frei, "Theological Reflections on the Accounts of Jesus' Death and Resurrection," 45-93.

23. See, e.g., J. Denny Weaver, "Narrative Theology in an Anabaptist-Mennonite Context," 172-73.

24. Again, it is important to recognize in a way that some of his follow-ers have not consistently done that Frei's account of narrative is intimate-ly related to his work on the identity of Jesus. See, e.g., Frei, *The Identity of Jesus Christ: The Hermeneutical Bases of Dogmatic Theology* (Philadelphia: Fortress Press, 1975); and "Theological Reflections on the Accounts of Jesus' Death and Resurrection."

25. Thiemann, *Revelation and Theology*, 110 (emphasis added).

26. J. Denny Weaver, "Narrative Theology in an Anabaptist-Mennonite Context," 176.

27. Lindbeck, *The Nature of Doctrine*, 100. For some of Lindbeck's scattered references to "ghettoization," see, e.g., 25, 77, 128-29. This is not to suggest that Mennonite theology is appropriately situated in the ghetto. Rather, what I am pointing to here is Lindbeck's strategy of appeal-ing to the mainstream in order to avoid ghettoization.

28. See, e.g., Friesen, "A Critical Analysis of Narrative Ethics," 244-46; and J. Denny Weaver, "Narrative Theology in an Anabaptist-Mennonite Context," 174-75.

29. Harry J. Huebner, "The Church Made Strange for the Nations," in *Echoes of the Word: Theological Ethics as Rhetorical Practice* (Kitchener, ON: Pandora Press, 2005), 101.

30. Such charges of sectarianism against narrative theology are by no means restricted to Mennonite theology. Rather, my point is that when objections are advanced by Mennonites against narrative theology, it is the charge of sectarianism that they characteristically raise. The standard Mennonite objection to narrative theology that I am describing relies heavily on the work of James Gustafson. See, e.g., James Gustafson, "The Sectarian Temptation: Reflections on Theology, The Church, and the University," *Catholic Theology Society of America Proceedings*, 40 (1985): 83-94. Such an indebtedness to Gustafson is most explicitly acknowledged by Holland, "The Problems and Prospects of a 'Sectarian Ethic': A Critique of the Hauerwas Reading of the Jesus Story," *Conrad Grebel Review*, 10:2 (1992): 162.

31. Holland, "How Do Stories Save Us? Two Contemporary Theological Responses to Story," 149.

32. See, e.g., Alain Epp Weaver's approving depiction of Gordon Kaufman's conception of the church as "part of a public community con-sisting of many particular groups in conversation on equal terms about how to evaluate and reconstruct their respective traditions" ("Options in Postmodern Mennonite Theology," 76). Also telling is Epp Weaver's appeal to Kaufman's understanding of religious language: "Although reli-gious language might once have found its proper home in the context of the church, today the meaning of religious terms is to be found in their

usage in the common discourse of Western languages" (74).

33. Friesen, "A Critical Analysis of Narrative Ethics," 239.

34. Ibid. It is significant to note that Friesen equates "rational discourse" with "public discourse." See also Holland, "How Do Stories Save Us?" who claims that narrative theology signals a "retreat from the public square into the world of the text" (151) that must be countered with a more public "dialogue with the radically other" (152).

35. John Howard Yoder, "Why Ecclesiology Is Social Ethics: Gospel Ethics Versus the Wider Wisdom," in *Royal Priesthood*, 110.

36. Ibid., 122. See also John Howard Yoder, "Armaments and Eschatology," *Studies in Christian Ethics*, 1:1 (1988): 51: "The believing community today participates imaginatively, narratively, in the past history as her own history, thanks to her historians, but also thanks to her poets and prophets."

37. John Howard Yoder, "On Not Being Ashamed of the Gospel: Particularity, Pluralism, and Validation," *Faith and Philosophy*, 9:3 (1992): 297. In a somewhat different context, he describes the church's "alternative consciousness" in terms of an "alternative narrative" (*Priestly Kingdom*, 94-95). Yoder makes this last point in the context of suggesting that "another view of what the world is like is kept alive by narration and celebration which fly in the face of the 'apparent' lessons of 'realism'" (94). The reference to "realism" here is to Niebuhrian "political" realism, and not the kind of epistemological or metaphysical realism that is more commonly discussed by the "narrative theologians."

38. Yoder, "On Not Being Ashamed of the Gospel," 290.

39. John Howard Yoder, "Sacrament as Social Process: Christ the Transformer of Culture," in *Royal Priesthood, 370*. Though not specifically in those terms, this same point also underlies the argument in "Walk and Word: The Alternatives to Methodologism," in *Theology Without Foundations: Religious Practice and the Future of Theological Truth*, ed. Stanley Hauerwas, Nancey Murphy, and Mark Nation (Nashville: Abingdon Press, 1994), 77-90.

40. Yoder, *Priestly Kingdom*, 36.

41. It is significant to note, however, that Yoder consistently emphasizes that his account of Constantinianism is not so much concerned with Constantine the man. Neither does he suggest that the so-called Constantinian shift was an instantaneous, once-and-for-all reversal. Rather, he uses "the name Constantine merely as a label for this transformation, which began before AD 200 and took over 200 years," nevertheless claiming that the "medieval legend which made of Constantine the symbol of an epochal shift was realistic." See John Howard Yoder, "The Otherness of the Church," in *Royal Priesthood*, 57; and *Priestly Kingdom*, 135.

42. See, e.g., Yoder, *Priestly Kingdom*, 135-36.

43. John Howard Yoder, "Christ, the Hope of the World," in *Royal Priesthood*, 198.

44. For Yoder's own account of the varieties of Constantinianism, old and new, see Yoder, *Politics of Jesus*, 141-44; and "Christ the Hope of the World," 195-97. For a helpful summary of Yoder's position, see Michael G. Cartwright, "Radical Reform, Radical Catholicity: John Howard Yoder's Vision of the Faithful Church," introduction to *Royal Priesthood*, 10-12.

45. See, e.g., Yoder *Priestly Kingdom*, 88, 143; "Christ, the Hope of the World," 200. See also Yoder, *Priestly Kingdom*, 85: "Let us name as definitional for beginning our characterization of the radical Protestant reformation the very notion of challenging establishment; i.e., of rejecting, or at least doubting fundamentally, the appropriateness of letting the Christian faith be the official ideology of a society, especially of the elite within a society."

46. Yoder, *Priestly Kingdom*, 92.

47. On the connection between Constantinianism and the relativization of Jesus, see Yoder, "Why Ecclesiology Is Social Ethics," 114. See also Yoder, *Priestly Kingdom*, 54, 88.

48. Yoder, *Priestly Kingdom*, 24, 36, 43, 46, 108, 136, 141; "The Otherness of the Church," 57; "On Not Being Ashamed of the Gospel," 295; and "Why Ecclesiology Is Social Ethics," 108-9. See also Cartwright, "Radical Reform, Radical Catholicity," 6-7. It is important to recognize that Yoder does not reject all dualisms as such. This is most clearly suggested by the prominence of the distinction between church and world in his work. Rather, Yoder is rejecting those dualisms which provide the framework for establishment epistemology. See Yoder, "Why Ecclesiology Is Social Ethics," 108-9.

49. See, e.g., Yoder, *Priestly Kingdom*, 115: "It seems self-evident from the majority perspective that this kind of [Anabaptist conception of] moral discernment must lead to a principled withdrawal from the exercise of certain social functions or from the 'use of power.' It is obvious that the systematic analysis of the advocates of the majority position would make this assumption, so that the choice must appear to be between involvement (which cannot be ultimately critical) and non-involvement. Then the mainstream tradition chooses involvement. The radical reformation perspective, however, refuses to stand that choice on its head and withdraw, but rather challenges the prior logical analysis." See also Yoder's rejection of the "epistemology of establishment" in "On Not Being Ashamed of the Gospel," 288-95.

50. Yoder, "Walk and Word: The Alternatives to Methodologism," 77-90, esp. 88. See also Yoder, *Priestly Kingdom*, 114.

51. Yoder, "Walk and Word," 82. See also Yoder, *Priestly Kingdom*, 7-8, 37, 113-16; "Sacrament as Social Process," 369; and "On Not Being Ashamed of the Gospel," 289.

52. Yoder, "Walk and Word," 89. See also Yoder, *Priestly Kingdom*, 114.

53. Anti-theory is most commonly associated with the work of Bernard Williams. Of particular importance is Bernard Williams, *Ethics and the Limits of Philosophy* (Cambridge: Harvard University Press, 1985). Much of the most relevant literature on ethical anti-theory has been collected in *Anti-Theory in Ethics and Moral Conservatism*, ed. Stanley G. Clarke and Evan Simpson (Albany: State University of New York Press, 1989). For a helpful secondary account of the anti-theory movement within contemporary moral philosophy, see Dwight Furrow, *Against Theory: Continental and Analytic Challenges in Moral Philosophy* (New York: Routledge, 1995).

54. Yoder, "Why Ecclesiology Is Social Ethics," 121. See also his account of the necessity of "perpetual reform" in *Priestly Kingdom*, 69-70.

55. Yoder, "Sacrament as Social Process," 372.

56. John Howard Yoder, "How H. Richard Niebuhr Reasoned: A Critique of *Christ and Culture*," in *The Authentic Transformation: A New Vision of Christ and Culture*, ed. Glen H. Stassen (Nashville: Abingdon Press, 1996), 75. See also John Howard Yoder, *Body Politics: Five Practices of the Christian Community Before the Watching World* (Nashville: Discipleship Resources, 1992), ix.

57. Yoder, "How H. Richard Niebuhr Reasoned," 75. See also Yoder, *Body Politics*, ix; and "Sacrament as Social Process," 369.

58. For Yoder's use of the terminology of "modelling" and "foretastes," see, e.g., Yoder, *Priestly Kingdom*, 94; "Sacrament as Social Process," 373; and "Why Ecclesiology Is Social Ethics," 106. See also Yoder, *Body Politics*, ix-x.

59. Yoder, *Priestly Kingdom*, 92. See also Yoder, *Body Politics*, ix.

60. Yoder, "Sacrament as Social Process," 364. See also Yoder, *Body Politics*, 20-21.

61. Yoder, "Sacrament as Social Process," 365-66; *Body Politics*, 20.

62. Yoder, "Sacrament as Social Process," 365; *Body Politics*, 20 (emphasis Yoder's).

63. Yoder, *Priestly Kingdom*, 117.

64. Ibid.

65. John Howard Yoder, "The Hermeneutics of the Anabaptists," in *Essays on Biblical Interpretation: Anabaptist-Mennonite Perspectives*, Text-Reader Series, vol. 1, ed. Willard Swartley (Elkhart, IN: Institute of Mennonite Studies, 1984), 11-28, esp. 21, 27-28. See also Yoder, *Priestly Kingdom*, 117-18.

66. John Howard Yoder, "Binding and Loosing," in *Royal Priesthood*, 353. See also Yoder, *Priestly Kingdom*, 117: "The free-church alternative . . . recognizes the inadequacies of the text of Scripture standing alone uninterpreted, and appropriates the promise of the guidance of the Spirit throughout the ages, but locates the fulfilment of that promise in the assembly of those who gather around Scripture in the face of a given real moral challenge." For a more extended treatment of the similarities between Yoder and Fish, see Mark Thiessen Nation, "Theology as Witness: Reflections on Yoder, Fish, and Interpretive Communities," *Faith and Freedom*, 5:1-2 (1996): 42-47.

67. Yoder, "The Hermeneutics of the Anabaptists," 27.

68. Quoted in Yoder, "The Hermeneutics of the Anabaptists," 27.

69. Yoder, "Why Ecclesiology Is Social Ethics," 102-26, esp. 110, 115, 120; "Sacrament as Social Process," 359-73.

70. Yoder, *The Priestly Kingdom*, 36: "The way of discipleship is the way for which we are made; there is no other 'nature' to which grace is a *superadditum*."

71. Yoder, "On Not Being Ashamed of the Gospel," 288.

72. Yoder is referring to Gustafson, "The Sectarian Temptation: Reflections on Theology, the Church, and the University," which, as noted in note 30 above, tends to lie behind the Mennonite account of the sectarian objection as well.

73. Yoder, "On Not Being Ashamed of the Gospel," 288-89.

74. Yoder, *Priestly Kingdom*, 40. See also Yoder, "On Not Being Ashamed of the Gospel," 289: "There is no non-particular place to stand."

75. This point has been most fully developed in John Howard Yoder, *For the Nations: Essays Public and Evangelical* (Grand Rapids: Eerdmans, 1997). See also Yoder, *Priestly Kingdom*, 55; and Cartwright, "Radical Reform, Radical Catholicity," 35.

76. Yoder, *Priestly Kingdom*, 75. See also 138. To the best of my knowledge, none of the sectarian objections against Yoder acknowledge his emphasis and discussion of this point.

77. Ibid., 139.

78. John Howard Yoder, "Meaning After Babble: With Jeffrey Stout Beyond Relativism," *Journal of Religious Ethics*, 24:1 (1996): 132.

Chapter 4
Radical Ecumenism, or Receiving One Another in Kuala Lumpur

1. Stanley Hauerwas, *In Good Company* (Notre Dame: University of Notre Dame Press, 1995), 169.

2. The allusion here is to Wittgenstein, on whom Hauerwas frequently draws. See Ludwig Wittgenstein, *Philosophical Investigations*, 3rd ed.,

trans. G. E. M. Anscombe (New York: Macmillan, 1968), §107: "We have got on to slippery ice where there is no friction and so in a certain sense the conditions are ideal, but also, just because of that, we are unable to walk. We want to walk: so we need *friction*. Back to the rough ground!"

3. See Rowan Williams, *On Christian Theology* (Oxford: Blackwell, 2000), 5-8, 146.

4. Ibid., 3.

5. bid., 5.

6. Ibid., 83-84.

7. Terry Eagleton, *Sweet Violence: The Idea of the Tragic* (Oxford: Blackwell, 2003), 165.

8. See John Howard Yoder, "The Nature of the Unity We Seek: A Historic Free Church View," in *Royal Priesthood*, 221-30.

9. Slavoj Zizek and Glyn Daly, *Conversations with Zizek* (Cambridge: Polity Press, 2004), 143.

10. Alain Badiou, *Saint Paul: The Foundation of Universalism*, trans. Ray Brassier (Stanford: Stanford University Press, 2003), 10-11.

11. Ibid., 53, 78.

12. Ibid., 95.

13. Yoder, *Politics of Jesus*, 228.

Chapter 5
Can a Gift Be Commanded? Political Ontology and Theoretical Closure in Milbank, Barth, and Yoder

1. John Milbank, *Theology and Social Theory: Beyond Secular Reason* (Oxford: Blackwell, 1990).

2. Ibid., 423.

3. See, e.g., John Milbank, "Can a Gift Be Given? Prolegomena to a Future Trinitarian Metaphysic," *Modern Theology* 11:1 (1995): 119-61. See also John Milbank, "Can Morality Be Christian?" in *The Word Made Strange: Theology, Language, Culture* (Oxford: Blackwell, 1996), esp. 225-28; "Grace: The Midwinter Sacrifice," and "Politics: Socialism by Grace," in *Being Reconciled: Ontology and Pardon* (London: Routledge, 2003).

4. Milbank, "Can Morality Be Christian?" 223, 226.

5. Such an objection is perhaps most appropriately associated with the work of Stanley Hauerwas. See, e.g., Stanley Hauerwas, "On Honor: By Way of a Comparison of Karl Barth and Trollope," in *Dispatches from the Front: Theological Engagements with the Secular* (Durham, N.C.: Duke University Press, 1994), 58-79.

6. See, e.g., Nigel Biggar, *The Hastening That Waits: Karl Barth's Ethics* (Oxford: Clarendon Press, 1993), esp. ch. 1, "Ethics as an Aid to Hearing." For a similar argument, see William Werpehowski, "Command

and History in the Ethics of Karl Barth," *Journal of Religious Ethics* 9 (1981): 298-320.

7. Biggar, *Hastening That Waits*, 17. For a similar argument, see Werpchowski, "Command and History in the Ethics of Karl Barth," 300-4.

8. Biggar, *Hastening That Waits*, 9.

9. Karl Barth, *Church Dogmatics* II:2 (Edinburgh: T & T Clark, 1957), 518.

10. See, e.g., ibid., 516: "It is the electing grace of *God* which has placed man under His command from all eternity" (Barth's emphasis).

11. Ibid., 518. See also 539: "It is in grace—the grace of God in Jesus Christ—that even the command of God is established and fulfilled and revealed as such"; and 557: the command of God "confronts us in the loftiness and dignity of the obligation which derives automatically from the gift that He has made us."

12. Ibid., 565. See also 548: "It is as God gives man His command, as he gives himself to man to be his Commander, that God claims him for Himself, that He makes His decision concerning him and executes His judgement upon him."

13. See, e.g., ibid., 606, 608.

14. Ibid., 517.

15. Biggar, *Hastening That Waits*, 16.

16. Barth, *Church Dogmatics* II:2, 527, 529.

17. See esp. Milbank, "Can Morality Be Christian?" 219, 226.

18. Ibid., 219.

19. Ibid., 226 (Milbank's emphasis).

20. Ibid., 221, 226.

21. Ibid., 226.

22. Ibid., 227.

23. Ibid., 226.

24. See, e.g., ibid., 228: "In the beginning there was only gift: no demon of chaos to be defeated, but a divine creative act; this virtue of giving was not required, was not necessary, and so was a more absolute good, complicit with no threat, which in relation to gift is an entirely secondary will to self-possession, to non-receiving of life and so to death."

25. Ibid., 226, 228. See also Milbank, "Can a Gift Be Given?" 135: "[The divine gift] is a gift to no-one, but rather establishes creatures *as* themselves gifts."

26. Milbank, "Can Morality Be Christian?" 226. In a similar vein, he claims that "[I]f supernatural, complete virtue is charity, gifts which are merely requirements or duties are not ethical or virtuous at all, and the command to give or love is supremely paradoxical" (ibid.).

27. Hans Urs von Balthasar, *The Theology of Karl Barth: Exposition and Interpretation*, trans. Edward T. Oakes (San Francisco: Ignatius Press, 1992), 245-47. See also Hauerwas, "On Honor," esp. 77-79.

28. Barth, *Church Dogmatics* II:2, 596, 663, 669. See also Biggar, *Hastening That Waits*, 24-25.

29. John Howard Yoder, "How H. Richard Niebuhr Reasoned: A Critique of Christ and Culture," in *The Authentic Transformation: A New Vision of Christ and Culture*, ed. Glen H. Stassen (Nashville: Abingdon Press, 1966), 75; and *Priestly Kingdom*, 92. See also John Howard Yoder, *Body Politics: Five Practices of the Christian Community Before the Watching World* (Scottdale, PA: Herald Press, 1992), ix.

30. John Howard Yoder, "Walk and Word: The Alternatives to Methodologism," in *Theology Without Foundations: Religious Practice and the Future of Theological Truth*, ed. Stanley Hauerwas, Nancey Murphy, and Mark Nation (Nashville: Abingdon Press, 1994), 77-90, esp. 88. See also Yoder, *Priestly Kingdom*, 114.

31. Yoder, "Walk and Word," 82. See also John Howard Yoder, "Sacrament as Social Process: Christ the Transformer of Culture," in *Royal Priesthood*, 369-72; "On Not Being Ashamed of the Gospel: Particularity, Pluralism, and Validation," *Faith and Philosophy* 9:3 (1992): 289; and *Priestly Kingdom*, 7-8, 37, 113-16.

32. Yoder, "Walk and Word," 89. See also Yoder, *Priestly Kingdom*, 114.

33. It is significant to note that Biggar himself stresses the need to disregard Barth's argument against system. See, e.g., Biggar, *Hastening That Waits*, 8-9, 26, 31ff. For an example of Barth's own rejection of system, see Barth, *Church Dogmatics*, II:2, 551.

34. Hans Frei, "Review of Eberhard Busch, *Karl Barth: His Life from Letters and Autobiographical Texts*," *Virginia Seminary Journal* 30 (1978): 45, as quoted in Werpehowski, "Command and History in the Ethics of Karl Barth," 300.

Chapter 6
Globalization, Theory, and Dialogical Vulnerability: John Howard Yoder and the Possibility of a Pacifist Epistemology

1. A word on globalization as "the context for this particular discussion" is in order here. This paper was originally presented at the International Consultation of Historic Peace Churches at the Bienenberg Theological Seminary in Switzerland, the theme of which was "Theology and Culture: Peacemaking in a Globalized World." As I understand it, this theme signifies two important and interrelated concerns: (1) an understanding of Christian pacifism as involving a commitment to a particular culture or counter-polis of some sort, and (2) a worry about the tendency of globalization to erode

local cultures and communities. Putting these concerns together produces the question of whether genuine Christian peacemaking is possible in a globalized world. My answer is that it is, but only because a non-universalist and radically particular conception of Christian pacifism provides a better way of negotiating the differences between local cultures than the reductive strategies of globalization which too often deny difference in the name of capital.

2. See *The Cultures of Globalization*, ed. Frederic Jameson and Masao Miyoshi (Durham, N.C.: Duke University Press, 1998).

3. Frederic Jameson, "Preface," in *Cultures of Globalization*, xi.

4. See Enrique Dussel, "Beyond Eurocentrism: The World-System and the Limits of Modernity," in *Cultures of Globalization*, 3-31.

5. The best discussion of these matters that I am aware of is Walter D. Mignolo, *Local Histories/Global Designs: Coloniality, Subaltern Knowledges, and Border Thinking* (Princeton: Princeton University Press, 2000).

6. See Edward Said, "Travelling Theory," in his *The World, The Text, and the Critic* (Harvard: Cambridge University Press, 1983); and "Travelling Theory Reconsidered," in his *Reflections on Exile and Other Essays* (Cambridge: Harvard University Press, 2000).

7. This sense of ambiguity within the discourses of globalization is nicely captured by Michael Hardt and Antonio Negri, *Empire* (Cambridge: Harvard University Press, 2000).

8. See Richard Rorty, *Consequences of Pragmatism* (Minneapolis: University of Minnesota Press, 1982), xiv.

9. John Howard Yoder, *The Christian Witness to the State* (Newton, KS: Faith & Life Press, 1964), 90.

10. John Howard Yoder, *For the Nations: Essays Public and Evangelical* (Grand Rapids: Eerdmans, 1997), 10.

11. For a further discussion of the way Yoder preferred to write "under assignment," see Stanley Hauerwas and Chris K. Huebner, "History, Theory, and Anabaptism: A Conversation on Theology after John Howard Yoder," in *The Wisdom of the Cross: Essays in Honor of John Howard Yoder*, ed. Stanley Hauerwas, Chris K. Huebner, Harry J. Huebner and Mark Thiessen Nation (Grand Rapids: Eerdmans, 1999), 404-5.

12. John Howard Yoder, "Meaning after Babble: With Jeffrey Stout Beyond Relativism," *Journal of Religious Ethics* 24:1 (1996), 134.

13. Yoder, "Meaning after Babble," 135.

14. John Howard Yoder, *Politics of Jesus*, 239.

15. The terminology of "mastering contingency" is suggested by John Michael, *Anxious Intellects: Academic Professionals, Public Intellectuals, and Enlightenment Values* (Durham, N.C.: Duke University Press, 2000), 77. In a more specifically theological context, this suspicion of the tendency to master the messy, contingent world of creatures by means of an imposi-

tion of "conceptual neatness" runs throughout the work of Rowan Williams. See Rowan Williams, *On Christian Theology* (Oxford: Blackwell, 2000), esp. 3-15, 146.

16. Yoder, *Politics of Jesus*, 228.

17. The relationship between Yoder and Hauerwas is far more complicated than this or any other summary statement (e.g., being for or against the nations) can adequately capture. Indeed, Hauerwas can (and should) be read as making the same kind of claim against methodological and idiomatic purity (also in the name of pacifism), even though he often makes such a reading harder by his preference for sweeping denunciations of liberalism. Hauerwas is not necessarily the best example of the kind of methodologism Yoder is against, but he is clearly the motivation behind many of Yoder's own examples.

18. Yoder, "Walk and Word," in *Theology Without Foundations*, 83.

19. Lisa Sowle Cahill, *Love Your Enemies: Discipleship, Pacifism, and Just War Theory* (Minneapolis: Fortress Press, 1994), ix.

20. Ibid.

21. Yoder, *Priestly Kingdom*, 143.

22. A similar argument, also offered in defense of Yoder, has been developed by Craig Carter, though more in terms of systematic theology than epistemology and the philosophy of science. See Craig A. Carter, *The Politics of the Cross: The Theology and Social Ethics of John Howard Yoder* (Grand Rapids: Brazos, 2001), 71, 127, 202, 235-36.

23. See Nancey Murphy, "John Howard Yoder's Systematic Defence of Christian Pacifism," in *Wisdom of the Cross*, 45-68.

24. For such an alternative reading of Yoder, see Stanley Hauerwas and Chris K. Huebner, "History, Theory, and Anabaptism: A Conversation on Theology after John Howard Yoder."

25. Yoder, *For the Nations*, 1.

26. Ibid., 3.

27. Ibid., 61. See also John Howard Yoder, "On Not Being in Charge," in *War and Its Discontents: Pacifism and Quietism in the Abrahamic Traditions*, ed. J. Patout Burns (Washington, D.C.: Georgetown University Press, 1996), 74-90.

28. Yoder, *Politics of Jesus*, 228.

29. Yoder, *For the Nations*, 42.

30. John Howard Yoder, *Priestly Kingdom*, 5. I thank Romand Coles for drawing my attention to the significance of this point.

31. To speak of tradition as an "argument extended in time" is to borrow from Alasdair MacIntyre, but it is a fitting way to capture Yoder's conception of tradition as well. See MacIntyre, *Whose Justice? Which Rationality?* (Notre Dame: University of Notre Dame Press, 1998), 12.

32. See Yoder, "The Authority of Tradition," in *Priestly Kingdom*, 63-79.

33. See, e.g., Yoder, "Radical Reformation Ethics in Ecumenical Perspective," in *Priestly Kingdom*, 105-22.

34. Yoder, "Patience as Method in Moral Reasoning: Is an Ethic of Discipleship Absolute?" in *Wisdom of the Cross*, 28.

35. Yoder, "Sacrament as Social Process: Christ the Transformer of Culture," in *Royal Priesthood*, 363.

36. Yoder, "'Patience' as Method in Moral Reasoning," 28-29.

37. Edward Said, *After the Last Sky: Palestinian Lives* (New York: Columbia University Press, 1999), 150 (italics in original).

Chapter 7
Patience, Witness, and the Scattered Body of Christ: Yoder and Virilio on Knowledge, Politics and Speed

1. See, e.g., Duane K. Friesen, *Artists Citizens Philosophers Seeking the Peace of the City* (Scottdale, PA: Herald Press, 2000), 33.

2. Ibid., 127, 217, 237.

3. See, e.g., Yoder, *Politics of Jesus*, 228, 232.

4. Yoder, *Priestly Kingdom*: 145. For a fascinating discussion of Yoder's critique of desire to seize God's will, see J. Alexander Sider, "'To See History Doxologically': History and Holiness in John Howard Yoder's Ecclesiology," PhD dissertation, Duke University, 2004, especially chapter 2.

5. Paul Virilio and Sylvère Lotringer, *Pure War*, 2d ed., trans. Mark Polizzotti (New York: Semiotext(e), 1997), 27.

6. Ibid., 35, 49.

7. Ibid., 13.

8. Ibid., 175.

9. See Paul Virilio, *Ground Zero*, trans. Chris Turner (New York: Verso, 2002).

10. Paul Virilio, *The Information Bomb*, trans. Chris Turner (New York: Verso, 2000), 144-45.

11. Virilio, *Ground Zero*, 12. Among other things, this recent work is an attempt to links the question of violence to the contemporary fascination with the "neo-eugenic" project of the technological self-perfection of human life.

12. Paul Virilio, *War and Cinema: The Logistics of Perception*, trans. Patrick Camiller (New York: Verso, 1984), 66, as quoted in John Armitage, "Beyond Postmodernism? Paul Virilio's Hypermodern Cultural Theory," *Ctheory* 23:3, [www.tao.ca/writing/archives/ctheory/0132.html].

13. Virilio, *War and Cinema*, 13, as quoted by Armitage, "Beyond Postmodernism?"

14. Virilio, *Information Bomb*, 12-13.

15. See, e.g., Virilio, *Pure War*, 34.

16. Ibid., 26.

17. Ibid., 99.

18. Ibid., 92.

19. Ibid., 26, 32.

20. Ibid., 94.

21. This tendency is perhaps best represented by J. Denny Weaver, *Anabaptist Theology in the Face of Postmodernity: A Proposal for the New Millennium* (Telford, PA: Pandora Press U.S., 2000).

22. Virilio, *Pure War*, 128.

23. Ibid., 62.

24. William Connolly, "Speed, Concentric Cultures, and Cosmopolitanism," *Political Theory* 28:5 (2000): 596.

25. Ibid., 597.

26. Ibid., 598.

27. John Howard Yoder, *For the Nations: Essays Public and Evangelical* (Grand Rapids: Eerdmans, 1997), 52.

28. See ibid., 61, 66-70 for a discussion of the "Jewishness of the case against 'taking charge' of the course of history" (68).

29. Ibid., 53.

30. Connolly, "Speed, Concentric Cultures, and Cosmopolitanism," 603.

31. Ibid.

32. See John Howard Yoder, "On Not Being Ashamed of the Gospel: Particularity, Pluralism, and Validation," *Faith and Philosophy* 9:3 (1992): 287.

33. John Howard Yoder, *When War is Unjust: Being Honest in Just-War Thinking*, 2d ed. (Maryknoll, N.Y.: Orbis, 1996), 5. For a further discussion of Yoder's stake in defending the integrity of the just war tradition, see Reinhardt Hütter, "Be Honest in Just War Thinking! Lutherans, the Just War Tradition, and Selective Conscientious Objection," in *The Wisdom of the Cross: Essays in Honor of John Howard Yoder*, ed. Stanley Hauerwas, Chris K. Huebner, Harry J. Huebner, and Mark Thiessen Nation (Grand Rapids: Eerdmans, 1999), 69-83; and Tobias Winwright, "From Police Officers to Peace Officers," in *Wisdom of the Cross*, 84-114.

34. Yoder, *When War is Unjust*, 50.

35. Ibid., 6, 63.

36. See Winwright, "From Police Officers to Peace Officers," 108-14.

37. See, e.g., Yoder, *When War is Unjust*, 71, where he argues that "the just-war tradition is not a simple formula ready to be applied in a self-evident and univocal way. It is rather a set of very broad assumptions whose implications demand—if they are to be respected as morally honest—that they be spelled out in some detail and then tested for their ability to throw

serious light on real situations and on the decisions of persons and institutions regarding those situations." See also the examination of the many different varieties of religious pacifism in Yoder, *Nevertheless*.

38. John Howard Yoder, "How Many Ways Are There to Think Morally About War?" *Journal of Law and Religion* 11:1 (1994): 84.

39. Yoder, *For the Nations*, 25.

40. Ibid., 24.

41. Yoder, "A People in the World," in *The Royal Priesthood*, 86.

42. See Yoder, *For the Nations*, 24, n. 22: "'Good news' is a kind of knowledge which is not known until one receives it, but then is received as good."

43. Yoder, *For the Nations*, 42.

Chapter 8
The Agony of Truth: Martydom, Violence, and Christian Ways of Knowing

1. David Bentley Hart, *The Beauty of the Infinite: The Aesthetics of Christian Truth* (Grand Rapids: Eerdmans, 2003), 331.

2. Rowan Williams, *On Christian Theology* (Oxford: Blackwell, 2000), 5.

3. Stanley Cavell, *The Claim of Reason: Wittgenstein, Skepticism, Morality, and Tragedy* (Oxford: Oxford University Press, 1979), 254. I owe this reference to Peter Dula.

4. A note on the themes of faith, freedom, and the university is on order at this point. This essay was originally presented at a conference entitled "Faith, Freedom, and the Academy," held at the University of Prince Edward Island, October 1-3, 2004. The overall theme of the conference was framed by the question of whether the university should be a place of "freedom *for* faith" or "freedom *from* faith." Put in those terms, this essay is an attempt to say "both" and "neither" at the same time, and in so doing to rethink the university by way of an examination of the question of the truth to which it takes itself as being dedicated.

5. Hart, *Beauty of the Infinite*, 441.

6. Dionysius of Alexandria, "Extant Fragments," trans. S. D. F. Salmond in *Ante-Nicene Fathers*, Vol. 6, *Gregory Thaumaturgus, Dionysius the Great, Julius Africanus, Anatolius and Minor Writers, Methodius, Arnobius*, ed. Alexander Roberts and James Donaldson (Peabody, MA: Hendrickson, 1995), 98.

7. See Thieleman J. van Braght, *The Bloody Theatre, or Martyr's Mirror of the Defenseless Christians*, trans. Joseph F. Sohm (Scottdale, PA: Herald Press, 1950), 737-38.

8. Boutzon le Heu, as quoted in Brad S. Gregory, *Salvation at Stake: Christian Martyrdom in Early Modern Europe* (Cambridge, MA: Harvard University Press, 1999), 104.

9. William T. Cavanaugh, *Torture and Eucharist: Theology, Politics, and the Body of Christ* (Oxford: Blackwell, 1998), 58.

10. Menno Simons, as quoted by Gregory, *Salvation at Stake*, 220.

11. Gregory, *Salvation at Stake*, 7 (emphasis added).

12. Carole Straw, "Martyrdom in its Classical Context," in *Sacrificing the Self: Perspectives on Martyrdom and Religion*, ed. Margaret Cormack, (Oxford: Oxford University Press, 2002), 40.

13. Michel Foucault, "Truth and Juridical Forms," in *Power, Essential Works of Foucault 1954–1984*, Vol. 3, ed. James F. Faubion (New York: New Press, 1997), 2.

14. Hart, *Beauty of the Infinite*, 443.

15. Gregory, *Salvation at Stake*, 132.

16. The reference is to Yoder, "The Otherness of the Church," in *Royal Priesthood*, 54-64.

17. Foucault, "Truth and Juridical Forms," 3.

18. Michel Foucault, "About the Beginning of the Hermeneutics of the Self," in *Religion and Culture*, ed. Jeremy Carrette (New York: Routledge, 1999), 159.

19. Foucault, "Truth and Juridical Forms," 8.

20. Foucault, "About the Beginning of the Hermeneutics of the Self," 179. James Bernauer summarizes Foucault's transition from subject as foundation to self as sacrifice as follows: "The aim of modern knowledges and practices is to foster the emergence of a positive self in which one recognizes and is bound to the self-knowledge defined through the categories of the anthropological sciences. Modern self-appropriation is the discovery of and attachment to that truth, as the firm basis for encounter with the world. Foucault contrasted the modern vision with those Christian practices which invited a renunciation of the self who was articulated as true. In his view, the key to the Christian's experience of self-discovery and subjectivity was located in the model of *martyrdom*" ("Michel Foucault's Philosophy of Religion: An Introduction to the Non-Fascist Life," in *Michel Foucault and Theology*, ed. James Bernauer and Jeremy Carrette [New York: Routledge, 2004], 90).

21. Michel Foucault, *Fearless Speech*, ed. Joseph Pearson (Los Angeles: Semiotext(e), 2001), 15-16.

22. This way of putting it is that of John Milbank, whose work itself relies heavily on that of Rose. See esp. Milbank, "The Midwinter Sacrifice: A Sequel to 'Can Morality Be Christian?'" *Studies in Christian Ethics* 10:2 (1997): 13-38; and "The Ethics of Self-Sacrifice," *First Things* 91 (March 1999): 33-38.

23. Gillian Rose, *Judaism and Modernity*, as quoted in Rowan Williams, "Between Politics and Metaphysics: Reflections in the Wake of Gillian Rose," *Modern Theology* 11:1 (1995): 8-9.

24. I owe the terminology of receptive generosity to Romand Coles. See Coles, *Rethinking Generosity: Critical Theory and the Politics of Caritas* (Ithaca, N.Y.: Cornell University Press, 1997); and *Beyond Gated Politics: Reflections for the Possibility of Democracy* (Minneapolis: University of Minnesota Press, 2005).

25. Gillian Rose, *Judaism and Modernity: Philosophical Essays* (Oxford: Blackwell, 1993), 4. It is important to recognize that the reference to "certainty" here is not to the familiar figure of Descartes but to the new ethics of Levinas and Derrida.

26. Williams, "Between Politics and Metaphysics," 13.

27. Gillian Rose, *The Broken Middle: Out of Our Ancient Society* (Oxford: Blackwell, 1992), 263-64.

Chapter 9
Christian Pacifism as Friendship with God: MacIntyre, Mennonites, and the Genealogical Tradition

1. Dawn McCance, *Posts: Re Addressing the Ethical* (Albany, N.Y.: State University of New York Press, 1996), 1.

2. An earlier version of this essay was presented at the conference, "Anabaptists and Postmodernity," held at Bluffton College, August 8-10, 1998. This also explains my use of the term "Anabaptism" in the introductory comments. Much mileage is often gained by distinguishing between Anabaptist and Mennonite. While such a distinction is often appropriate, it bears no rhetorical function in the discussion that follows. This essay is written against the background of debates in contemporary Mennonite peace theology. Reference to "Anabaptism" is simply in deference to the title of the conference. I thus limit my use of the term to the introductory comments, preferring the term "Mennonite" in the title and the remainder of the essay.

3. Alasdair MacIntyre, *After Virtue*, 2d ed. (Notre Dame, IN: University of Notre Dame Press, 1984), 155.

4. Ibid., 156.

5. Ibid.

6. Alasdair MacIntyre, *Whose Justice? Which Rationality?* (Notre Dame, IN: University of Notre Dame Press, 1988); *Three Rival Versions of Moral Enquiry: Encyclopaedia, Genealogy, and Tradition* (Notre Dame, IN: University of Notre Dame Press, 1990).

7. See, e.g., Saint Thomas Aquinas, *Summa Theologiae*, trans. Fathers of the English Dominican Province (New York: Benziger Brothers, 1948), II-II, 23, 8. See also II-II, 23, 4, ad. 1.

8. Aristotle, *Magna Moralia*, 1213a22-24, as quoted in John M. Cooper, "Aristotle on Friendship," in *Essays on Aristotle's Ethics*, ed. Amélie Oksenberg Rorty (Berkeley: University of California Press, 1980), 320.

9. Aristotle, *Nicomachean Ethics*, trans. Terence Irwin (Indianapolis: Hackett, 1985), 1159a7-9, 1158b32-36.

10. Aquinas, *Summa Theologiae*, III, 79, 2; III, 79, 4, ad. 1.

11. MacIntyre, *Three Rival Versions of Moral Enquiry*, 143 (emphasis added).

12. For a helpful discussion of Nietzsche on friendship, see John Coker, "On Becoming Great Friends," *International Studies in Philosophy* 25:2 (1993): 113-27; as well as Jacques Derrida's sustained commentary on Nietzschean friendship in *The Politics of Friendship*, trans. George Collins (New York: Verso, 1997), esp. 26-45, 281-90.

13. We are told that the incomplete and unpublished fourth volume of Foucault's *History of Sexuality* was to deal more extensively with the politics of friendship. Nevertheless, some of Foucault's thoughts on friendship are available in several interviews and shorter reflections on his later work. See, e.g., Michel Foucault, "Friendship as a Way of Life" and "Sex, Power, and the Politics of Identity," in *The Essential Works of Michel Foucault, 1954-1984*, vol. 1, *Ethics: Subjectivity and Truth*, trans. Robert Hurley et al., ed. Paul Rabinow (New York: New Press, 1997).

14. Derrida, *The Politics of Friendship*, 232.

15. Ibid., 65, 240, 295.

16. Ibid., 306.

17. See, e.g., Jacques Derrida, "Heidegger's Ear: Philopolemology (*Geschlecht* IV)," in *Reading Heidegger: Commemorations*, ed. John Sallis (Bloomington: Indiana University Press, 1993), 164-64.

18. Ibid., 168.

19. Ibid., 174.

20. Ibid., 194.

21. Ibid., 196.

22. Ibid., 168.

23. Jacques Derrida, "The Politics of Friendship," trans. Gabriel Motzkin *Journal of Philosophy* 85 (1988): 641. See also "Heidegger's Ear," 197. The related themes of *aporia* and *polemos* run throughout Derrida's discussion of friendship. See, in particular, "Heidegger's Ear," 203-16.

24. Derrida, "Heidegger's Ear," 174.

25. Instrumental in the development of such a reading is the work of John Caputo, e.g., *The Prayers and Tears of Jacques Derrida: Religion without Religion* (Bloomington: Indiana University Press, 1997).

26. Jacques Derrida, *The Gift of Death*, trans. David Wills (Chicago: University of Chicago Press, 1995), 31, 33.

27. Ibid., 2, 83.

28. Ibid., 87.

29. Ibid., 25, 33, 41.

30. John Milbank, *Theology and Social Theory: Beyond Secular Reason* (Oxford: Blackwell, 1990), 4-5.

31. Ibid., 376.

32. Ibid., 5.

33. Ibid., 279.

34. Ibid., 417.

35. Ibid., 416.

36. For a helpful discussion of the sense in which, for Milbank, a Christian ontology of peace is rooted in the practices of charity/friendship with God and forgiveness, see David Toole, *Waiting for Godot in Sarajevo: Theological Reflections on Nihilism, Tragedy, and Apocalypse* (Boulder, CO: Westview Press, 1998), 73-75.

37. John Milbank, "Enclaves, or Where is the Church?" *New Blackfriars* 73:861 (1992): 349.

38. Milbank, *Theology and Social Theory*, 421.

39. Ibid., 418.

40. Ibid., 422.

41. Toole, *Waiting for Godot in Sarajevo*, 76.

42. See John Milbank, *The Word Made Strange: Theology, Language, Culture* (Cambridge, Mass.: Blackwell, 1997), 123-68.

43. I owe this way of putting it to Scott Bader-Saye, *Church and Israel After Christendom: The Politics of Election* (Boulder, CO: Westview Press, 1999), 154 n. 55.

44. Milbank, "The Name of Jesus," in *The Word Made Strange*, 149.

45. For a similar argument, though in a very different context, see Bader-Saye, *Church and Israel After Christendom*, esp. 52-69, 134-48.

46. Milbank, "Name of Jesus," 150 (my emphasis).

47. Ernst Troeltsch, *The Social Teaching of the Christian Churches*, trans. Olive Wyon (Louisville: Westminster/John Knox Press, 1992), 39.

48. "Radical Orthodoxy" is the preferred name for the "new" theological movement that Milbank and others represent. See John Milbank, Catharine Pickstock, and Graham Ward, eds. *Radical Orthodoxy: A New Theology* (New York: Routledge, 1999), esp. 1-20.

49. John Howard Yoder, *Christian Attitudes to War, Peace, and Revolution: A Companion to Bainton* (Elkhart, IN: Goshen Biblical Seminary, 1983), 186.

50. Frederick Christian Bauerschmidt, "The Word Made Speculative? John Milbank's Christological Poetics," *Modern Theology* 16:4 (1999): 423.

Chapter 10
Curing the Body of Christ: Memory, Identity, and Alzheimer's Disease By
Way of Two Mennonite Grandparents
   1. Carl Elliott, *A Philosophical Disease: Bioethics, Culture, and
Identity* (London: Routledge, 1999), xxii.
   2. David Keck, *Forgetting Whose We Are: Alzheimer's Disease and the
Love of God* (Nashville: Abingdon Press, 1996), 48.
   3. For a helpful exploration of this temptation in a very different context, see William T. Cavanaugh, *Torture and Eucharist: Theology, Politics,
and the Body of Christ* (Oxford: Blackwell, 1998).
   4. Harry Huebner, *Church as Parable: Whatever Happened to Ethics?*
(Winnipeg: CMBC Publications, 1993), 173.
   5. Ibid., 172.
   6. Ibid., 173.
   7. Michael Ignatieff, *Scar Tissue* (Toronto: Viking, 1993), 53.
   8. Keck, *Forgetting Whose We Are*, 28.
   9. Ibid.
   10. Ibid., 32.

Chapter 11
Image, Identity, and Diaspora: The Ethics of Visual Culture in Charles
Taylor and Atom Egoyan
   1. See, e.g., Michael Hardt and Antonio Negri, *Empire* (Cambridge,
MA: Harvard University Press, 2000), 59, 138. See also Kenneth Surin,
"Marxism(s) and 'The Withering Away of the State,'" *Social Text* 27
(1990): 45-46: "The [capitalist] institutional assemblage whose 'idea' is
the state today serves to incorporate and neutralize all movements of
resistance, the undertaking of this role being one of the necessary conditions for the realization of surplus value."
   2. W. J. T. Mitchell, *Picture Theory: Essays on Verbal and Visual
Representation* (Chicago: University of Chicago Press, 1994), 13.
   3. Charles Taylor, "Overcoming Epistemology," in *Philosophical
Arguments* (Cambridge, MA: Harvard University Press, 1995), 2-3.
   4. Ibid., 7, 11-12.
   5. Ibid., 7-8, 12-13.
   6. Ibid., 8, 13.
   7. This way of summarizing Taylor's objection to ethical theory also
relies on Michael Stocker's influential essay, "The Schizophrenia Modern
Ethical Theories," *Journal of Philosophy* 73 (1976): 453-66. Although significant differences between Taylor and Stocker remain, their criticism of
the enterprise of ethical theory is strikingly similar.

8. Taylor, "Overcoming Epistemology," 477 (emphasis added).

9. Ibid., 12.

10. For a helpful summary of Kant's ethics in these terms, see Romand Coles, *Rethinking Generosity: Critical Theory and the Politics of Caritas* (Ithaca, N.Y.: Cornell University Press, 1997), 24-74.

11. Charles Taylor, *Sources of the Self: The Making of the Modern Identity* (Cambridge, MA: Harvard University Press, 1989), 516. For a more extended discussion and defense of his conception of strong evaluation, see Charles Taylor, "What is Human Agency?" in *Human Agency and Language: Philosophical Papers I* (New York: Cambridge University Press, 1985), 15-44.

12. Taylor, *Sources of the Self*, 75 (emphasis added).

13. For a more in-depth discussion of these themes, see Scott Bukatman, "Videodrome," in *Spectacular Optical*, ed. Sandra Antelo-Suarez and Michael Mark Madore (New York: Trans>arts.cultures.media, 1998), 55-60.

14. Richard Porton, "The Film Director as Philosopher: An Interview with David Cronenberg," *Cineaste* 24:4 (1999): 6.

15. Marc Glassman, "Emotional Logic [An Interview with Atom Egoyan]," in Atom Egoyan, *Speaking Parts* (Toronto: Coach House Press, 1993), 44. This is actually Egoyan's description of an earlier film, *Speaking Parts*, but it is even more fully realized in *Exotica*, which had not yet been made at the time of this interview.

16. Lawrence Chua, "Atom's Id [An Interview with Atom Egoyan]," *Artforum* 33:7 (1995): 26.

17. Carole Desbarats, "Conquering What They Tell Us Is 'Natural,'" in Carole Desbarats, Daniele Riviere, Jacinto Lagiera, and Paul Virilio, *Atom Egoyan*, trans. Brian Holmes (Paris: Editions Dis Voir, 1993) 22, 27.

18. *Calendar*, as quoted in Peter Harcourt, "Imaginary Images: An Examination of Atom Egoyan's Films," *Film Quarterly* 48:3 (1995): 11.

19. For Egoyan's own account of this notion of camera as character, see Egoyan, *Speaking Parts*, 51. See also Daniele Riviere, "The Place of the Spectator," in *Atom Egoyan*, 98.

20. Ron Burnett, "Introduction," in *Speaking Parts*, 18. For Egoyan's own account of this ambiguous, nonmoralistic attitude toward technology, see Richard Porton, "Family Romances: An Interview with Atom Egoyan," *Cineaste* 23:2 (1997): 12.

21. See Burnett, "Introduction," 11.

22. For this way of describing the "diasporic condition" that Egoyan's work articulates, see Paul Virilio and Sylvère Lotringer, *Pure War*, rev. ed., trans. Mark Pilizzotti (New York: Semiotext(e), 1997), 65.

Chapter 12
Between Victory and Victimhood: Reflections on Martyrdom, Culture, and Identity

1. "The Martyrdom of Polycarp," in *The Acts of the Christian Martyrs,* ed. Herbert Musurillo (Oxford: Clarendon Press, 1972), 13.

2. "The Martyrdom of Pionius," in *The Acts of the Christian Martyrs,* 165.

3. Ibid., 139.

4. Ibid., 143 (emphasis in original).

5. For example, Pionius's lament, "Would that I were able to persuade you to become Christians," is met with the derisive response, "You have not such power that we should be burnt alive." See "The Martyrdom of Pionius," 145.

6. See, e.g., ibid., 145, 159.

7. Ibid., 163.

8. Ibid.

9. Ibid., 165.

10. For a helpful discussion of the genealogy and transformations of the word *culture,* see Terry Eagleton, *The Idea of Culture* (Oxford: Blackwell, 2000).

11. Ibid., 6.

12. Elizabeth Castelli, *Martyrdom and Memory: Early Christian Culture Making* (New York: Columbia University Press, 2004), 33; see also p. 173.

13. Ibid., 4.

14. Ibid., 17, 198.

15. Ibid., 198.

16. Ibid., 4.

17. Ibid., 40.

18. As evidence for this claim, Castelli cites John Wagner, ed. *The Big Book of Martyrs: Amazing But True Tales of Faith in the Face of Certain Death* (New York: Paradox Press, 1997); DC Talk and the Voice of the Martyrs, *Jesus Freaks: Stories of Those Who Stood for Jesus: The Ultimate Jesus Freaks* (Tulsa, OK: Albury Publishing, 1999). One might also mention Susan Bergman, ed. *Martyrs: Contemporary Writers on Modern Lives of Faith* (New York: Orbis, 2002). In addition, it would be interesting to explore the appearance of the rhetoric of martyrdom in the recent "rap wars" between East and West Coast rappers that resulted in the deaths of 2Pac Shakur and Notorious B.I.G., among others. Recent discussions of the suicide bomber are too numerous to mention, but see David Brooks, "The Culture of Martyrdom," *Atlantic Monthly* (June 2002); and Joyce M. Davis, *Martyrs: Innocence, Vengeance, and Despair in the Middle East*

(New York: St. Martin's Press, 2004). Among recent academic treatments, see Brad S. Gregory, *Salvation at Stake: Christian Martyrdom in Early Modern Europe* (Cambridge, MA: Harvard University Press, 1999); and Daniel Boyarin, *Dying for God: Martyrdom and the Making of Christianity and Judaism* (Stanford: Stanford University Press, 1999); as well as the extensive bibliography provided by Castelli.

19. Michael Hardt and Antonio Negri, *Multitude: War and Democracy in the Age of Empire* (New York: Penguin, 2004), 346 (emphasis in original).

20. See Gillian Rose, *Mourning Becomes the Law: Philosophy and Representation* (Cambridge: Cambridge University Press, 1996). For a helpful discussion of this emphasis in Rose's work, see Rowan Williams, "Between Politics and Metaphysics: Reflections in the Wake of Gillian Rose," *Modern Theology* 11:1 (1995): 3-22.

21. The language of "uncoupling," along with the connection to Paul, is drawn from Slavoj Zizek, *The Fragile Absolute: or, Why is the Christian Legacy Worth Fighting For?* (London: Verso, 2000), 123-30.

22. Readers familiar with the work of John Milbank will recognize his influence here. And while my reading of martyrdom owes much to Milbank, I seek to distance myself from traces of the logic of security and control that seem to remain in his work.`

23. Rowan Williams, *Lost Icons: Reflections on Cultural Bereavement* (Edinburgh: T&T Clark, 2000), 109. This is also reminiscent of the French political philosopher Alain Badiou, who claims that contemporary culture has recently become dominated by a "victimist conception of man." See Badiou, *St Paul: The Foundation of Universalism*, trans. Ray Brassier (Stanford: Stanford University Press, 2003), 6.

24. Slavoj Zizek and Glyn Daly, *Conversations with Zizek* (Cambridge: Polity Press, 2004), 140-41.

25. Ibid., 141-42. See also Zizek, *Fragile Absolute*, 107-13.

26. Williams, *Lost Icons*, 147.

27. Rowan Williams, *Christ on Trial: How the Gospel Unsettles Our Judgement* (Grand Rapids: Eerdmans, 2003), 107 (emphasis added).

Chapter 13
Putting Ourselves in Question: The Triumphal Entry and the Renunciation of Triumphalism

1. See Herbert McCabe, "The Genealogy of Christ," in *God Matters* (Springfield, IL: Templegate Publishers, 1991), 246-49.

2. Rowan Williams, "Palm Sunday," in *A Ray of Darkness: Sermons and Reflections* (Boston: Cowley Publications, 1995), 46.

Index

The Author

Chris K. Huebner is Assistant Professor of Theology and Ethics at Canadian Mennonite University in Winnipeg, Manitoba. In addition to teaching in the area of theology and ethics, he also contributes to the departments of philosophy and peace and conflict transformation. His writings are primarily in the area of philosophical theology and can be located at the intersection of politics and epistemology, with a special interest in questions of peace and violence.

He has published a number of essays in academic journals and is an editor of *The Wisdom of the Cross: Essays in Honor of John Howard Yoder* (Eerdmans, 1999; Wipf & Stock, 2005).

Huebner earned his PhD in theology and ethics from Duke University in 2002, under the supervision of Stanley Hauerwas. His dissertation, "Unhandling History: Anti-Theory, Ethics, and the Practice of Witness," was an examination and defense of John Howard Yoder's "methodological non-Constantinianism."

Born in Winnipeg, Manitoba, Huebner is married to Rachel Klassen Huebner, and they have two children. They attend Charleswood Mennonite Church in Winnipeg.

Chris Huebner displays John Howard Yoder's intent to cultivate the patience needed to keep dialogue alive, as he develops a trenchant theological critique of prevailing notions of freedom, culture, and interpretation. In a powerful homage to his mentor, he shows the alternative path of self-criticism needed to liberate a world suffused by religious strategies intent on dominating. There can be no other way once we appreciate that knowledge is not ours to possess but only to seek—with others and through disagreement, as exemplified in the "knowledge of Christ."

> —David Burrell,
> Hesburgh Chair of Theology and Philosophy,
> University of Notre Dame

Huebner's challenging work brings Yoder's convictions into conversation with postmodern philosophy and theology, demonstrating the importance of keeping the church central for Christian ethics and reminding us that disruptive discipleship means vulnerability, not control.

> —Gayle Gerber Koontz,
> Professor of Theology and Ethics,
> Associated Mennonite Biblical Seminary

A Precarious Peace is intelligent, at times elegant, and unremitting in its depiction of the church as a counter-polis, gifted with witnesses and martyrs and a distinctive voice, but resistant to the frozen embrace of a theology captured by method and harnessed to rootless abstraction. In his analyses of gift and violence and friendship and war, and in his conversations with thinkers as various as Alasdair MacIntyre, Paul Virilio, and John Milbank, Chris Huebner shows how theology should be done: with all the passion due the occasions that prompt it. The proximate inspiration for this work, as befits a North American Mennonite of the twenty-first century, is John Howard Yoder, and Yoder would approve his progeny. But Huebner's range and voice makes what he has to say relevant to Christians of all stripes, and among the many virtues of the book is that it shows, without trying to, the increasing insignificance of denominational divisions for the intellectual work of the church.

> —Paul J. Griffiths,
> Schmitt Chair of Catholic Studies,
> University of Illinois at Chicago